LOOKING FOR AMERICA

Books by Richard Rhodes

Fiction

HOLY SECRETS
THE UNGODLY

Nonfiction

LOOKING FOR AMERICA
THE OZARKS
THE INLAND GROUND

RICHARD RHODES

LOOKING FOR
AMERICA

A Writer's Odyssey

DOUBLEDAY & COMPANY, INC.
GARDEN CITY, NEW YORK
1979

Portion of "Hungerfield," copyright © 1952 by Robinson Jeffers, from HUNGERFIELD AND OTHER POEMS, by Robinson Jeffers. Reprinted by permission of Donnan C. Jeffers and Garth S. Jeffers.

Some of these essays originally appeared in periodicals: ALWAYS ON THE STRECH: A WESTERN VOYAGE, CREDENCES OF SUMMER and BORROWED FINERY (as PACKAGED SENTIMENT) in *Harper's Magazine;* ONCE A YEAR ON LABOR DAY (as $8884.42 A SECOND) and THE DEATH OF THE EVERGLADES (as THE KILLING OF THE EVERGLADES) in *PLAYBOY Magazine*, Copyright © 1971 by Playboy Enterprises, Inc.; SEX AND SIN IN SHEBOYGAN, A GREAT RIVER PASSING FOREVER: THE MISSISSIPPI (as THE MISSISSIPPI) in *PLAYBOY Magazine*, Copyright © 1972 by Playboy Enterprises, Inc.; COMING DOWN SNOW MOUNTAIN (as A VERY EXPENSIVE HIGH), STRUNG OUT ON BLAST in *PLAYBOY Magazine*, Copyright © 1974 by Playboy Enterprises, Inc.; LOATHE THY NEIGHBOR in *PLAYBOY Magazine*, Copyright © 1975 by Playboy Enterprises, Inc.; THE DEMONS OF GERALD FORD, THE GREAT MEMPHIS PORNOGRAPHY TRIALS (as "DEEP THROAT" GOES DOWN IN MEMPHIS) in *PLAYBOY Magazine*, Copyright © 1976 by Playboy Enterprises, Inc.; HOW I RODE WITH HAROLD LEWIS ON A DIESEL FREIGHT TRAIN DOWN TO GRIDLEY, KANSAS, AND BACK and THE LAST KENNEDY in *Audience*, Copyright © 1971 by Hill Publishing Company, Inc.; A LITTLE WORLD MADE CUNNINGLY and SKYWRITING (as THE SKYWRITING PROCESS) in *Audience*, Copyright © 1972 by Hill Publishing Company, Inc.; J. ROBERT OPPENHEIMER, SHATTERER OF WORLDS (as "I AM BECOME DEATH . . ." THE AGONY OF J. ROBERT OPPENHEIMER) in *American Heritage*, Copyright © 1977 by American Heritage Publishing Co., Inc.

Library of Congress Cataloging in Publication Data

Rhodes, Richard.

Looking for America.
1. United States—Civilization—1970
—Addresses, essays, lectures.   2. National characteristics, American—Addresses, essays, lectures.   I. Title.
E169.12.R48   973.92
ISBN: 0-385-14473-3
Library of Congress Catalog Card Number 78-18554

For
David Butler
Lawrence Gonzales
Robert Kotlowitz
and especially
Arthur Kretchmer

CONTENTS

FOREWORD

Some years ago I left regular employment and went out looking for America. I had grown up on city streets and on a working farm. I had gone to college and studied the history of ideas—European ideas. I had served in the military and married and fathered children and hidden from myself too long within a large, benevolent corporation. I had lately published a book about the Middle West. I wanted to look farther afield. I wanted to live by my wits, such as they are. I wanted to explore.

This book is one result. It contains a significant part of a decade's work, the best of that work except for the novels. Much of it was written for hire, but I did not consider myself a hireling. I chose most of the subjects, and the editors who encouraged me and supported me published what I wrote. I continue to be grateful for that confidence. It meant I could report without indirection what I saw.

What I saw was not necessarily what others saw in America in the 1970s. Vietnam is hardly here, and almost nothing of Watergate. I realize that some will believe such omissions immoral. But good men and women were attending those important examinations, men and women with skills different from my own. I chose instead to look for landscapes, patterns, technologies, the beast in the jungle, the masks of men. I hoped to approach the riddle of who we are and why we came here and what we intend to do. My models were not the new journalists or the old, but Emerson and Whitman and Thoreau.

There is such a creature as the American mind. It is adaptive, opportunistic, vernacular, transcendental, raw. We are a culture of hunter-gatherers more than we are pastoral or agricultural. We find and use and move on. Much of our uncertainty about resources today arises from that distinction. William Carlos Williams thought we chose the mercantile avenue of conquest over the primitive, the Indian. In major ways we did, but beneath the mercantile the primitive persisted, and finally the two modalities combined. Combined successfully as biology measures success: a nation of tinkers and pathfinders and craftsmen, two generations out of the woods, we lead the world into the twenty-first century, our achievements and our evils alike enlarged.

That is a little of what I learned, but I cannot capsulize here a decade of search. The essays that follow are arranged by categories, not chronologically. They are frequently personal, and personal themes recur. I wheeled in the Donner Party more than you may like, because I was writing a novel about it and found its miniaturization of the American Dream compelling. I wheeled in my mother's suicide, looking to exorcise it. I wheeled in the Osage Indians, figures from a frieze on the wall of my private golden age, which is at least as sentimental as your golden age. Work is always autobiographical, one reason why I examine here so many kinds of work.

I know of no other written form so extemporaneous as the essay. It is a spiral rather than a circle, by definition unfinished. It has been too much an indulgence of gentlemen, and so has lost repute, but it is an old and honorable form, invented at a time when men believed an individual sensibility, an individual intelligence, could be a useful and sometimes revealing measure of the world. That belief abides in the United States: the United States is an essay itself.

I went out looking for America. What follows is one level, one horizon, of what I found.

Bonner Springs, Kansas—
Kansas City, Missouri
1969–1978

I have come to believe that this is a mighty continent which was hitherto unknown.

Journal of the Third Voyage
CHRISTOPHER COLUMBUS

I
OUT IN THE COUNTRY

"*Always on the Strech*":
A Western Voyage

*All ages and all sects are found to undertake this long tedious
and even dangerous Journy for some unknown object never to be
realized even by those the most fortunate. And why? because the
human mind can never be satisfied never at rest always on the
strech for something new some strange novelty. . . .*

JAMES CLYMAN

James Clyman, a man at home in the western wilderness before
any map maker charted it, wrote the ironic and tender words into
his journal while sitting beside a fresh grave in Kansas in the summer of 1846. The grave held the body of an elderly woman who
had come down by wagon from Illinois bound for California.
Clyman had met her son-in-law farther west, at Fort Laramie, an
old friend who fought with him and with Abe Lincoln in the
Black Hawk War, James Frazier Reed. Of Scottish and Polish descent and only a year earlier a prosperous Chicago businessman,
Reed had sold out his business interests, commissioned a huge,
two-story wagon his daughter Patty christened the "Prairie Parlor
Car," and with his wife and children and mother-in-law and
teamsters set out for California. In Independence he joined up
with the wagons of George and Jacob Donner, two Illinois
farmers, and with other wagons going west, to make a train.
Some then called it the Donner-Reed Party; the Donner Party, we
call it now.

Clyman could not have known, as he wrote beside the grave in

Kansas, the horrors that the Donner Party would meet at the barricade of the Sierra Nevada (could not have known that of eighty-three who reached the mountains just as the first blizzard of Sierra winter broke only forty-eight would survive, that Reed would kill a man and be banished and out of his banishment build an army of rescue to save those who banished him, that some among the party would descend to cannibalism to spare themselves certain starvation, or that the Donners would give their name to the great pass of California emigration), but he knew his own dangerous journeys through the mountains and knew his own restless searching for strange novelties and knew the American temper. Today's Interstate 80, straightened somewhat, still follows the Donner trail from Salt Lake City to Sacramento. So does the flight by jet. We are still emigrants west on the long trail, still unsettled, still exploring. Only two generations separate us from the Donner Party's excursion of 1846, and one generation more returns us to the American Revolution. Some among the Donner Party were children on our first Fourth of July. One of the Donner Party's grandchildren is alive today. Once a year she visits Sutter's Fort to see the doll her mother, Patty Reed, carried secretly down from the death camp in the Sierra.

Clyman's generic, *always on the strech*, became Thoreau's specific. "Eastward I go only by force," the isolate New Englander wrote in *Walden*, "but westward I go free." He thought his forests extended to the setting sun, but larger landscapes lay west. Ten thousand years before a New England pond became our metaphor for life lived in the natural world, a great lake covered western Utah, southern Idaho and eastern Nevada, and the land that is now Salt Lake City bubbled a thousand feet below the surface of the water. Then the level of the lake's water fell below the level of its outlet and it began to dry up, leaving, today, salty Utah Lake and the Great Salt Lake to preserve its bitter dregs. The shoreline of Lake Bonneville, as it came to be called, still runs for hundreds of miles high up on the mountainsides. Emigrants used that shoreline in places for a natural road. Early explorers mistook Lake Bonneville's salty remains for an inland extension of the Pacific Ocean and searched in vain for a salt river flowing west. They found none, did not for years comprehend that west of Utah rivers do not flow, as rivers ought, to the sea, but spread out into alkaline sinks where their waters evaporate into the desert air. Clyman knew, another strange novelty.

And earlier still, a massive faulting of the earth's crust forced the edge of Nevada down below California and thrust up the Sierra Nevada, sheerest of mountain ranges. Gabriel might have raised it there, barricade before paradise. Who today would walk across those mountains? Yet farmers and businessmen did, and so did their children, only a child and a grandchild ago.

Old geology. It should remind us of where we are, and how recently we came here, and how tentatively we have settled. The astronauts' clever photographs are deceiving; from any near vantage, our planet isn't small. We live on its surface as ants might live in a penthouse garden, relying on its first six feet of soil to sustain us, tunneling not much farther down for our minerals and oils. We live on the broad floors of old seas, or crowd together on shores worn away from ancient hills, or watch the sun rise late and set early among high mountains that are yet mere cracks in the earth's thick mantle, and below that mantle churns an ocean of oceans of basal magma and molten iron. Oozing up from cracks deep in the floors of our seas, those heavy liquids move our continents around as easily as flowing water moves autumn leaves, on a scale of time that we can measure but cannot, short of memory as we are, comprehend. The earth was here before us, and will remain after we are gone. We are not poisoning it; we are only poisoning that part of it that sustains us on its surface. For some unknown object never to be realized even by those the most fortunate.

Joseph Smith of New York discovered America, a place of latter-day saints. He could not believe so rich a continent had no human past. The visions came easy, the visits with the angel, the stone box half buried on a hillside, the plates of gold and brass. Easy, easy to record them, even tedious as they crowded on. The history of a people from 600 B.C. to A.D. 421. How they left Jerusalem, wandered the wilderness, built a boat, sailed to America, founded cities and nations. How Christ came here and showed the people his wounds and delivered again his parables, his sermon on the mount. The people straying again from grace and God destroying their great cities and roads and farms. The plates sealed up in the box on the hillside. A few of the people surviving, forgetting their knowledge of iron and the wheel, becoming savages, becoming Indians. Their traces in the lower

continent, the Aztecs, the Incas. An entire human history in the
New World sprung from Smith's visions and then the evidence
concealed, God flinging a city to the bottom of the ocean or underneath a mountain with a flourish of Smith's pen. It is as if
William Blake sat in upstate New York envisioning his *Prophetic
Books*, but Blake had no church rich in property and followers
grow up to honor him. It needed Americans to believe such visions, to become latter-day saints. It needed a history of the land
they would occupy large as the land itself and Jesus brought over
on a thunderbolt to bless it.

The Saints marched into Utah on a trail the Donner Party cut.
Cut, twenty able-bodied men, swearing and sore, through the
Wasatch Mountains, and gave up cutting three miles before they
were through, forced their oxen and their wagons up a steep
canyonside rather than cut more. The Saints came over the mountains to a desolate valley where one lone tree grew beside a lake of
salt, a valley desolate enough, Brigham Young hoped, that no one
would ever bother them again. Smith murdered in Illinois in the
Carthage jail, riots in Independence, riots in Illinois. The Saints
made the desert green, a fertile hideout.

A pall of smoke suspended on the cold lake air covers the Great
Salt Lake, waste from the smelting stacks of the Kennecott Copper Corporation dug like an amphitheater for giants into the hills
at the lake's south shore, waste from the stacks of a steel mill
twenty miles down the road, waste from automobiles moving
steadily up and down the valley. The guide at the beach says no
one can touch Kennecott Copper, the state's biggest taxpayer.
Nor the steel mill, apparently. You could buy this state for a million dollars, an attorney in Salt Lake City says, gone dreamy on
Coors beer. The lone tree the Saints found in the valley, a
businesswoman says, was chopped up and sold in pieces to raise
funds. Her son will be a missionary for two years, carrying the
story of the Saints to the gentiles beyond the valley. Kennecott
Copper's two stacks could be filtered for less than twenty million
dollars.

The Wasatch gleam with snow, a landscape of glory for the city
socketed into their foothills, fine houses on the foothills, a golden
temple in the heart of the city. *This is the place*, Brigham Young
said when he saw it, fresh from a briefing with Jim Bridger. Fish
from the mountain streams die in the Salt Lake and wash up on
its shores: trout, catfish. Only brine shrimp live in the lake, thou-

sands of tons seined out annually and boiled up to make tropical
fish food for America and the world. The Donner Party camped
on the lake's south shore by twenty curious wells, holes in the
ground filled to the brim with fresh water that filled up again
when you dipped water from them. A man from California told
the party to cross the desert straight instead of going around. The
Saints, coming over the next year, crossed no desert, stayed east of
it and made their portion green. Copper ore is sold at the beach
of the Great Salt Lake, and jars of perfectly spherical sand, and
crystals of salt. On an island in the lake a pleasure palace sits
empty and rotting, its great roller coaster long ago burned down,
and on another island buffalo and antelope forage on the edge of
the strange water. In the city, on a weekend, a party of married
couples getting away from home and children check in at our
motel and lie long afternoons beside the blue pool eating pizza
and drinking beer. We ask one of the couples to dinner in our
room, order hors d'oeuvres, and some unknown chef, bored on a
Sunday night in Salt Lake City, makes up a mammoth tray of
shrimp and olives and rolled ham and cheese and fresh salads. It
is dinner enough, and the talk is good of Saints and sinners. Beside the gray and turgid lake you lick salt from the back of your
hand and find no seashells on the shore. Its salinity reached its
maximum in 1958. It is fresher now, a little fresher.

Kennecott Copper muzzles in the earth, throwing back humps
of black slag. On a holiday, they close the liquor stores in Salt
Lake City. The Wasatch water the valley, keep the golf courses
green, guard the eastern flank. Moroni and Mormon, dead Americans now become angels, keep watch. Here Christ will come again
in glory and lay the gentiles low.

On the Great Salt Desert, lakes of our imagining float above the
black highway and spread across the white salt to our north and
south. On the Great Salt Desert, William Eddy of the Donner
Party saw twenty William Eddys stumbling before him on the
second day, and the oxen's feet broke through the salt crust to the
bitter waters of the sinks. They knew then, the people of the
Donner Party, must have known, knew what was in store for
them. They crossed the desert in September, following the Californian's misleading trail, and saw their two-day forced march
stretch into three and then into four. James Reed lost his Prairie

Parlor Car and all his goods and most of his oxen. The shoreline of Lake Bonneville looked ironically down. At a new rest station in the salt flats two highway engineers who knew their history well pointed out Pilot's Peak to us, the peak toward which the Donner Party had driven, then walked, then stumbled and run, knowing at last that water was even farther from them than that distant hill.

The desert spreads inviolate beyond the highway. The trails of the Donner wagons still scrape it in their antique ruts. It is a giant bone, the earth's skull scalped and bleached by the Indian sun, and the air above it shimmers with the hallucinations a dying skull might bleed. It humbles men now; once it broke them, revealed to them, earnest of the crossing, the crouching animal inside their own skulls.

To leave that landscape, to drive up into treeless and sage-covered hills, and to encounter then, at the Nevada line, a flourishing casino, was to see again how we perch, birds on a twittering machine, atop the surface of the earth. In a land of endless sun we found people pale as cave dwellers pulling and pulling on the tireless and cynical levers of chromed machines. Children hang so on their mothers' arms, receiving as irregularly a coin or two of quiet. We ate quickly and drove ahead, crossing most of Nevada the same day. The highway rolls out straight as a wire until it approaches a mountain, curves then around it in a faultless curve and runs straight again to the next mountain. Ground squirrels, nothing better to do, fling themselves at your car, and occasionally a small town exits off the interstate. Painted cattle guards police the exits, but no cattle can be seen, or even sheep, only the gray sage, only the red mountains that serrate the state, the mountains around which the Donner Party wandered desperate and dry for half of October while the nights grew cold. In Nevada, small towns paint their names gigantically on mountainsides, the interstate narrows to two lanes and creeps through the centers of towns to sustain the trade, and outside the towns there is land to burn if anyone cared to burn it. The Sierra, the continent's western barricade, robs Nevada of water and robs it thus of life. And since Americans live there, they respond by bringing in the shining machines that supply Nevada with its greatest natural resource, gambled coin. Nevada maintains its perfect highways because they lead to only two places, to Las Vegas and to Reno, both sited just below the Sierra to entice Californians eastward over the mountains again. By such craft the state has achieved what few other states in the Union have even dared to consider: it has preserved much of itself as a natural wilderness, free even today from the heavy taint of man.

We watered at Winnemucca. My daughter bought an Indian headdress, we ate, we slept, and then we went on, soon to meet the Truckee River, east of Reno, a silver latchstring hung out all the way from Lake Tahoe to guide us, if the great wire of the highway wasn't enough.

The Truckee winds and twists and turns, a rush of clear water descending to arid Nevada from Lake Tahoe, that sample Bonneville high in the Sierra. In the Donners' day, explorers thought the river was outlet to what was then called Truckee Lake, the lake to which the Donners later gave their name and around which they camped that fatal winter of 1846. Truckee, kindly Indian chief, one of Nevada's original settlers, told parties of emigrants to follow the river to the high lake; beyond the lake rose the pass over which thousands of Americans would cross to California. Now the river is Truckee, and the little logging town just east of the lake is Truckee, and the lake is Donner and the pass is Donner, though it might as well be Gold or Silver or Emigrants' for all the history it has seen. Tragedy has its reward, poor enough pay for the suffering the Donner Party endured. Truckee Meadows, where the party camped too long so they could recruit their hungry oxen, is now Reno, and hardly a blade of grass in sight, but higher up the older landscape remains much as it was a hundred years ago, altered only by the broad fills and cuts of the interstate. Beside the highway, at a point three miles west of Truckee, rest still the remains of one cabin's worth of Donner emigrants, a little hatch of a bronze marker clamped down over their heads, and the cars and trucks speed by. So we live, in layers, never having been a people to fool with skulls, *memento mori*, on the mantelpiece.

We stayed at Lake Tahoe, in a pleasant cabin with an electric-blue roof, all but alone at the end of the winter off season. The lake exacts its tributes, a body of water nearly a thousand feet deep, so clear and blue that you can see the Sierra's granite boulders thirty feet below the surface in the sloping bottom off the shore. A Sierra lake is no child's wading pool, certainly not this huge one filled up from the base of the mountains. Fifty years ago, entrepreneurs carted two ocean-going steamships up the mountainside and assembled them at Lake Tahoe. Both now lie sunk at the bottom of the lake, ocean-going or not. One imagines Tahoe in wintertime, gray and chill while the Sierra snowstorms batter it and pile fifteen feet of snow on its shores, its waters a frigid 39 degrees. The Donners were wise not to have visited it; with their luck they would have fallen in. But in early summer it blooms into beauty, its shores yellow with pine pollen. On one of its beaches my children built a city of miniature rivers and houses and cars, a water-soluble imitation of what developers with the best of intentions and an eye for harmonious design are doing to Tahoe's North Shore now that the South Shore is a meretricious wasteland of casinos and bars. The North Shore outran its sewage-treatment capacity a year ago and has lately held up building permits until new plants can be installed. In ten more years it will be a rim of condominiums, another American place sacrificed to our urge to get away from it all.

In the meantime, Tahoe contends with its hippies, the *avant-garde* of the away-from-it-all. They linger by the roadsides, their bedrolls on their backs, listlessly thumbing rides they do not expect to get from automobiles they only formally disavow: they could hardly wander without them, unaccustomed to the work of walking. They seem, there in the cold mountains, most forlorn, acting out guerrilla theater on the roads and beaches, skirmishing at the safe edges of an invisible war, the boy shuffling down the middle of the road grudgingly moving to the grade to let a car go by, the boy sticking out his tongue next to the restaurant window at the businessman glaring at him from inside, the young teen-age girls bravely following their older men and bearing because they must the angry or lustful stares of the middle-aged men who pass them on the sidewalks. They live as they live because it is possible to live that way in America today despite their rhetoric of revolution. Theirs is no revolution but a marginal retreat, a simple and old-fashioned pulling of fat off the continent's incredible bounty. Their sadness, their despair, their lack not only of power but even of the knowledge of how to achieve it or of interest in the achieving, testify to their acceptance of the world as it is. They exist in a state of psychic hibernation, awaiting some better age.

Each day, I drove over a mountain from Tahoe to Truckee and

beyond Truckee to Donner State Park, wondering, as I have wondered since I began thinking of the Donner Party as some archetypal America in a minor mode, what led this inexperienced group of prosperous farmers and businessmen to brave so terrible a journey. California's fertility could not have been enough: they lived in fertile Illinois and Missouri to begin with.

Then I paced off the distance between the cabins. The Donner Party reached Truckee Lake in the first hours of a snowstorm that would bury the pass in thirty feet of snow, and the ground around the lake in fifteen. They found a cabin left behind by young Moses Shallenberger two years before, when he had been forced by similar snow to camp at the lake for two lonely months. They built, as quickly as they could, an addition to that cabin and two other cabins nearby. They panicked; they knew their doom; they huddled together there on the mountainside. Yet two of the three cabins at the lake are spaced more than seven hundred feet apart, and the third more than a mile from its nearest neighbor.

But assume for the sake of argument that the families that built those cabins so far apart did so from motives of distrust. George and Jacob Donner, two brothers who had lived and worked side by side all their lives, certainly had no reason to distrust each other. Forced to halt a few miles away from the other families, at Alder Creek, with no time to build cabins, they yet chose to set up their tents more than four hundred feet apart, across the creek. They could have gathered wood for only one fire, could have cooked one common meal, could have shared the work of nursing. They chose not to, driven even in their extremity to put distance between themselves. It makes no sense unless their need for territory was vaster than ours, and if you accept that assumption then you must also accept the assumption that some subtle process of erosion, some anonymous compulsion of nerve and blood and insensibility, has released us from their need for territory and enabled us to live in crowded cities and breathe poisoned air and jostle each other almost beyond endurance. And taught us to prefer it.

Nor can the process be reversed (though it might be modified) even if the people in our cities already knew the lifetime of skills necessary to live off the land. Having been, as a child, something of an amateur pyromaniac, I have liked lately to daydream of a benevolent nationwide conflagration, government-sponsored and

-approved, in which we all get together and burn down our cities and start over.* But we couldn't start over, if only because we have completely polluted our national water supply.

I had the advantage of the fishermen and campers who go to Donner State Park, for I had visited it before, in books, when no polite ranger guarded its gate, and I could people it with ghosts: Moses Shallenberger trying manfully to eat coyote and giving up in disgust; Patty Reed playing with her doll and eating strips of rancid hide pulled off the fire rug; Louis Keseberg, dark Bavarian, growling in his cave of a cabin mumbling human bones; Patrick Breen coldly refusing others food and noting the progress of madness and death like a recording angel; and over them all, the white burial of the Sierra snow. Oh, they were modern enough, people who decided, having read a book and heard a story or two, to go to California, a journey they undertook as casually as one might say, Let's go to the lake, or Let's go into town, when in fact they might have said Let's go to Tibet or the Amazon, they were that innocent of what such a journey entailed, that convinced that God in his wisdom would preserve anyone American by birth or American by choice from harm. And on the way they bickered, they quarreled, they accepted bad advice because the source of the advice had a necktie on, they—many of them—refused to share with each other when the need was upon them, and so half of them died most horribly of exposure and starvation. Yet they were also not modern, revealed the coarse soil of their birth, the toughness of the rural tradition in which most of them grew up: of eighty-nine people, half of them children, forty-one dead before they achieved the winter passage, none committed suicide: preferred slow death by starvation to suicide, preferred cannibalism to suicide. That fact alone must stagger us today with its implications of strength and of trust in the ultimate benevolence of life. There is no reason to believe we lack that strength and trust today, though we might have to dig for it. We may well need it before we are through.

In San Francisco, come down from the mountains late on a Wednesday morning, we checked into a motel at the edge of

* A similar vision, it seems, animates the Japanese architect Kenzo Tange, whose master plan for Tokyo, a city of some 12 million souls, proposes tearing the entire thing down and building a new one.

Chinatown and, as soon as we could, boarded a cable car for Fisherman's Wharf. The afternoon was to be the children's, but it became ours also. Even in early June, the wharf was crowded with tourists come to eat shrimp and crab and to play in that adult playground. On the sidewalks, protected by wooden roofs, vendors sold paper cups of shrimp and displayed pale coral crabs. Green lobsters struggled to find footing on beds of shaved ice, and over it all blew the air of the salt and iodine sea. Behind the row of restaurants, on the wharf itself, fishermen coiled their lines in wicker baskets. Near the launch ramp, where a dredge worked to deepen the channel, a charter boat loaded long-haired Indians for the ride to Alcatraz, the island they claimed and temporarily occupied. An outdoor stand on the wharf behind them expelled gusts of garlic, so that they seemed launched on an aromatic breeze to their labor of reclamation. "Did you see the Indians?" asked our Italian waiter at Alioto's, as any Westerner might have asked any stranger come into town a hundred years ago. Yes, said the children, gravely coiling spaghetti onto soup spoons, we did. They seemed disappointed that Alcatraz's free occupants had no feathered headdresses on, an oversight in their education I have worked to correct.

After lunch we boarded—receiving ticket stubs from a bearded sailor—the *Balclutha*, a nineteenth-century iron square-rigger now permanently docked at the wharf. She whaled; she traded; she grained; she fought her way around Cape Horn; she made the Alaska run and carried tall timber to the shipyards of New England; she ran aground off the Alaskan coast; finally the San Francisco Maritime Association fitted her out as a floating museum. My midwestern children, who had never been aboard anything larger than a twelve-foot sailboat before, made her their own. They rang the ship's bells, pulled the great wheel, winched the anchor winch, and clattered through the decks to the hold, still stocked with wooden crates and ballast barrels. The *Balclutha* shone with varnished railings and hand-pegged floors and smelled of pitch and brass and hemp and iron. She must have been a fine ship for sailors, built in Scotland after that country's forests were gone, her great iron mainmast buried like a challenge thrown down from heaven to the very basilica of the hull. Melville's massive blubber hooks hung on one deck, and a once-obscene bas-relief from naughty San Francisco leaned nearby, a nymph and satyr disporting sans genitalia, their mutilation decreed by a decency committee long ago. Whatever their public image, the Victorians of America and of Europe were in some ways far less prudish than we. Which of us could cut up a whale, or live at night with the smell of our own urine and night soil urging up from under our beds? They lived—the sailors, the fishermen, the drivers of oxen and dealers in trade—harder than we, and did it younger. Their portraits—the *Balclutha* displayed many—they took seriously, men in black with mustaches and beards grown early to hide their youthfulness, frowning as manfully as they could muster out at the varnished wooden box of the camera. If they seem larger than life now, it is because they tried to be larger than life then, braving the deserts and mountains and seas they crossed, braving the loss of their young to any disease that casualed by, braving surgery without anesthesia and love driven through a convention of last names between even man and wife. Yet the *Balclutha* would have given them security within her iron hull; she floats today, docked next to the feeble tin machines parked on the street, as a monument to a time when a few things at least were built to last.

We left her reluctantly, my wife and I, both of us in love with the sea. The children raced down the ramp under the baleful eye of the salty ticket taker, and after more sidewalk touring we stopped to drink at a German bar where a black myna predictably named Blackie perched in a cage above the smoke whistling at the patrons and obviously convinced that he was in charge, since after all he hung high above the rest of us, Father Mapple in ecclesiastical black with a sermon or two in his craw. An entertainer in lederhosen played an electronic accordion, and standing at the bar, a young German, blond and blue-eyed and muscular, put his dimpled chin in the air and closed his eyes and not so much heard as smelled, breathed, the polkas and Edelweissen and Danubes the accordion evoked. He might have been standing in an Alpine ski lodge in 1938 savoring empire. Along the way to the bar the children had acquired monumental all-day suckers; they licked them gravely and looked around to eyes that honored their sun-bleached hair. Most of the people in the bar were heavy, filling the narrow chairs and bar stools to overflowing, yet the heaviness implied muscle as much as fat, and who were these people transplanted from Bavaria to San Francisco drinking deeply of the Old Country on a sunny Wednesday afternoon? If Fisherman's Wharf were in Disneyland they would have been animated plastic Germans with coloring too high along the cheeks and a tendency to practical jokes, but this was San Francisco and the people were real.

On, then, on this tour of people's museums, to the Wax Museum, with figures courtesy an imitator of Madame Tussaud's. We might have visited many uplifting places in San Francisco, I know, but we were savoring the vernacular this trip.

Whatever recent judgment the outside world has rendered, in the museum you may still adore Jack and Jackie, Jack standing there next to George Washington looking like Peter Marshall delivering a Senate prayer, Jackie plain in a black suit, white gloves in hand, her hemline unfashionably below the knee, Eleanor bravely behind Franklin seated in a chair, and in the limelight, between the flags of the presidency and the nation, Lyndon Baines Johnson. Nixon, so far as Tussaud's is concerned, hasn't yet arrived. One wonders what expression his anonymous creator will choose to give him. Lyndon looks oriental, and surprisingly without guile—not a very good likeness, all in all.

And the other saints of the people's pantheon: Brigitte holding up a towel to her naked front, her wax butt peeking behind from a mirror; Liz, looking fifteen years younger and not half so glorious as she looks today, in the time of her time, seated with her five husbands resurrected around her, all holding uncharacteristically empty champagne glasses; Einstein and Freud, Mussolini and Hitler, Willie Mays and Joe DiMaggio, Al Capone and a federal agent dressed like Humphrey Bogart; Winston Churchill staring out at us (*then* they come alive, when their glass eyes look at you directly, and they slip in and out of existence in the space of a blink like those optical illusions we all found in comics and schoolbooks as children, and you catch your breath and for a moment believe that Winnie really is alive behind the glass). We, the people, we worship *size*, the space a man or a woman takes up in the universe, fair or foul. Let the children enjoy their Long John Silvers and Sleeping Beauties: grown, we invent giants and monsters and princesses too, whatever claims we may have made, these recent modern years, to sophistication and maturity and even to ennui.

The museum has its basement, just as we do, just as the Donner Party did, that place where fantasy runs into nightmare,

except that the basement is as real for the race as it was for the
Donners, pure violence acted out in the name, usually, of the
Higher Law. In the museum, heads roll from the guillotine to
make official the French Enlightenment, the rack stretches another Spanish heretic in the name of the Church, a man screams
silently from the double hook on which he hangs live in the name
of Allah. Beside such horrors, electrode-studded Boris Karloff
seems an old and trusted friend, the Wolf Man in need of a
shave, the Mummy, as he always seemed to me, the patient of a
physician or a nurse who went too far. My son is furious not to be
allowed to see these ultimate demonstrations of man's inhumanity
to man, but I who do not believe in censorship find myself forbidding him the material for more nightmares than he can whip up
on his own.

It is a most allegorical museum, we discovered then, because up
from the basement of horror, past the street level of distinguished
and notorious humanity, we ascended on carpeted stairs to a hall
of religions, there to be treated, with music appropriate to a California mausoleum, to the religious leaders of the ages: irritable
Moses examining a tablet of commandments, Buddha in his garden, Christ at the Last Supper (holding, as do the Twelve, an
empty glass tumbler of the sort motels provide) and, in another
diorama, delivering the Sermon on the Mount to an unlikely
collection of auditors: a turbaned African, a pale and aged Nordic
who might have fled from a Bergman set and shriveled under a
Bergman curse, a blue-eyed American girl, the peoples of the earth
gathered together as if Norman Rockwell had cast them for the
part. It is enough for us; we leave the way we came, a wax guard
directing us to the exit.

On then, to placate the boy, to Ripley's Believe It or Not Museum, and here, as on the *Balclutha,* I am home. So many American children, in those days that seem now so long ago, during and
before World War II, grew up on Ripley's and Richard Hallibur-
ton and Tom Swift. Ripley's was not some Pre-Cambrian game of
trivia to us, but the only kind of history we respected, a history of
fabulae, a history of the follies and monstrosities of mankind. We
knew, listening to the grownups talk Depression and then war,
that the world was strange and more than a little bizarre; Ripley
brought the truth home to us in concrete examples we could trust.
Believe it or not? Of course we believed it, as we believed the tales

we heard of the horrible offspring of a blond woman explorer and a gorilla, a half-human blond man-ape still roaming the African jungle, or of the suppression of Tucker's futuristic car by a jealous General Motors, or of the appearance of flying saucers in the sky. And here it all was, the calf with seven legs, one of them growing out of its back; the skeleton of a two-headed child born in Philadelphia and encased now in glass in Ripley's Museum after who knows what dark transactions with the mother who birthed it or the medical school that mounted it; shrunken heads courtesy the Jivaros, including the head of an oriental missionary (I saw one once that looked like a tiny Albert Schweitzer); a wax dummy of an English boy who aged eighty years in his first six and died, bearded and palsied, at the age of seven; drinking bowls made of human skulls; exotic carvings from the Mysterious East.

And most interesting of all to me now, the folk art of the recent American past, a room in Ripley's that ought to be labeled WHAT WE DID BEFORE RADIO AND TELEVISION. We didn't do much more, although we did it more intricately: we carved 364-foot wooden chains from a solid pine board, or fleshed out a full-color Last Supper painted in postage stamps, or dried apples to create wizened doll faces, or made typewriter paintings, fish-scale flowers, nut sculptures, or stitched clothes for fleas. You cannot visit Ripley's without concluding that the human animal will do almost anything to fill time. It isn't the Puritan ethic; it's the way our brains work. The Orientals keep as busy, if Ripley's ponderous oriental collection is any measure: grow giants who write fairy tales and midgets with thirteen-foot queues, drill holes in their heads to carry candles on the nightwatch, construct prayer wheels to add up chits in heaven, carve ivory or cherry-tree roots. Their occupations were hallowed by tradition, ours were not, which is perhaps why we traded them in so willingly for newer pastimes, for garage sales and decoupage and Carson and Cronkite. A reasonable trade, I suppose: what do you do with a 364-foot wooden chain?

San Francisco, it seemed to me after our afternoon's wanderings, is well on its way to becoming a city that adults might bear, and where a few, tucked away on the sides of Telegraph Hill, might even live. The Chinese, proud and individualistic and adaptive people that they are, have had the best of it and may even keep it, but the casual visitor realizes quickly enough that the city is alive around him and intends to stay that way, cable cars and incredible 40-degree grades and all. Below the city they have stopped filling in the harbor, and within the city itself, life is as good as city life can be. A brother of mine who lives in Los Angeles speculates that people who want privacy and room may well, in the next half century, have to adapt themselves to life in the Canadian wilds or north of the arctic circle, but perhaps not; perhaps we will live in our suburban wastelands and pilgrimage, periodically, to enclaves of reality like San Francisco, where, by then, they may have decided to add more cable cars and ban the automobile entirely, and where, in the sun of day and the fading light of evening, grownups may happily play.

We had come west, we thought, to visit, but no American ever went west to visit: he went west to find a wilderness of his own. We found ours at last, three hours south of San Francisco, but to understand what we found you must understand what wilderness once was, in California and in America. John Muir, knowing that it was already behind him, described one version of it:

> When California was wild, it was one sweet bee-garden
> throughout its entire length. . . . Zones of polleny forests,
> zones of flowery chaparral, stream tangles of rubus and wild
> rose, sheets of golden compositae, beds of violets, beds of mint,
> beds of bryanthus and clover, and so on, certain species
> blooming somewhere all the year round. . . . The Great
> Central Plain of California, during the months of March, April,
> and May, was one smooth, continuous bed of honey blooms, so
> marvelously rich that, in walking from one end of it to the
> other, a distance of more than four hundred miles, your foot
> would press about a hundred flowers at every step.

This is one wilderness today, one wilderness 1970, where at last we came: Punta de los Lobos Marinos, point of the sea wolves: Point Lobos, a state reserve just south of Carmel-by-the-Sea, on the Monterey Peninsula, down the coast from San Francisco: 1,250 acres that one literate visitor called "the greatest meeting of land and water in the world." You drive through a simple entrance into pines. The cool air forces your windows down. A ranger takes your car fee and gives you a brochure. You drive a

shaded road, slowly, thinking yourself in an ordinary park, and
then a wary but unfrightened doe stands suddenly in the road before you, looks back over her fawn shoulder at your car, nuzzles
the dust of the roadway, casually moves on. At a circle of gravel,
you park, get out, take a foot trail toward the point. Wildflowers
grow so thick that you cannot see the ground and the surf crashes
through narrow caves and canyons to break before you far from
the shore. Sea otters bark from their island off the point, and at
some seasons, the brochure says, you may watch gray whales glide
past you to a union far to the south, a union that is no concern of
yours. The blue sky races mirages of sail overhead, puffs angling
on a fleecy tack. Ground squirrels feed from your hand. The rare
Monterey cypresses, gnarled by ocean storm, black out fantastic
shapes against the sky, a man erect dancing with three naiads, a
lust of matted hair, skeinings of branches, gray-bleached skeletons
of tangled limbs. Red rocks layered with charcoal, the strata of
dried oceans, rise up to remind you of the planet's age, carvings of
rock subtler and bolder in their random creation than the boldest
and most subtle carvings of men, and, breaking against them,
carvings of water, the spume flashing in the sun, that humble you
with their indifference to permanence, their casual indifference to
passing time.

You leave the rocky point and return to the path, and realize
then that in this wilderness of 1970 you are bound within wire-
edged walkways, pledged not to pick one flower or disturb one
stone, to harm no creature, to smoke no cigarette, hardly to
breathe if you can help it. And realize that we are now what we
always were: creatures who should not be allowed to touch a wilderness because, having touched it, we will destroy it if we possibly can. So we are not of the wilderness, however much you, I, all
of us may yearn for it. We are not Indians gliding through the
forest. We are, whatever the evolutionists may say, some yet
unexplained separate creation, most bloody and until recently
most unbowed. The Indians whom Sutter sent out to help the
Donner Party across the mountains, Luis and Salvador, drew
apart from the Forlorn Hope, the first gang of Donners to cross
the winter pass, when they saw the Hope eating each other: could
not comprehend a race of people who would sink even in starvation to what the Indians thought such depravity: and for their
gentle qualification Luis and Salvador were shot and eaten in
their turn.

And wired away now from our wilderness, realizing as a murderer must realize after the act of murder how completely we have destroyed what we most deeply loved, we decide that the time has come for the destroying to stop. Because now, Donners all, we understand that we are destroying the one creature who really matters: ourselves, each other, the man or woman or child or children we love. The water is full of mercury and arsenic, the air of monoxide and lead. DDT builds up in our bones, and radioactive iodine in the glands of our children. And the wilderness is guarded by wires.

And now that we know we are truly destroying ourselves, the images all go to green, having been red before as a night battlefield flared by fatal shells. Now we go to green, become conservationists, docile and humane. Now we are signatories of the whole earth. It has got to be the irony to end all ironies, this docile greenness lately sprung among our consciences. Our very teeth, incisors and canines and bovine molars, attest our ambivalence. The Donners didn't brave the Sierra for bravery's sake, nor for glory's; they merely thought it their natural right to ride into wild California and make farms and factories where there had been no farms and factories before. They strike terror in us even today because they didn't, as we have for two hundred years routinely done, merely rape the wilderness that spraddled before them, but suffered it like animals.

Whatever the Sierra Club says, the wilderness won't save us, is not the preservation of the world, is something to love and protect as we do our other pets, but won't preserve us. We will make the continent a garden, not a wilderness, or we will make it nothing at all. Because we want to get on with facing the real wilderness, the only one that has ever challenged us, the wilderness of our own brains. *That* is the one that is always on the strech. It promises Sierras that beggar imagining.

"A Great River Passing Forever": The Mississippi

Of time and the river: all who have sought the Mississippi have found something more, have found their own sources and outlets, as if the river were a god or the oracle of a god. Mark Twain as Huck Finn, on the church of his raft: "It was kind of solemn, drifting down the big still river, laying on our backs looking up at the stars, and we didn't even feel like talking loud, and it warn't often that we laughed, only a little kind of a low chuckle." T. S. Eliot, St. Louis boy englishing his childhood awe: "I do not know much about gods; but I think that the river/Is a strong brown god. . . ." William Carlos Williams, tough baby doctor sprawling loose before the New World, the New World for him a goddess in wondrous bloody lust baiting priapic De Soto: "And in the end you shall receive of me, nothing—save one long caress as of a great river passing forever upon your sweet corse." De Soto's men, fearful that the Indians would discover by their leader's death that he was not the god they thought him to be, cased him like a nut in a hollowed cottonwood log and dumped him into the river, where he perhaps became a snag, became a towhead, became an island midstream and then was duly washed away to the Gulf, detritus of conquest, discoverer dissolved by the flood he discovered, as are we all. No man steps twice into the same river. Not even his own.

> I'm wukin' my way back home,
> I'm wukin' my way back home,
> I'm wukin' my way back home, Baby.
> I'm wukin' my way back home.
> Timber don't git too heavy fo' me,

An' sacks too heavy to stack,
All that I crave fo' many a long day,
Is yo' lovin' when I git back.

The Mississippi River drains nearly half the contiguous United States. Its tributaries head as far east as Pennsylvania and New York, as far north as Minnesota, as far west as the Continental Divide in Wyoming and Montana. It carries the runoff of 1,245,000 square miles of land into the Gulf of Mexico. If you count the Missouri as its main branch—Twain makes the point at the beginning of *Life on the Mississippi*—it is the longest river in the world. In places, more than a mile wide and as much as two hundred feet deep. Muddy, but not so muddy as most of us imagine: though it annually transports some four hundred million tons of silt and gravel downstream, slowly working to level the continent, its volume of water is so tremendous that all those tons of earth represent an average of only six hundred parts per million of its total load. That is a tenth of the Missouri River's average. China's Yellow River, by contrast, often carries a weight of earth greater than the weight of its water. In low water, above the mouth of the Missouri at St. Louis, the Mississippi is sometimes as blue as the Danube. It is turbid not because of mud but because it carries suspended within it tiny grains of sand that efficiently reflect sunlight on the wavelengths of the human eye.

Nor is the Mississippi busy at delta-building, as the Nile was before the Aswan High Dam choked it, as the Tigris and Euphrates are today at the rate of 160 feet a year. The Mississippi's delta forms not outward but downward: such is the weight of the alluvium it has deposited into the Gulf below New Orleans that it has depressed the earth's crust there, and continues to do so today, tilting the block of crust downward and uplifting the coastal lands in the state of Mississippi. Numbers can hardly compass the volume of water the Mississippi carries. Bank-full, the lower river can handle one million cubic feet of water *per second*, and could water tens of thousands of New Yorks.

It heads in Lake Itasca, in northern Minnesota (though some have argued, successfully I think, that if early explorers had entered the North American continent from the west, they would have counted the headwaters of the Missouri River, in Montana, as its source—until St. Louis, the Missouri is the longer and more powerful stream). Unlike most rivers, within a few miles of leaving Lake Itasca the Mississippi begins meandering, wandering back and forth in its bed in a pattern dictated by the slope of the land and its composition, a pattern shaped by complicated pressures of water and earth into one of the simplest of all mathematical forms, the sine wave or connected S curve. It picks up the Wisconsin River—French explorers used the Wisconsin as a short cut to the Mississippi from the Great Lakes—then the Missouri, then the Ohio, the St. Francis, the Arkansas, running full and powerful now, then the Yazoo, then down into the bayou South and past New Orleans and another hundred miles out its three delta passes to the sea. A pantheon of smaller rivers enter it all along its way. It is not the Father of Waters but the Collector of Waters. From the Appalachians to the Rockies and over into Texas, from the Canadian border to the Gulf Coast, everything that rains from the sky, everything we pour and flush and drain, eventually runs into the Mississippi. The Great Sewer, one early observer named it who saw the dead trees and the black, bloated bodies of drowned buffalo it freighted by. It is the Great Sewer in spades today.

Once it emptied into an ancient river called the Teays. Ice-age glaciers pushed it south, connected it with the Ohio, and it found outlet into a belly of flat land that reaches up almost to St. Louis, the Mississippi Embayment, in ages past the farthest inland extension of the Gulf of Mexico. Down the middle of the Embayment, down a depressed line of bedrock called the Mississippi Structural Trough which is covered today with three thousand feet of alluvial soil, the Mississippi River ran in full course to the sea.

If huge natural forces are gods, the Mississippi is one of our greatest gods, and its mark is on our past. Relic species of fish and wildflowers that are found in the Missouri Ozarks do not occur again until the Appalachians. They are divided from themselves by the river, which also divided the dense forest that once covered eastern America, the pelt of God, from the prairies and plains of the West. Anonymous Mongolians who crossed the Bering Straits twenty thousand years ago, and discovered North America, first looked at the river through human eyes, stalking mastodon into the Embayment out of Ozark hills. It drowned De Soto's corpse and thwarted La Salle's visionary dreams. It defined the Louisiana

Purchase for Thomas Jefferson. Lewis and Clark poled it; Zebulon Pike explored its western reaches; it was turnpike and waterway to nineteenth-century America. Vicksburg's blood ran into it and the blood of Union men.

It nurtured the genius of Samuel Clemens. He returned to it joyfully, as a man returns to an oasis in an ill-favored land. "The Mississippi is well worth reading about," he began *Life on the Mississippi*, in words so understated they hardly make a sound. "It is not a commonplace river, but on the contrary is in all ways remarkable." He was not a man to gush. He saved his emotion for a later moment when he might explain indirectly what he felt for the river, he who had been a river pilot until the Civil War with its attendant dangers cut short his career: "Your true pilot cares nothing about anything on earth but the river, and his pride in his occupation surpasses the pride of kings." Like Huck, he lit out for the Territory, leaving the river behind. For the rest of his life he struggled with that decision, and more than once its consequences brought him low. Men who love a god must love him entirely. That is the least worship the god demands who might as easily claim your life.

The Mississippi has claimed lives, tens of thousands of them: De Soto's was only a marker after all. Count drowned *voyageurs*, their canoes overloaded with beaver pelts; count keelboat men coursing down drunk from Ohio; count escaping slaves and exploding steamboats and sailors cannoned out of gunboats in the Civil War. Count the victims of the river's huge floods. Three hundred thirty thousand people were rescued from roofs and treetops during the Flood of 1927, the flood Herbert Hoover called "the greatest disaster of peace times in our history." Count all the dead and you still have not begun to measure the river, but at least you may begin to know it as more than the steadfast Ol' Man of *Showboat* fame.

And know this also about the river: that unlike every other alluvial river in the world, it does not build up the land. The Yellow, the Po, the Nile build valleys to ever-higher elevations by washing the hills where they head into the valleys downstream. The Mississippi does not, because it is so large, because it is so deep. Even its continually changing meanders, once the river has cut through their necks and run on by, fill back in. You can see them from the air all along the Embayment, the snaking vines of the past river, memories of past courses solidified into soil as if they never were. The Mississippi is not an American citizen, has not settled here; like an oracle in this also, it is a traveler, it is only passing through.

Pollution threatens the lower river, pollution from the farms and towns and cities and industrial parks upstream, pollution from sixty refineries and steel mills and chemical plants at Baton Rouge—threatens, potentially, the Gulf of Mexico itself, which may die someday as Lake Erie died—but pollution is not the primary paradox of man's work on the Mississippi. That paradox is subtler, as befits a god. A paradox of first choices and last things. The river must be controlled if people are to live on its vast floodplain. But the river cannot be controlled. Not entirely. The price would be too high, and the effects unknown. The river is big as Nature herself. That is the paradox, that Nature is larger than any man-made controls, and includes them.

In Vicksburg, Mississippi, years ago, in grudging response to the Flood of 1927, which upset all their calculations, the U. S. Army Corps of Engineers built their Waterways Experiment Station. Civilian engineers had argued successfully that gauging the river, as the Corps in the past had done, wasn't enough to understand it, nor leveeing the river enough to control it: they must model it and try out their works on the models before they built them on the river itself. German prisoners of war built the most comprehensive of the river models at Jackson during World War II. Good duty, the colonel in charge of the Vicksburg Station says today. The Germans still hold reunions from time to time to admire their giant toy. Another model, now defunct but serviceable in its time, occupies an area the size of a football field at the Vicksburg Station. You can step across the Mississippi on the model as easily as you would step across a ditch. The Mississippi lady who guides you on the tour must call up first and ask the pump house to turn the river on. Here is Vicksburg, a short hike down the model is Natchez, and down farther the Atchafalaya flows in from the west. Trees of green wire tower above the river on concrete islands and along the *batture*, the land riverward of the levees. The levees themselves are scaled disproportionately high. They look like the walls of medieval forts. The model is a moment in the river's life, and it serves its purpose, but more subtle models await us indoors.

Today, to model the river, the station works on a larger scale along shorter sections. Inside buildings whose tin roofs cover an acre of land, garden bulldozers gouge out buff clay. To known measurements of the river, tinsmiths make templates that guide workers who build up the river bed by hand, flooring it with sand or powdered coal that duplicates the silt on the bottom. City water from Vicksburg pulses up over headbays and flows downstream, meandering, changing course as the real river changes, and into this model river the engineers insert locks and dams and jetties and watch the water flow. Engineers in rubber waders walk the river, clipboards in hand, or negotiate miniature barges through model locks with radio controls. It is reasonably accurate work, and it has saved American taxpayers millions of dollars among the billions that the Corps's work on the river has cost, but it catches the imp of fancy. It left me fancying that all our military men might live at stations mapped wtih giant games, and that the station compounds might be fenced with high cyclone fencing, the barbed top wires facing in. The Waterways Station has modeled Asian rivers in its time, and may model the Mekong Delta one of these days, if there is any delta left to model. Models cannot reproduce bomb craters, or the corpses of the Asian dead, no matter how many might litter the banks. There are degrees of madness: playing with models would be one of the lesser degrees if the models were not expanded again outward into the real world.

In one of Waterways' buildings stands a model of Niagara Falls. "We used this model to save the Falls," says the lady guide. Upriver from the falls stretches a power dam. "They shut off the Falls at night"—she means the real ones, not the model—"and store up water in the reservoir above the dam. They turn the Falls back on during the day for the honeymooners. Oh, and leave them on until the lights go out, about ten o'clock. They don't want to spoil the scenery for the tourists." She would be certifiable if her statement weren't true. The Engineers shut off Niagara Falls at night and turn them on by day for tourists. To generate electric power.

They would shut off the Mississippi if they could. Since they can't, they have set out to pave it. Dams on its upper reaches and tributaries, levees and diversion channels on its lower stream, contain all but the most enormous of floods. That work is nearly complete, and it cost us far more than it cost to go to the moon. But the Mississippi *meanders*, to its own whim, and a shifting channel threatens the expensive levee works and complicates shipping, so the Corps means to hold the Mississippi to its present bed. To that end, in low water, boats leave stations along the lower river laden with asphalt and concrete mats and fit them against the banks of the river where it works to cut those banks away, on the outside curves of its meanders. And mile after mile on the lower river, jetties jut out into the water, their ends marked with red buoys, deflecting the flow back within the channel. The channel still shifts, but its shifting is at least partly controlled, and river pilots who once rememorized the river every trip now have some assurance that it will flow approximately where it flowed before. But the process of adjustment goes on: engineering is a matter of adjustment, and of adjustments then upon adjustments; the tolerances are coarse, and the adjusting must go on, insuring a future for the Corps.

Men who turn Niagara Falls on and off like a tap aren't likely to leave the Mississippi River alone. A massive challenge elicits from such men a massive response, as we saw in Vietnam. Is it perverse of me to imagine that the Corps would bomb hell out of the river if they thought it would do any good? They planned as much for the successor to the Panama Canal until the Nuclear Test Ban Treaty scotched their plans. They were going to blast out a new canal with atomic bombs. Hell of a lot easier than dredging. Sorcerer's apprentices, the Corps, and seldom a sorcerer nearby to call a halt.

Here is a model of New York, Long Island, the coasts of Connecticut and New Jersey, and over there is a tide generator and fans to imitate the freshening wind blowing in from the Atlantic that mixes the salt with the less-than-sweet. Here is San Francisco-Oakland, there the Arkansas and the Red and the Rio Grande. They are modeling artificial harbors to be built up and down the California coast to accommodate supertankers. They are planning a navigable waterway into the heart of Texas. They never modeled Florida, more's the pity. The scale of that beleaguered shallow peninsula is too subtle to duplicate on less than the original itself.

But from building to building, indoors and out of doors, the Mississippi lady returns you again and again to sections of the Mississippi. It has been the Corps's greatest challenge, and its greatest reward, more dams, more jetties, more and more asphalt mats, higher and higher levees, and still today not controlled, still evading the turn of the magic tap. For that at least we may be thankful.

"One who knows the Mississippi," wrote Samuel Clemens more than a hundred years ago,

> will promptly aver—not aloud, but to himself—that ten
> thousand River Commissions, with the mines of the world at
> their back, cannot tame that lawless stream, cannot curb it or
> confine it, cannot say to it, Go here, or Go there, and make it
> obey; cannot save a shore which it has sentenced; cannot bar its
> path with an obstruction which it will not tear down, dance
> over, and laugh at. But a discreet man will not put these things
> into spoken words; for the West Point engineers have not their
> superiors anywhere; they know all that can be known of their
> abstruse science; and so, since they conceive that they can fetter
> and handcuff that river and boss him, it is but wisdom for the
> unscientific man to keep still, lie low, and wait till they do it.

It may once have been wisdom to keep still and lie low, but it is not wisdom any more. The mentality that fetters and handcuffs rivers is the same mentality that threatens to pollute the ocean and poison the air and salt the land, and the unscientific man finds more science walking beside a creek than the engineers yet teach in their schools, and he had damned well better not keep still if he and all the others like him want the earth to survive. The day of abstruse science is over, because nature is more abstruse yet, and evolved her academies over millions of years, and took short-term calculations of benefit into account and proved them wrong, made lush valleys into deserts and pushed ocean bottoms up into mountaintops and long ago worked her adjustments out. They can be modified, but they cannot be ignored.

Only consider one line of the Corps's work, one of its upriver dams. Silt that once the river carried away to the sea now piles up behind the dam. Imagine the extent of that silt, already one-third up on some dams, a hundred years from now. When it fills the reservoir, where will the floodwater go then? Ah, but the Corps is aware of that problem. It will solve it tidily: it will build another dam upstream. But upstream are not deep-carved canyons suitable for a dam but prairie and plain where the water spreads out across four, five, ten times as much land, and good land, too. The new dam is wider, the new lake shallower, and the silting there proceeds faster than it did in the canyon reservoir below. The threat, however, is removed for another generation. Where will the water go then? The Corps builds for today, not for generations unborn. The problem is here, in flooding now, not there, in silt-filled reservoirs fifty years hence. Thus the Corps's mentality matches the mentality of the industries that refuse to stop polluting because the river or the lake is not yet thoroughly dead, or because their competitors haven't stopped, or because the facts aren't all in, or because the cost is high and the dividends to stockholders correspondingly low, or because it's cheaper to advertise their concern.

There is a limit to adjustment. We are near that limit. We will have to do more than flatten our tin cans and exchange our detergents for soap and carry our bottles back to the store. We will have to do more than lie low. The river leads the way, past battlefields and unnamed graves.

Behind a bluff overlooking the Mississippi River at Vicksburg, trenches and redoubts now softened by green lawn barricade the town, marked with memorials of white marble glaring in the delta sun. The Mississippi ran red with blood, a guide says (it runs red today at Baton Rouge with bauxite waste from an aluminum-smelting plant—lead in that waste, and mercury, cyanide, ten or twenty other poisons—*in trace amounts*, the company environmentalist demurs). At Vicksburg, Grant unleashed the dogs of modern war, siege, trench and mine, espionage and flank attack and blockade, and the citizens of Vicksburg ran to tunnels cut back into the hills of wind-blown loess on which their besieged city was built.

The battlefield, now a National Military Park, is silent today, the enormous delta trees hardly moved even by the wind of summer, silent as a battlefield in the midst of battle when the ears can bear no more of gunshot and cannonade. Here ran a trench; there artillery boomed from behind earthworks guarded by sharpshooters; nothing now but mounds that might be burial mounds and the sod sealed over like skin grafted to hide an ugly scar.

With elegant foppery, the generals of the War of the Potomac lined up Union and Confederate opposite each other in open fields and marched them forward in European style, while ladies and gentlemen of Washington carriaged out to picnic and to watch, and men were merely pawns, firing and retreating in line, firing and retreating in line, until the setting sun stalemated the game and battle broke off to wait for picnic weather.

Grant had the sternness of his conviction, Grant counted the lives of common men precious, but he also had the stain of technology and could batter Confederate wives and children into tunnels, to make a point. Modern war is no worse, though technology has amplified it into bombers at fifty thousand feet and hungry, fatal mercenaries. Its paradox is the same as the paradox of the Engineers' work on the river, because both think somehow to improve human life with technology, but both are partial technologies that do not take the organism of nature, including man's own nature, sufficiently into account. Replace men with cannon, but pound the enemy's homes. Bind the river with dams and levees, but forget the silting of the reservoirs and the danger of settlement on floodplains, and pollute the river and the Gulf with metals and with oil.

Behind the Vicksburg bluff, closest to the river, lies the national cemetery marked with rows and rows of the anonymous dead, each body or fragment of body celebrated with a numbered brick of marble or a headstone inscribed UNKNOWN. The Army buried the dead together in shallow graves after the battle. They would have moldered there forever, but pigs rooted up the corpses at Shiloh. Country pigs rooted at the national conscience and the national cemetery system was hurried into law and at Vicksburg 16,600 corpses were unmatted and laid out in individual plots with no more identity than the earth that covered them. There is something cynical about this green and peaceful cemetery where between the numbered bricks the spaces for the bodies seem all too small. The men were buried in common while the war raged on and only later did the rooting pigs call us back to do the anonymous bones some minor honor. Twain found more to respect at Vicksburg than I. "Everything about this cemetery suggests the hand of the national Government. The Government's work is always conspicuous for excellence, solidity, thoroughness, neatness. The Government does its work well in the first place, and then takes care of it." But the dead lay unnamed at Vicksburg, and who in good conscience could repeat Twain's words today?

After Vicksburg, I visited another grave, searching for sources, a grave on a bluff like Vickburg's overlooking the Missouri River, a grave I had not visited for twenty years: my mother's. She died of a gunshot wound, by her own hand, during the despair of the Depression, in 1938, when I was one year old. Hers was a ghost I had never laid to rest, have only begun to lay to rest now, and like the soldiers' graves, her grave seemed too small to contain the enormity of her loss. I searched for most of an hour before I found it down a hillside, a wilted peony on the stone dropped there by someone who had visited the cemetery earlier that day and wept not only for her own dead but also for the dead whom no one had yet seen fit to mourn with flowers. But the name was carved on the stone, and the word WIFE, and the dates 1908 and 1938 with a hyphen between to call forth to those who mourned her the meaning of her years, if meaning there was. More at least than a number. More than the word UNKNOWN. How the families of the Vicksburg dead must have grieved to wander over the freshly sodded earth of the Vicksburg National Cemetery, after the speeches of dedication were done, and find no identification at all, and find only a field of corpses conveniently separated and numbered like parts in a warehouse. The government does its work well in the first place, and then takes care of it.

Of all the Corps's civil works, the Mississippi remains the most recalcitrant, will not be bound, and you must see that engineers do not sleep peacefully with the flood of the river roaring in their ears, must even dream of it sometimes who pride themselves on never dreaming at all, dreams being the very antithesis of order to an engineer, the very stuff of madness, though in truth they serve to keep us sane.

Think of Mark Twain, the public man who intended to make his mark on the world with a machine called the Paige typesetter, a machine with eighteen thousand moving parts in which he invested two hundred thousand dollars of Sam Clemens' earnings as a writer. He believed it would revolutionize typesetting; he intended it to make him a Whitney or a Rockefeller. It was a glorious machine, as machines go. It was Twain's mechanical man, and his undoing, which secretly he knew. It bankrupted him and

sent him around the world to play the clown at lectures when he
might have been home writing books. It was the node of his
neurosis, the focus of the division within himself. All his life he
was divided between the rewards of manipulating human beings
and the satisfactions of understanding them. Mark Twain worked
his machine; Sam Clemens visited the river.

Or think of the hills outside Vicksburg, hills of dense, deep
loess cut down vertically fifty feet or more to make room for highways and roads, cut so dramatically that you feel, driving between
the cuts, as if you were driving through a battle trench. Above the
cuts, the lush delta foliage laps at the edges like the water of the
river itself and the vines reach over for root they only barely cannot find. Change the angle of the cuts only a few degrees and the
vines would race down the hillside and lock across the road and
break it up and carry it away to the river and dump it in. Would
do that in the name of an order that has nothing to do with asphalt or the dozer blade. The dead at Vicksburg know, waiting
there underground impatient for Judgment Day and the return of
their names, and from seeds dropped over their corpses they have
pushed up live oaks and magnolia trees that sometimes encase the
stone markers themselves, seizing them within their trunks as the
law seizes evidence in a raid. So the river cuts at levees, its ten
million pressures resolved into sine waves as elegant as the paths
of missiles, and as unswerving.

                                            . . . almost forgotten
        By the dwellers in cities—ever, however, implacable,
        Keeping his seasons and rages, destroyer, reminder of
        What men choose to forget. Unhonoured, unpropitiated
        By worshippers of the machine, but watching, watching
                and waiting.

That is the river T. S. Eliot saw, the real river, the one Sam
Clemens could not deny, though Mark Twain urged him to, to
pay for his machine.

Steamboat on the river: the *Delta Queen*, met at night by one of
her stores boats run out from the wharf at Vicksburg. Passing us
first as we supplied a diesel tug, lit up like a distant carnival with

lights run around her decks, her glorious red paddle wheel slapping the water behind her and her steam whistle tooting twice as she beat on by. Straining up the river at five or six miles an hour, hugging the banks, staying out of the sweep of the channel, the pilot alert in the night to the Corps jetties buried under high water, his spotlight searching the water and the flooded banks. She is not as elegant as the old steamboats were, but she is the most elegant boat on the river today, a visitor to the Mississippi who made the Mississippi her home.

She was built in California for the Sacramento River trade; ran from Sacramento down to San Francisco in the last years of the custom that Johann Augustus Sutter began on Mexican territory 130 years before; served honorably, painted drab, as a ferry in World War II; was then crated and towed down the California coast and through the Panama Canal to New Orleans and then up to Cincinnati and a home berth. Plies the river now on weekend excursions for the young and on week-, even month-long excursions for the old who can afford the passage and the time. Charged with ghosts that enlarge her pacific pleasures of card games and quiet dancing and calliope hikes around the decks into something somber, stately, and irredeemably antique: ghosts of ages gone, ghosts of a time in American life when we made choices we must now unmake.

The Civil War ruined the river trade, discovered the uses of rails overland, changed the orientation of the continent from north-south to east-west, prepared us for industrialization. The Civil War put millions of men in ready-made clothes for the first time in their lives, gave them interchangeable rifles, taught them to eat out of cans, forced them to march together who always before had marched separately to different drums.

We might wish the South had won. The South fought to defend slavery, and in that it was terribly, tragically wrong; but the South also fought to defend the rural and the local, the homemade, and we must wish today it had won that battle even as we are glad it lost the other. Those today who defend the wilderness, the natural, against technology gone berserk, the Sierra Clubs and the Environmental Defense Funds, are only fighting the battle again, against worsened odds. The *Delta Queen* struggles to beat upstream where diesel barges laden with oil easily pass her by: the defenders of the environment could do worse than to take her for their standard. She is old and inefficient; her only excuse for being on the river is the excuse that she is scaled to human scale, and does not destroy.

By daylight, from her deck, because the water is high and the Corps's works submerged, you see the river as De Soto or La Salle must have seen it, brown water and willow-grown banks, and from Vicksburg to Memphis, a passage of two days and nights, hardly any work of man in sight. A single skunk pushing through the brush on shore can fill the boat with its fierce musk. In the early morning the pilot whistles deer to break across glades at the water's edge. Implacable mosquitoes swarm aboard at dusk as if they had waited like the passengers for the dinner gong. The sun sets red into the green willows as if it were setting into the sea.

If he had poled up the river instead of marching to it overland, De Soto would have thought the continent uninhabited. De Soto brought pigs to America, pigs that would later root up the dead at Shiloh. He fed his men from the river and knew its teeming life, catfish big as a man, paddlefish with snouts like ocean swordfish and mouths baleened to catch river plankton, their white meat fine as sole, their dark meat of a taste like the backwaters of the river under the banks late at night, a taste as yet unnamed.

Indians rowed out to challenge De Soto in forty-foot canoes hollowed from entire cottonwood trees, and since he came not to know the river but to dominate the men who lived on its flanks, he knew how to respond. The river he did not attend: it was only another obstacle. Crossing it must have put him in a fine funk; even on a boat the size of the *Delta Queen* you sense its aloofness to the parasites and symbiotes it carries on its back. It is as much a wall as Melville's Whale, and beyond that wall lurks nature itself. The paddle beats the water into successive vertebrae, peak and trough and peak and trough falling away behind, and you wonder in awe how many forms water can take, has taken, will take in centuries to come before it closes over us for the last time.

Charles Eads, the engineer who bridged the Mississippi at St. Louis in 1874 with a bridge the Corps said could not be built, the engineer who opened up the river's passes below New Orleans so that ocean-going ships might enter it from the sea, walked as a young man on the bottom of the Mississippi under a diving bell of his own construction, walked on the bottom of that rushing river some two hundred times. He heard the gravel, gravel big as cannonballs, bouncing off the bottom and arching up and jetting down to bounce again. He learned the might of the river and what it was made of, learned how to control it well enough that his bridge still stands and his passes are still open, but he must also have locked the river away in the cellar of his mind and never known the sleep of childhood again. You come back to earth and feel that nothing you do afterward will ever measure up, one of the astronauts is reported to have said. That is how Eads must have felt. To walk the bottom of the Mississippi is to have been buried under the waters of half a continent, baptism worthy of a Christ. Merely to work upriver on a boat, giant arms out of steam cylinders cranking the paddle wheel behind you, is to know something of that experience, to feel something of that dread, or else why, in the middle of the night, when the pilot of the *Delta Queen* abruptly cut the engines and the rhythm of the paddle dropped to a funereal meter half an octave below, did a crowd of passengers appear on deck in their nightclothes apprehensively started out of sound sleep?

The pilots know. They have pushed through the wall. As they beat up the river through the long day, the view is plain, water and trees, the boat shifting westward or eastward to avoid the channel, the water flowing on. Enlarge the Vicksburg models to full scale and in theory you control the river itself. But up in the pilothouse of the *Delta Queen*, Captain Howard Tate, the hired pilot, thirty-five years on the river and not, he says, enamored of it at all, is constantly at work at the two long steering arms that have replaced the big pilot wheel, adjusting them this way and that as if he were threading an invisible maze. He points to a line of water—that's a jetty—to a bulge of water—that's a shoal— threads behind an island to take advantage of its lee—all but brushes the trees on one bank—stays clear from shore on another. The water is alive with obstacles and dangers, including the works of the Corps. Tate is a pilot and knows them all, runs the boat through the night, in shifts with other pilots, as surely as he runs it through the day. Twain said all there is to say about the skill of Mississippi River pilots. I need only add that they are still there, on the river, doing their extraordinary work, but I must also add, by way of drawing a time line for us all, that there aren't five of them left under fifty years of age. One of those, not yet thirty, is captain of the *Delta Queen* this sailing, and was born on a

houseboat with a paddle wheel behind. He counts himself one of
the Chosen, modestly. He ought to: he is. "I wonder," wrote the
Trappist monk Thomas Merton, "if there are twenty men alive
in the world now who see things as they really are. . . . I don't believe that there are twenty such men alive in the world. But there
must be one or two. They are the ones who are holding everything
together and keeping the universe from falling apart."

Of time and the river: William Carlos Williams: "It must be realized that men are driven to their fates by the quality of their beliefs." Long ago, at the turning of the Civil War or perhaps before, we chose money and its technology as the mode of belief
with which we would deal with the continent we intended to
dominate, at whatever cost to our lives. Our fate today, pollution
and decay, is the fate we were driven to by that choice, a choice of
abstraction over association, of the mechanical over the living, as
at Vicksburg's siege. If the river awes, inspires, even terrifies, it
does so because it still runs half wild, splitting a continent in two,
and sometimes, on the river, all the works of our civilization seem
to fall away behind the screen of trees, leaving a space of room on
a carnival boat to assess those works for what they are.

They are ways we have attempted to cope with a world that
overwhelmed us, but coping is no longer enough, nor could it be.
The nineteenth century did not know it was merely coping. It
thought it had the world in hand. Our fate, our threatening fate,
has been to suffer the working out of that arrogance.

But the quality of our belief is changing, and today, two by
two, we board the carnival boat for other destinations. One of the
great historical shifts in sensibility is under way: it is what we will
be remembered for, not our technology and our wars. The ecology
movement is part of it, a vital part. That movement, preoccupied
with deadlines, has not yet had time to study its sources, has not
yet looked much beyond romantic naturalists like John Muir and
Henry David Thoreau and Aldo Leopold. Eventually it will locate
those sources among old gods, in religions older than Christianity
that worshiped the incredible and benevolent complexity of the
natural world. Humility is the quality of belief our sensibilities
today are seeking, the spirit that puts human worth before techno-
logical progress, love before manipulation, the local and related
before the universal and borrowed. And most of all, reverence for

life, reverence for life before pride of domination. Wars call us home: we have fought Nature for five hundred years, but she has no more yielded to our arrogance than Vietnam. Cannot be forced to yield, because the field is hers, the weapons and the combatants themselves subject to her laws. Clemens marked the vision at the end of *A Connecticut Yankee*. He choked his Yankee on the poisoned air of the battlefield where lay the dead of the industrial civilization he had created to bring Utopia to a world that has never needed Utopia, the Garden being already at hand.

Amid the century's carnage it has sometimes seemed too late. It must have seemed too late to men of the middle ages, when a third of Europe died of plague. It was not too late then: the light of the Renaissance broke through. It is not too late now: the rivers, the Mississippi River first among them, remain to remind us: that, like men if they have the courage to change, if they can move on from old graves and the rust of old arrogance, rivers run through roots, down to the restoring sea.

> *I'm wukin' my way back home,*
> *I'm wukin' my way back home,*
> *I'm wukin' my way back home, Baby.*
> *I'm wukin' my way back home.*
> *Timber don't git too heavy fo' me,*
> *An' sacks too heavy to stack,*
> *All that I crave fo' many a long day,*
> *Is yo' lovin' when I git back.*

The Death of the Everglades

The old man saw the lizard slip from under a bush in front of the drugstore where he had gone to test his blood pressure and saw it sprawl on the flagstone path beside the sidewalk and hunched toward it propping himself with his cane. He raised the cane over his head baring his teeth and jammed the cane down and pinned the lizard to the flagstone tearing its belly out and it twisted over, its four infant hands clutching the air and its mouth opening and closing and the man jerked the cane up and jammed it down and jammed it up and down until he had mashed the lizard into the stone. The black tip of his cane smeared now, the old man looked uneasily around and breathing hard set the cane to the walk staining the white stone red and lurched away, teeming Florida jerking across his narrowed eyes.

He didn't understand.
That the lizard was harmless?
Yes.
But he did understand. It wasn't harmless.
A lizard?
It was a fuse running back into the swamp. He put it out.
One of many fuses then.
We put them out whenever we can. They mean us no good.
They mean us no harm.
They mean us no harm. They mean us nothing at all.

The Everglades, the wilderness Everglades that was once the wonder of the world, is not dying. It is already dead. The shell is left, the shell of a wilderness, and should be saved. We save shells. They are symmetrical and can be understood. The silent things that live inside them are not symmetrical and cannot be understood. They must be taken for what they are or destroyed. They do not care if they are taken or not. They live and die in silence. The old man raged. The lizard never said a word.

I am not cynical. I am not wedded to death, though at one time I thought I might be. I do not know Florida as well as the men and women who live there who would save it from itself, but I know land, and know when it is failing. South Florida will be a garden or it will be a desert. It will never again be a wilderness. It is not a wilderness now. It is the rag left over when the wilderness wears away.

Amerigo Vespucci named this western continent with a name better than his own. In a letter to Lorenzo de Medici he called it a New World. It tore men's eyes open. They could not believe what they saw. On their maps they shrank it into comprehension. Leonardo da Vinci, the most visionary of Renaissance men, drew the New World as a string of islands. Jacques le Moyne, the first artist to visit North America, drew Florida smaller than Cuba and located the Great Lakes in Tennessee.

Men came to the New World to plunder. Later they came to live. They could choose to move through the wilderness and make it their own or they could choose to push it back before them, destroying it as they went. Having money and courage but lacking the genius that might transform them into a new kind of people, they chose to push the wilderness back. They chose to remain European, with European notions of land ownership and European beliefs in man's authority over the natural world. That is why, though we think of ourselves today as American, we do not think of ourselves as an American race. We are separate from one another. We are Italian or Polish or Black or Wasp. The only people in America who feel they belong to the land, and so to each other, are the people we call Indian. They are the people who made the wilderness their own.

You can easily locate the places that pass for wilderness in the United States. The United States Geological Survey has not yet found time to record them on its most intimate series of topographical maps, the 7½-minute series, scaled one inch to two thousand feet. Barrens of western Nebraska, Wyoming, Utah, Nevada, have not yet been mapped for the 7½-minute series. The Everglades from Lake Okeechobee to Cape Sable has not yet been mapped for the series, though a jetport almost rose on the edge of the Big Cypress Swamp, though most of the Everglades has been leveed and ditched for water storage, though canals have been cut for new towns near the Big Cypress' Fakahatchee Strand, though acres of Nike missiles point toward Cuba from the center of the national park. The Everglades is still officially a wilderness, but it has already been pushed back. It teemed once with life. It teems no more.

"How shall I express myself," the traveler William Bartram wrote from upper Florida in the eighteenth century, "to avoid raising suspicions of my veracity? Should I say the river (in this place) from shore to shore, and perhaps near half a mile above and below me, appeared to be one solid bank of fish, of various kinds, pushing through this narrow pass of the St. Juan's into the little lake, on their return down the river, and that the alligators were in such incredible numbers, and so close together from shore to shore, that it would have been easy to have walked across on their heads, had the animals been harmless?" Bartram saw alligators twenty feet long, with bodies, he said, big as horses'. The longest recorded in the twentieth century was thirteen feet.

Birds, countless millions of birds, came to Florida once from all the reaches of the world, so thick in the sky that they darkened the sun, so thick in the shallow rookeries that their droppings turned the brown water white for miles. At the height of Florida's trade in egret plumes, eighty years ago, one Jacksonville merchant in one shipment sent 130,000 egret skins to New York. The birds come now in shrunken numbers, fewer than fifty thousand of them a year, and many do not stay. Some species will never be seen again. They are extinct, and to understand the dead finality of that word you must imagine what you would feel if you were the last human being alive anywhere in the world.

The first pictures of wilderness America to reach Europe were Jacques le Moyne's drawings of savage Florida. For a time, Florida *was* the New World to European eyes. William Bartram's *Travels* fired the imaginations of the English Romantic poets, of William and Dorothy Wordsworth and of Samuel Taylor Coleridge. Coleridge read Bartram and dreamed of building a utopia in Florida. Young men in groups of twelve would sail there and work only half a day and discuss philosophy in the long afternoons. Coleridge never left the English Lake District, but Bartram's Florida worked its way into his opium dream and came out *Kubla Khan:*

> *Where Alph, the sacred river, ran*
> *Through caverns measureless to man*
> *Down to a sunless sea.*

Alph was a Florida spring. But the caverns proved treacherous. They were caverns of time, and we moved through them as if the only lives that concerned us were our own.

We took the land and made it ours. "After we had strooken sayle and cast anker athwart the River," wrote an early French explorer of Florida, "I determined to goe on shore to discover the same." Religion strengthened him. He was only a little lower than the angels. He was lord of the earth. The men who planned the Everglades jetport felt the same. "We will do our best," one of them wrote, "to meet our responsibilities and the responsibilities of all men to exercise dominion over the land, sea, and air above us as the higher order of man intends." You can hear the Great Chain of Being rattling in there, the old medieval hierarchy of stone and plant and animal and man and angel and God. The preservationists who fought the jetport down heard only greed, but the old belief in the sovereignty of man impelled men to discover America and justified our existence here for three hundred years. Those who hold that belief today cannot understand why others do not. They smell subversion.

"How," asks a broadside circulating these days in South Florida, "can anyone legally stop a useless land from becoming a community of churches, schools, hospitals, universities, playground parks, golf courses, and beautiful homes where thousands of precious children will be born and raised to be useful citizens?" That the swamps and floodplains are not useless, that they collect and store and purify all the water South Florida will ever have, that the worst thing that could happen to the region would be the addition of more thousands of precious children to its present load, are not assertions easy to prove.

"Before this century is done," Peter Matthiessen writes in the Sierra Club book *The Everglades*, "there will be an evolution in our values and the values of human society, not because man has

become more civilized but because, on a blighted earth, he will
have no choice. This evolution—actually a revolution whose violence will depend on the violence with which it is met—must aim
at an order of things that treats man and his habitat with respect." Nowhere in America is the conflict more directly engaged
than in South Florida. If its primeval wilderness is gone, its ecosystem is not yet irrevocably damaged. Birds still sing and trees
still grow. There is something left to save, a water supply and a
way of life. New and terrifying problems have not yet displaced
the old. Miami is not yet New York, nor Okeechobee Lake Erie.
But how much time remains for South Florida is a question on
which few people agree.

The Everglades was once a vast and grassy river. It began in the
flood-and-hurricane spill of Lake Okeechobee and flowed south
and southwest a hundred miles to merge with the ocean above
Cape Sable, on the southwestern tip of Florida. Sawgrass and
water and peat muck, a river fifty, seventy miles wide, bound on
the east by a limestone ridge and on the west by a broad and
shadowed cypress swamp, it looked like a marsh, but the water
flowed sluggishly down. One foot of falloff in ten months. An
inch and a little more a month. From new moon to new moon in
the summer the land might receive thirty inches of rain and fill
up like a tipped bowl. Alligators spread out then to feed, and deer
and the panthers that harvested them found refuge on hammocks,
tree islands shaped like longboats that interrupted the monotony
of sawgrass. In the late summer and early autumn, hurricanes
thrashed the sawgrass and tore the tops off the royal palms. The hurricanes dropped the last of the rains the land would see until summer came again. The water crept down the land or evaporated away
in the sun or transpired away through the pores of green plants and
trees. Disappearing, it concentrated the life that swarmed within
it, mosquito fish and killifish and crayfish and the larger predators
that lived on them, and the birds came to feed in the broth and
reproduce. The water level dropped lower and lower and alligators
dug out holes, tearing the grass and the peat away with their tails,
making room not only for themselves but also for a seed crop of
fish and turtles and frogs that would grow to populate the land
when the next rains came. The first thunderstorms of late winter
brought fire that burned away the old cover of sawgrass. On the

higher land, the fire destroyed brush and the shoots of hardwoods but left behind the corky, fire-resistant pines.

When the water that flooded over Okeechobee reached the mangrove estuaries that lined the coasts, it mixed with seawater, stirred by the tides. The brackish solution that resulted from the mixing was a thousand times more fertile than the sea itself, haven for adolescent pink shrimp whose shells gave the roseate spoonbill its color, haven for young fish that men would later hook for sport and net for food. Crowds of crocodiles swarmed in the deltas of mangrove rivers, the only place in North America they were ever found. The mangrove forest itself was one of the largest in the world, trees that reclaimed the land from the sea, trees denser on their islands and peninsulas than any rain forest.

Aboriginal Indians lived on the mangrove coast and hunted the Everglades, men who came down from the continental wilderness and exchanged their buckskins for breechclouts of woven palm engorged in back with the tails of raccoons, women who bared their brown breasts and hung their bellies with Spanish moss like tropical growths of pubic hair. They piled up mounds of feasted shells that later whole farms would occupy, roared out to slaughter the fat manatee, dug coontie root and learned to wash it free of its alkaloid and pound it into white flour, harvested the land and the ocean and threw the waste over their shoulders and moved on. In other mounds, they piled up their dead without ceremony until a dream of death came down the peninsula from the interior of America and then they saw through to the other side and began to leave tokens in the graves of those of their blood who would pass over. The idea of death brought an idea of life and they flowered out in decoration, scratched patterns on their pots, carved wooden deer heads with knives made from the teeth of sharks, pushed smoothed knucklebones through their earlobes, took scalps and arms and legs from their enemies. And these, the Calusa and Tequesta, greeted the Spanish when they arrived. Greeted the Spanish with poisoned arrows and night hatchetings, but within a hundred years all of them were gone, killed by new diseases or shipped off to slavery in Cuban sugar fields.

The Everglades was not fit to live on, not fit to farm. White men left it alone while they tackled the northern wilderness. They pushed all the way to Oregon before they began to look seriously at the young peninsula that reached farther south than any other land in the United States. In the late nineteenth century sporadic efforts at drainage began. A muck dike went up along the lower rim of Lake Okeechobee to stop the spill of water and farmers moved in with cattle and sugar cane. Where the Everglades peat was exposed to the sun it began to oxidize, crumbling from fertile muck into gray silica-brightened ash that fed nothing. It is still oxidizing today, and will be gone, the work of five thousand years, in a few decades more. America's winter vegetable garden, Florida people call it.

The Okeechobee dike held the lake water back, but it was no match for hurricanes. One hit the lake in 1926 and drove the shallow water through the dike and killed three hundred people determined enough to try to make their living on a floodplain. A worse hurricane hit in 1928, and this time rescue workers stacked the bodies up like cordwood and burned them because there was no place to bury them in the flooded ground. Two thousand people died. Herbert Hoover came to Florida to survey the destruction. The new levee he caused to be built stands today. It began the federal-state program to control the lake and the Everglades below, although most of the canal work wasn't started until the late 1940s, at about the same time that President Truman announced the creation of a new national park at the lower end of the state.

Today only the part of the Everglades that lies within the national park—6 per cent of its original area—escapes direct control, and even that 6 per cent depends during the dry season on water draining into it from spillways on the Tamiami Trail and from a canal on the eastern edge of the park. The Everglades south of Okeechobee for a distance of twenty-five miles is farmland. Three water-conservation areas now lie where most of the Everglades ran before. They are surrounded by canals and levees. The Central and Southern Florida Flood Control District, the FCD, using stations constructed by the Army Corps of Engineers, pumps water into the water-conservation areas for storage in dry times and pumps water out of them to the ocean in times of potential flood. They are maintained as wilderness areas, and as many people visit them for hunting and fishing and airboating annually as visit the national park. But they are only historically Everglades, because the water flows through them now only at the behest of man. Nor are they particularly effective for storage. One scientist estimates that all the rain water they catch is evaporated or transpired away before it can be used. They are essentially shallow lagoons. It was in these areas that the worst of last winter's fires burned. It was in one of these areas, in 1966, when flood followed five years of drought, that the stress of high water killed thousands of deer. People blamed the Corps of Engineers. The Corps of Engineers correctly pointed out that the water-conservation area where the deer were killed had not been designed for wildlife preservation but for water control.

The park suffered during the same drought. Lacking the rainfall that supplies it with 80 per cent of its water, it needed the flow south from Okeechobee, but the spillways on the Tamiami Trail were closed. The Engineers explained that they had not planned the water-conservation system to feed the park.

Hurricanes in the 1920s, fires in 1945, flood in 1947, severe drought in the early 1960s, flood in 1966, more fires in 1970 and 1971—South Florida and the Everglades have had their woes. But cycles of flood and drought have always worked their changes on the South Florida landscape. The difference today is that men are there, men who are working their changes too.

The jetport controversy has been resolved. Forty thousand flights a month still use the single training strip north of the Tamiami Trail above Everglades National Park, but the training strip will be moved and the jetport built elsewhere in Florida, on a site where the natural order has already given way completely to the man-made. It is worth remembering that the preservationists' victory was only a relative victory. The jetport has not been canceled. It will only be moved, to a place where it will cause less damage because the damage has already been done. That is what rankles the landowners of southwestern Florida. They have held their land for years, paid taxes on cypress swamp and wet prairie and everglades, waited their turn while the Gold Coast yielded up its wealth. The jetport would have sustained a major city. A government far away, an Interior Secretary from Alaska, a President from California, denied them their dream. Gave it away to other landowners. Encouraged by wilderness activists and hordes of newsmen, just such people as Spiro Agnew warned against.

The dream of city building, the dream of land bought at one hundred dollars an acre and sold for twenty golden thousand, has not faded. The jetport released energies in South Florida that will not easily be discharged. Twenty-five years ago the same land-

owners watched a new national park devour huge areas of Dade
and Monroe counties. They say bitterly today what they must
have thought bitterly then, that the Park is *already larger than
the state of Delaware.* They mean, *how much land does a park
need?* And not a notably scenic park at that, a water park, a
biological park, a park for alligators and birds and gumbo-limbo
trees. Then the jetport, a second chance. Lost because it would
damage the park. Then, in 1970, the possibility that a leg of Interstate 75 might be cut from Naples to Miami to replace the Tamiami Trail. A panel of scientists and engineers recommended
that no road at all be built. Florida's Secretary of Transportation
compromised on Alligator Alley, which runs from Naples straight
to Fort Lauderdale and avoids most of the Big Cypress. But even
the new highway won't do landowners much good, because it
will probably have few access roads.

Having successfully expelled the Everglades Jetport, preservationists are fighting today to save the Big Cypress Swamp from
development. Only from the Big Cypress does water still drift
freely into the park. The preservationists would like the federal
government to buy half a million acres north of the park to protect its western water supply, a water supply that amounts to 15
per cent of the park's total water resources but 40 per cent of its
dry-season flow. Burdened with deficits, the Nixon administration
would prefer to preserve the land without buying it by converting
the Tamiami Trail into a scenic parkway and federally zoning the
swamp around it for recreation only.

The landowners, the big ones, are fighting back, and fighting
the harder because they know this fight may be their last chance.
Much of the Big Cypress was originally intended to be included
in the park. It is still raw today, but development is beginning.
New towns are going up on its western edge. A Miami real estate
firm is selling land within the park itself for "waterfront estates,"
land still privately owned because Congress has not yet provided
funds to buy it. Oil companies would like to drill in the Big Cypress, laying down access roads that would further alter its sheet-
water flow and encourage development. Speculators are dredging
out canals. If the Everglades Jetport was yesterday's South Florida
controversy, the Big Cypress is today's.

You can walk in the Big Cypress if you don't mind getting wet.
Roberts Lake Strand is surrounded by Loop Road 94, in the heart

of the land the preservationists hope Congress will buy. It is one
of the smaller strands in the Big Cypress and one still unmarred
except for the scars of old logging and the deprivations of boy
scouts in search of cypress knees. The strand begins at roadside, a
screen of brush and cypress trees. If you do not know the swamp
you do not enter it easily, no more easily than you would parachute for the first time from a plane. Panthers. Water moccasins.
Alligators. The water creeps over your shoes. Firm bottom, sometimes bare limestone pitted with solution holes dissolved out over
the centuries by plant acids, more often a tangle of leaves. Cool
water, brown but entirely clear. Small plants like green stars grow
on the bottom. You can drink the water. It tastes of plant decay,
but no more so than most Florida water. The cypress trees close
overhead and sunlight breaks fitfully through. Lichens grow on
the tree trunks, gray-green, bright green, even pink, and moss soft
as velvet, wet home for things too small to see. On the cypress
branches sit air plants like isolated pineapples, their pointed leaves
cupped to catch rain. Some of the air plants catch enough water
to support life, natural aquariums with a crawfish and a tadpole or
two up there in the trees. The nooks and crannies of life, a tadpole in an air plant on a cypress in the swamp. You realize you
will not be attacked by predators and you relax, enjoying the cool
water in the summer heat. You slog back into the swamp and farther back, heading toward a pond, passing a few cut stumps, then
big trees never cut, trees that have grown in silence since before
Columbus' first voyage, trees towering like the columns of cathe-
drals up to the sun. And rooted in the water, in the slow south-
ward flow.

The pond is in a clearing, one of the water holes around which
the cypresses grow. It is still choked with grass from the winter
drought. The grass will die, flooded out by summer rain and
thrashed down by alligators. You wade to your waist in the water
now, taking caution in the dense grass. Ahead of you, out of sight,
frogs bleat and jump. The distance is exact, an exact defensive
boundary. Cross the boundary and you throw a switch and the
frogs bleat and jump. The grass is indifferent. It has grown and
seeded. It has done its job. It hangs in bunches on your legs.
From time to time you reach under the water and push the grass
behind you. You are making an alligator trail. You are an alligator
pushing through lime grass in the Florida sun. You reach the edge
of the pond and climb over a floating log and re-enter the cypress

shade. You could walk into eternity in a cypress swamp. It has no corners. It is not abstract and knows no titles or plats. It flows and changes in patterns we only dimly begin to understand. The South Florida ecosystem has been studied seriously for less than thirty years.

If you find bogeymen in a cypress swamp, then you put them here. It is only itself, green in tooth and claw. It is what we left behind, territorial frogs and silent trees. You could live here if you took the trouble to learn how. An alligator might get you. There are worse deaths. Death means nothing and less than nothing here. Death leads back to life as surely as a circle turns in upon itself. If you died, the moss would still hang from the trees and the air plants still sit like comic birds nursing along a tadpole or two. The resurrection ferns, come summer and summer rain, would still resurrect. The gods who designed the swamp had a sense of humor. They put air plants on the trees and gray-green pads of periphyton in the water and they canceled death. The periphyton is spongy and slippery. You can mold it like clay. It feeds small things that feed larger things that eventually feed alligators, and the alligators belch and bed down in cypress ponds. Gar hover like broken branches. Leaves float by. A spider shakes its web strung on struts that reach high up into the trees. Cypress knees bend above the water. They might be shaggy ladies offering an accommodation. "How could anyone want to tear this beautiful place down?" asks my guide, a friend of the earth. How could they not, with its old mysteries scratching at their souls? It denies them their sovereignties. It reminds them that life, all life, their own life too, is a swarm of molecules thrown up momentarily in fantastic shapes and washed down and thrown up again, like waves breaking forever against a shore. Cowering behind antique metaphysics, believing life a constitutional right and death an obscenity, most of us find such reminders hard to cherish.

As love does when it decays, the debate over the future of the Big Cypress Swamp is rapidly resolving into a power struggle. Those who believe some wild land should be preserved in America, for itself and as a hedge against the unknown effects of massive ecological change, are fighting to preserve the Big Cypress. Those who believe the land is infinitely bountiful and was put here for human use are fighting to develop the Big Cypress. Wedged between the two positions is the tender science of ecology, and it is no more capable of taking a clear stand than a child is capable of deciding between parents in a divorce.

Joe Browder, Washington secretary to the Friends of the Earth and the one man more responsible than any other for bringing the Everglades Jetport to national attention and national censure, believes that Big Cypress development would be a catastrophe. "Failure to protect that portion of the Big Cypress that supplies water to Everglades National Park," he has written, "would, in addition to destroying the existing natural values in much of the Everglades, decrease water supply and increase water demand in southwest Florida to such a degree that additional pressures would be placed on the other major Everglades watershed, the sawgrass glades managed by the [Flood Control District]. The extra water demand would diminish the supply available for urban, industrial, and agricultural users in southeast Florida, and would further stimulate the conflict between all other users and Everglades National Park."

Landowners in Collier County, the county in southwestern Florida that includes most of the Big Cypress, completely disagree. They believe the water is plentiful, the swamp useless and dangerous, development desirable, and water into the park merely a matter of aiming a few canals its way. Their plans, they have said publicly, "could make this park into a living garden for wild life and plant life the year around." It is that already, but never mind.

The facts, so far as they are known, fall somewhere between.

The Big Cypress is presently an unusual and largely undamaged South Florida swamp, most of it privately owned. All of its water comes from rain. The rain that falls on the Big Cypress recharges the fresh-water aquifer that supplies water for human use on the southwestern coast of Florida. It is the only natural water supply available to the coast. When the aquifer is full, water left standing on the ground drifts slowly down into the coastal portion of Everglades National Park, maintaining the life there under natural conditions.

If the Big Cypress were drained, its ecology would be altered from that of a swamp to that of dry land. Most of the life that thrives there now would die away. So would the coastal estuary. The park would take its water from canals, and the canals would certainly change and might permanently disrupt the ecology of the land within the park itself. The park's chief biologist, William Robertson, thinks the effect of development "highly unpredictable" but probably damaging.

The water-resources division of the United States Geological Survey, in a report prepared for Interior Secretary Walter Hickel before he departed Washington, implied that controlled development of the Big Cypress would cause some damage to the park but would not seriously impair the Gulf Coast's water supply. "No estimate is available," the report said, "of the total water-supply potential of [the western Big Cypress]. The present total water use in those areas is insignificant compared with the quantity evaporated, transpired, and discharged through the canal systems."

Draining the Big Cypress, then, would deliver up an enormous tract of land for human use. It would destroy the Big Cypress itself. It would turn the park into a giant zoo, an ecosystem that would look natural to casual visitors but would in fact be artificially maintained through canals. Pesticides used for mosquito control in the new towns north of the park would take their toll on the park, but the effects would be long-term. Any adverse effects on the Gulf Coast water supply would also be long-term.

The question of the Big Cypress becomes a long-term question, though it must be answered now, before development proceeds any further: what kind of future do the people of South Florida envision for themselves? And that question is part of a larger dilemma: what kind of future do all of us in America envision for ourselves? Assuming that we have a choice, do we want to live entirely in cities under artificial conditions or do we want a little of the natural world around us?

The larger dilemma begins to answer itself not in the speeches of our leaders but in the actions of individual citizens moving forward along parallel lines. We laid out the land long ago, in square sections that looked logical on a map but had nothing to do with the natural divisions of the land itself and little to do with the interests of the people who lived on it. Nowhere did the fine Enlightenment minds that devised our Constitution fail us more completely. Over the grid of sections, they fitted a Balkanized grid of political institutions, of townships and counties and states. Each had its particular sovereignties. Each developed its particular structures of power, some informal, some legally constituted. The old boundaries worked when the nation was poor in people and overrich in resources. They worked when those who differed from the established authorities had at least the possibility of moving on.

They are strained almost to breaking today, and the points of stress locate problems the entire nation is scrambling to solve. Our cities need money because their legal boundaries no longer define the metropolitan areas in which we live, areas that may well cut across city, town, village, county, and even state lines, areas chopped up into small authorities that drain away tax money to duplicate services the city has traditionally supplied. Citizens in nearly every state struggle with state legislatures still gerrymandering to give dominance to rural interests. Pollution control continues by law to be the responsibility of state and local governments, while pollution blows across state and county lines. The shape of our political institutions no longer matches the shape of our purposes and our need.

Consider Florida. The Everglades, which is all one watershed from Okeechobee to Cape Sable, is divided into three counties, a state-federal water conservation district and a national park, each with its own priorities of water and development.

The Big Cypress Swamp is being developed by men who have no legal or political responsibility to consider the ultimate effects of that development. The area of the Big Cypress that preservationists would like the federal government to buy is situated in Monroe County. Most of the large developers live in Collier County or in Miami. The Monroe County seat is in Key West, two hundred miles away across Florida Bay.

Lake Okeechobee supplies water for Miami and most of Florida's Gold Coast. The water that feeds Okeechobee and is beginning to pollute it with pesticides and fertilizers rushes down the channelized Kissimmee River from farms and towns to the north, farms and towns that draw their own water supply from sources other than the big lake.

The list could be longer, and it could be duplicated anywhere in America. It demonstrates a failure of responsibility on the part of institutions that no longer fit our needs but are unwilling to rearrange the authority they have held so many years. But we have never been a people to let institutions stand in our way. When they have not worked, we have either abolished them or left them to die of neglect while we moved on to others that could do the job we wanted done. That is why a few activist men and women could work through the courts, the press, the television networks and the lobbies of Congress to convince a President that he should personally cancel one county-sponsored jetport. That is why Congress, not the state of Florida or the governments of Collier and Monroe counties, will probably find some way to buy or otherwise control the Big Cypress Swamp. But that is also why the battle to save the wild lands, in South Florida and elsewhere, has been so difficult for those who believe land deserves its day in court as surely as people do: because the idea is new and the institutions that will make it work are still being shaped.

The battle may be won, if there is time. No one knows how much time is left. However abstractly we divided the land, and however much we may want today to redivide it into shapes more consistent with its natural patterns, it has never been attendant to our laws. It changes with the certainty of the old laws of chemistry and physics. We can misuse it, if that is what we are doing, for an unknown length of time before it fails any longer to serve our needs, but when that time is up it fails suddenly and totally and without much hope of recovery. Poisonous algal blooms have already appeared at the northern end of Lake Okeechobee. Miami imposed water rationing last winter. "The Everglades," says Arthur Marshall, an ecologist at the University of Miami who has studied South Florida for eighteen years, "has all the symptoms of environmental stress and approaching catastrophic decline."

Perhaps it has. The men who believe the Lord gave us land to build on aren't worried. "Look at the Dutch," one of them, Ben Shepard, a commissioner of the Dade County Port Authority, said recently. "They completely destroyed the ecology of their land and yet it's supporting human life satisfactorily. The Dutch are some of the best-adjusted, prosperous, happiest people today." It probably does him no justice to recite John Maynard Keynes's jape at such men. "Practical men," Keynes said, "who believe themselves to be quite exempt from any intellectual influences, are usually the slaves of some defunct economist." Because Florida, having everything else, also has its own little Netherlands: Key West.

Key West. A waterless island of fossilized coral surrounded by the sea. If the continent were water and the water land, Key West is where all the sweetness and bitterness, all the honey and sour acids of our complicated American lives would drain. The southernmost point in the United States. Land's end. Old glory and present decay. Haven for disgruntled Cubans paddling the ninety miles from Havana in rafts of canvas and old inner tubes. Tourist trap meringued with Key Lime pie. Swabbies' town clipped to a drab naval base where black submarines cruise the harbor like sharks. Where developers reclaim land from the sea, the dying mangroves stinking of sulfur. Where an aquarium displays ocean fish in narrow tanks, white fungus blinding their eyes. Hemingway's home and Audubon's shrine.

Some of Key West's water comes from the Everglades. When the Navy decided to settle permanently on the island, it ran a pipeline down the Overseas Highway to supply it with water. Before the pipeline came in, the natives collected rainwater in cisterns behind their houses or bought it from commercial cisterns that dotted the island like small-town Mexican jails. With its population growing today in response to the tourist trade, Key West has gone to desalinization. Westinghouse built it a nuclear-powered desalinization plant, the largest of its kind in the United States. If we run out of water we can always distill the sea. With water, the motels in Key West may fill their swimming pools for tourists who come to see the turtle stockyards or to bend an elbow in Hemingway's favorite bar hung with parachute canopies and open to the street. And no one can complain of ecological damage, because there isn't much you can do to a dry Florida key once you've kicked out the dwarf Key deer. There ought to be no wilderness here at all except the wilderness of the sea, but even here the wilderness intrudes like a hypodermic injecting blood into a dying man.

Hemingway's house hangs back on a side street, a wide, gracious house surrounded on four sides with gardens and tropical trees, a huge banyan, shading palms, a royal poinciana with all its fired flowers burning. Cats prowl the corridors and sleep under the trees. Here the man lived for twenty years, tightening down the screws on his inner life even as his public life thickened with poisonous fame, writing less and less well. Describing love with the naïveté of a schoolgirl. Hunting Nazi submarines in the Caribbean. Converting heroism into mere bravado by dividing it from its vital source, the idea of death, his best and only theme, the theme he avoided more and more. Avoided until it killed him.

He was a hunter and a fisherman. He tried to come to grips with the land and the sea and at his occasional best he succeeded as well as anyone ever has, but to hunt and to fish is only to use the natural world, and to recover that world in all its intimacy you must be used by it, must give yourself up to it as nakedly as any Indian. He could not. He walked the narrow catwalk to his study over the garage and sharpened his pencils and fought to find feelings he progressively lost because he could not bear the crowd of fantasies that came with them. "There is no timber," an Irish playwright once wrote, "that has not strong roots among the clay and the worms." You must be buried alive like a seed or a larva to grow up into the sun, and to write about that growth you must willingly bury yourself alive over and over again. Paralyzed by private grief, Hemingway wielded his shovel clumsily over his own grave. Below his study, so they say in Key West, in a rusted steel safe, Hemingway's last wife found the manuscripts he had locked away there from prying eyes. She would publish them after his death to add a few thousand years more to his trial in purgatory. He bent to the wilderness and it devoured him.

Audubon owned no house in Key West, but he stayed in one that is more than a match for Hemingway's. It is a shrine today, decked out with expensive antiques that command more attention than they deserve. The house belonged to a Key West salvager named Geiger, a plump, bespectacled old scholar and hypocrite who made his living hauling in the lucrative stores of ships wrecked on the coral reef east of the island. Key West was a wealthy town when Miami was still an Indian village, and the islanders weren't above rearranging reef markers to keep it that way. Captain Geiger salvaged with the best of them and got rich on the proceeds.

Down one day came Audubon to work up the Florida birds. The captain housed him, Audubon a rare bird himself. Once, in New Orleans, broke, months from home and marriage bed, he accepted a beautiful courtesan's commission to paint her portrait. He hauled his palette to her backstreet house and found her naked before him on a couch. She lay naked for ten long afternoons while he stared and cartooned and oiled. It was the most difficult commission he ever accepted, he told a friend later.

He brought the same compaction of frustrated lust to his birds. They perch life-size on the pages of the enormous elephant folios displayed today in Captain Geiger's house. Audubon's eye raped them alive, tore them free from the clay and the worms. They rend their prey or fix the water at their feet with high metabolic intensity or poise to leap from the paper and claw out your heart. He saw the wilderness through them, made them transparent as any lantern slide. Their hollow, whistling bones and their racing wings beat from the interstices of the creamy paper against which they were thrown. Making them, building them up with remembered motions of the eye and the hand that first described them alive in the Everglades, he lived with the fear that trickled sweat down his back and pushed through to the swarming mystery beyond. The Aztec priests who never cut their hair and never knew a woman molded seeds and fresh human blood and black dirt into idols in black rooms off the main halls of their temples, and Audubon, sweating in an upstairs parlor at raffish Captain Geiger's house in Key West, molded seed and blood and black dirt into birds and discovered the essential Florida, the Florida that not even the most ardent preservationist dares speak of, the Florida that sent William Bartram into paroxyms of hysterical bliss and Samuel Coleridge into opium dreams. Why, the wilderness is insane. It destroys us with pluralities. It skins off our flesh and shows us branching vessels and twitching meat and bubbling fluids and bones round and sturdy as tree trunks. The alligator in its drying pond chews up its young, the wild boar breeds moaning with its mother, the panther licks its wet member, the mantis eats the male it has coupled with, the strangler fig chokes to death its guardian tree, the shrimp feasts on rot and the buzzard on decay and the proud eagle on carrion, and we see into ourselves and are horrified to live in such a world, a world that so mirrors our own depths, that delights in acts we have thought depraved, have worked from the beginning of our consciousness to fence in and legislate away. We wear pants and write laws and turn over the earth and only at the climax of our feverish couplings do we dimly sense how far we have removed ourselves from the moment-by-moment ecstasies of any animal's ordinary day. And that is one reason to keep what is left of wilderness in this civilized land, not to fish and hunt but to see the complexities that lay dormant within us, the possibilities we have not yet understood, because Shakespeare and the old Indian tales and the myths of Greece and Rome together do not begin to reveal as many metamor-

phoses as one walk through a cypress swamp or one descent into a
coral reef. Audubon knew, and pushed through his fear to the
other side and came back bird-maddened and showed us what he
saw, the Florida that pulses inside. And for his trouble he is
enshrined today on a barren Florida key fed by foul water
recovered from the ocean. That is Key West, a little Netherlands.
We can convert the whole continent over if we choose. Look at
the Dutch.

When we came to Florida, my wife and two children and I, we
took a house on the white beach at Naples, and we returned to it
now by air from Key West like birds returning to an old and favored nest. At Naples the land meets the sea casually. Nothing
there of rugged coast or coral reef. You must swim out seven miles
to find a depth of thirty feet. No undertow will claim you, or any
shark. Deceptive shallows, as Florida with its imperceptible sea-
weed tilt is deceptive, a beach itself dropping slowly into the
water, a ramp on which the smallest creature may generation by
generation crawl out onto the land. We came from the sea, by degrees teaching our flesh to wrap the sea inside it. It courses
through us every day of our lives, reddened now with hungry iron.
We never returned. The fish left the sea and returned, most of
them. Their blood, like ours, is less salty than sea water, because
while they lived in the estuaries or in fresh water the sea increased
its load of salt leached from the land. The shark, with his bitter
blood, never left the sea. He is old and well adapted. Older still
are the airless bacteria that lie at the bottom of the lakes we have
poisoned and the most terrible of disease organisms we suffer, bot-
ulism and tetanus and gangrene. The airless bacteria evolved before the fresh wind blew across the face of the world,
evolved in vapors of methane and a saltless world of water. And
learned to encyst themselves against the deadly oxygen that gives
us life. Learned to wait their turn in a world gone wild with life.
They wait now and will always be waiting, until sun and fresh air
sting them no more.

Florida summer oppresses. Sweat collects. Clothes do not dry.
You move in an invisible cloud of steam smelling sea metals and
the dust of palm trees. Sun on the white beach reverses colors in
your eyes. At low tide in the early evening, beachcombers pull
piles of Naples starfish from the wet sand and lay them out on
towels to dry, to die. My son flushes an ivory crab from its hole. It

stands high on jointed legs, its eyes like black pearls glued to its carapace, and it turns in little jumps to face the boy as he moves. It is a head without a trunk jumping on jointed legs. It skitters sideways and collects itself and runs away to dig another hole and wait in the shadow inside and the boy is awed to silence.

Near sunset, the pier down the beach that reaches out a thousand feet into the Gulf fills up with fishermen. Young people with long hair, elderly couples in pale blue shorts and yachting caps. A hunchback whose shrunken legs dangle over the rim of his wheelchair. A fat woman with curlers in her cropped gray hair smoking a pipe, her enormous breasts hanging loose beneath a dirty tee shirt. Fish flop on the pier and lie still, one silver eye fixed on the moon. Schools, universities of bream flash among the pilings, bream enough to repopulate the ocean if it were ever in need, bream that sound the water like an orchestra of harps as they jump and dodge the predators that chase them. A black ray, one of its wings chopped off for bait, stains the pier. The tension of the fishermen smells like boiling lead. They have come out to catch fish in the low tide. Men cast their lines and reel them up. Boys drop lines between the floor boards and lie on their bellies peering into the darkness below. A woman baits the four prongs of a hook as big as a man's fist. Back on the land, a mosquito-control truck pumps mists of Dibrom through the streets and Naples disappears like Brigadoon. Brown pelicans, birds as comic and serene as Polynesian girls, birds that look like benevolent pterodactyls, circle the water beside the pier and casually fold their wings and dive and bring up fish no fisherman can touch. And fly a little way off and settle on the water and flip the fish in the air and swallow them.

The sun thickens to a giant red ball. It touches the water and flattens out at its base. The lead tension holds, vibrating like a dulled gong. At the moment of the sun's setting, everyone on the pier stops fishing and looks up to watch, pulled alert by an old compulsion. The water and the sky turn pink. The red ball grows, careless of the energy that gives everything in the world its single life. It drops into the ocean, feeding the water. Something breaks inside. The sea has eaten the sun. A few at a time, the fishermen reel up and walk away. The Dibrom settles on trees and houses and Naples returns to life minus mosquitoes. Out of sight in the swamp, in the sawgrass, living mosquitoes sniff the air, the males searching nectar, the females seeking blood.

Florida night. The thunderstorms of late afternoon have blown away. The sun has set and the fishermen are gone. The moon is down. On the porch of our house I am drinking bourbon and talking to a friend of the earth. It is our last night in Forida and we are ready to return home because Florida has come to seem some enormous conspiracy of contentious men and pregnant silence and I need distance to sort it out. The friend of the earth believes the wild lands will be saved because they must be if he is to find any peace in the world. Bitter at the confusion of my own life, I believe they will be turned and plowed and paved so that homes can be built where children will grow up guarded from the stews of birth and the stink of death, out of sight of the real life of the world. He is optimistic and his optimism makes no sense. We have everywhere destroyed the wilderness, raging and whimpering as we went. Yet he believes we will put aside our old autocracies and become natural democrats.

My wife remembers then a time, as a child, when she found a shell on the Naples beach and took it to her Victorian grandmother, who told her to throw it into a pot of boiling water to clean it out. A child, she did, and something alive shot out of the shell and flailed its legs in agony up to the roiling surface of the water and died, died as terribly as anything can ever die. She understood later what it was, a hermit crab. She would never again clean out a shell. The friend of the earth remembers a time when he was lost in the mountains of New Mexico and feared that he would die. He walked out in three days without food, marveling that he felt, after the first day, no hunger, only the compulsion to put one foot in front of the other lest he lie down and give up. He is camping in the same mountains as I write.

We are a wild species, Darwin said long ago. We were never scientifically bred. We are a various and colorful pack of mongrels, and the wilderness made us what we are: it is the place from which we came, and the place, clay and worms, where we shall go. For most of the life of man we could not live with that knowledge. Rather than live with it we pushed the wilderness away from us as a child pushes away the mother who would smother him with complexity. We go into the wilderness today, what is left of it, to find out who we are, but that is not the reason we should preserve it. We should preserve it because we need to know now, and our children and our children's children will need even more to know later, that we are not finally compelled by our raging and whimpering always and forever to destroy, that we are not entirely wedded to death. We need to leave a little food on our plates to prove that we are not impoverished. We need magnanimity, more today than we have ever needed it before.

At midnight we wade into the Gulf, my wife and the friend of the earth and I, into one small shore of the sea. The sky is clear and filled with stars, constellations we can see, formations we have never named, galaxies and suns too far from us for any except spiritual vision. They glow over the swamp, over the Everglades, over the great ramp of land that rises out of the water to cause men contention they have not yet decided how to still. Shall there be homes on the land? Oil pumped out of it? Water drawn up to wash away sweat and the spendings of the night? Shall old lizards crawl through muck there, green moss riding on their backs? And birds nest, and the used shells of their eggs drop down through the branches to float on the brown water? The things that live there, in the grass and in the swamp, will not know nor care what we do. They will go on as they have gone or they will not go at all. They do not choose. They only live. And the sharks circle forever, waiting for their prey.

The sea water glows around our bodies as we move: night plankton: they come alive with light in the moving water we make, dots, sparkles, flashes, flares. We stare under water at a flood of stars glowing around the tips of our fingers, lighting our kicking feet and our stroking arms. They were here all along in the bright day and we did not know. We swirl them into light and they decorate us, imitating the stars above, microscopic things glowing in the water like the giant stars reduced by incomprehensible distances to points of white in the black sky. The stars in the sky and night plankton making stars in the water wherever we go: layers, and layers under layers down into the very center of things, and layers there too small to see, and layers below those layers until the head swims and still more layers then. We are no more divided from the world than the water itself is divided. When we damage the world we damage ourselves. If we destroy it we destroy ourselves. A piece at a time, we think, a part at a time, but the world has no pieces and does not come apart. Wherever we put our hands, points of energy trail off from us like the tails of comets. The tree that falls without sound falls within our hearing.

Loathe Thy Neighbor

For a long time I wanted to move to California, and now I don't want to any more. For a long time the whole country wanted to move to California, and now it doesn't want to any more. These several changes of mind go together.

California has been a dream for so long, and we have dreamed of California for so long, that we hardly even any longer notice the mechanism. The audioanimatronic men and women, the vinyl surf, the polyurethane clouds move grandly on the stage; caught up in their verisimilitude—or, rather, their lack of verisimilitude, because it is their difference from us that attracts us—we ignore the whirring of the ordinary gears and the slap-slap of the ordinary tapes running out in the pit below.

The place to go to start thinking about California is the books of Joan Didion. Didion is a "native daughter," as she puts it. She grew up in and around Sacramento; she lives in Malibu. I've never met her, and I don't think I want to. Her writing is so intense that I suspect she is like the Emily Dickinson of whom an acquaintance wrote, "I never was with anyone who drained my nerve power so much. . . . I am glad not to live near her." Didion's writing drains your nerve power too, and the only reason you forgive her is that it so obviously also drains her own. Didion is California's Cassandra: she always tells the truth, and it is never the truth California wants to hear. You and I, for example, have sometimes naïvely thought of California as Eden. Didion tells us a darker truth: that Californians also think of California as Eden. "It is assumed," she writes—assumed by Californians—"that those who absent themselves from its blessings have been banished, exiled, by some perversity of heart. Did not the Donner-Reed Party, after all, eat its own dead to reach Sacramento?"

I know a little about the Donner-Reed, the Donner, Party:
sometime ago I published a novel about the Donner Party that
was as historically accurate as the records would allow. The
Donner Party, you will recall, was that group of pioneers from Illinois, Missouri, Tennessee, Ireland and points between that attempted a new route to California in 1846 and was trapped in the
Sierra Nevada below what is now called the Donner Pass for five
months, during which time most of its members lived off the dead
rather than starve to death. The Donner Party is usually thought
of as the archetypal pioneer diorama, despite the fact that our pioneer forefathers didn't make a practice of eating their companions. The Donner Party occupies a special, dual place in the California mentality, as Didion goes on to show: "We were taught,"
she writes, "that they had somewhere abdicated their responsibilities, somehow breached their primary loyalties, or they would
not have found themselves helpless in the mountain winter . . .
would not have given way to acrimony, would not have deserted
one another, would not have *failed*."

Well, by any mortal standards, they didn't fail. More than half
of them made it through the snowbound Sierras in the middle of
the worst winter in thirty years. Nor did they fail at re-
sourcefulness, as their willingness to live off the dead shockingly
demonstrates. For their courage they are usually, and rightly,
claimed by Californians as fine examples of the state's early pioneer stock. The state even maintains a museum devoted to them,
as well as to the other early pioneers, in Donner Memorial State
Park, near Truckee. Where they "failed," really, was in discretion.
They didn't keep their mouths shut, so to speak. They brought
contumely down on proud California heads. California would prefer that you admired its missions, which Indian slaves built, rather
than the Donner Party. Didion once more: "It is characteristic of
Californians to speak grandly of the past as if it had simultaneously begun, *tabula rasa*, and reached a happy ending on the
day the wagons started west." That scenario isn't likely to welcome
a story as grotesque as the Donners'. Californians chewing
corpses: the very thought revolts. Why would they need to? "December in California is as pleasant as May," the guidebook, written by a Californian, informed the Donners, the same guidebook
that led them astray across a route the Californian was promoting
but hadn't personally tried.

We—my wife, my son, my daughter, and I—packed up to go out to California on vacation a while back, to look around, having not found peace of mind in Kansas, having found cold in winter and heat in summer and commerce and small talk. People might live better in California, we thought, because California is said to be a better place to live. We packed our bags and found someone to sit with the dog. Promised the kids a visit to Disneyland. Had lunch before we left with a man who has spent his life fixing up the Midwest, trying to make it livable. He thought the idea of changing your life by changing your residence—the idea that has moved people to California for three hundred years —was laughable. "You can't escape any more," he said, laughing. "There's no escape anywhere. You might as well stay here." I said we'd see.

We arrived in Carmel, on the Monterey Peninsula, where we had rented a house, just before sundown one day, shivering in the unaccustomed chill of an ordinary summer evening by the northern sea. We picked up the key and bought groceries and some of that good California wine and let ourselves in. Fog streamed through the pines. We found wood and built a fire and settled back and toasted our luck, luck to be in California. Did we like Carmel, the sea, the cypresses, the fog, the white sand? We talked of living there one day. It was the best of the California we knew. The only drawback was that even small houses in Carmel started at forty thousand dollars, with no view. We didn't talk about that. We made small talk with wine. Picking our place.

We awoke to cold mornings and turned the furnace up and after we were warm we walked down the hill, down Ocean Avenue, through the town to the white-sand beach, and watched the breakers and listened to them beat. Dogs ran the beach with handsome middle-aged women following them or elderly men in jodhpurs and riding boots, ordinary neighbors. Girls braving the cold in bikinis played Frisbee with boys in chopped jeans. The fog drifted away like smoke clearing a battlefield to reveal Point Lobos, the wild point of land south of Carmel Bay. Point Lobos is a state reserve, a jut of land where visitors are confined to narrow trails by edgings of wire and poison oak and so a place where wildflowers thrive and deer wander and sea lions bark from protected islands offshore and the cold surf breaks clean on pebble beaches of granite and Monterey jade. Edward Weston spent years photographing Point Lobos, and his photographs of its skeined kelp and Monterey cypresses and eroded coves have been compared, somewhat fatuously, to Beethoven's last quartets. I will give California Point Lobos.

Point Lobos attracted another artist to the Monterey Peninsula years ago, a man who is now dead, a man who is revered in Carmel as saints are revered in Italian villages, the poet Robinson Jeffers. Jeffers hardly ever came down to town, yet he was unwittingly Carmel's seignior, first proof of its dedication to the finer things of life and its disdain for the common. Jeffers was born in Pittsburgh, Pennsylvania.

He and his wife, Una, found Carmel in 1914. The town was young and wild then and you could buy an acre of shore line for one hundred dollars instead of the twenty thousand dollars or so it would cost today, undeveloped. Jeffers had an income and could afford to live where he chose. He chose Carmel, convinced with his wife that they had "come without knowing it to our inevitable place." Over the years, he built a house and a stone tower on Carmel Point, hauling great rocks up from the shore, wrestling the wrack. The house and tower still stand, occupied now by one of his sons.

Jeffers loved the landscape and seascape of the bay and the peninsula and the points. At the same time, he was intensely shy, almost phobic, of people. He felt so good about the place where he lived, and so bad about people, that he combined the two feelings into a philosophy that threads haughtily, chillingly through his poetry:

I must not even pretend
To be one of the people. I must stand here
Alone with open eyes in the clear air growing old,
Watching with interest and only a little nausea
The cheating shepherds, this time of the demagogs and the
*   docile people, the shifts of power,*
And pitiless general wars that prepare the fall;
But also the enormous unhuman beauty of things; rock, sea and
*   stars, foolproof and permanent,*
The birds like yachts in the air, or beating like hearts
Along the water: the flares of sunset, the peaks of Point Lobos. . . .

But because pain stood in the way of Jeffers' pleasure with people, he displaced that pleasure onto nature. Found his beauties there. Notice that he could afford to buy the best view. It is, I think, the basic, generic, archetypal California shuffle: you move to California and buy a little beauty, buy a little space so you can have a little grace, and the neighbors be damned.

Not everyone: tens of thousands of Californians moved there because they thought they could find a better job, but that hasn't gone too well lately, and when the jobs are off, you can divide the ordinary Californians from the shufflers. The judgment of the executive director of the Sierra Club, Michael McCloskey, a hard man, was: "We are in favor of zero population growth at the earliest feasible time." Just like that: where the elite meet to eat. It isn't accidental that the Sierra Club was founded in California, which already has more national parks than any other state. It isn't accidental that California these days, having noticed that people, ordinary folks, are moving in among its natural beauties, has decided abruptly to close up shop, discourage immigration, cancel development, as Oregon began doing years ago. (Historically, Oregon was the first Beautiful Place in the American West: people migrated there before they began migrating to California in any numbers. One recalls Dick Tuck's answer to Robert Kennedy when Kennedy asked him what they should have done to win the Oregon primary in 1968: Tuck said they ought to have airlifted in a few ghettos.)

California is the state, above all others in the United States of America, Florida included, where people move who covet the best view, who believe that art, beauty and truth can be bought. People like that don't make the best neighbors. Jeffers would have preferred to be alone on his point, as he grumbled in one of his poems: "This beautiful place defaced with a crop of suburban houses. . . ." The word for that attitude is greed, and it is greed no less for being masked as nature worship. The people in those suburban houses also like the view. And are, in turn, greedy on their own behalf. For all its beauty, Carmel is in some ways a silly town, a town of tourist shops and tourist shopkeepers pretending to be a town of Bohemians, as the adherents of the counterculture were called when Carmel was young. The artists and writers who settled in Carmel in its early years settled there because it was cheap. It is hardly cheap any longer. But the town struggles to keep such "charm" as it has left, and for the past several years, that struggle has taken the form of a battle over an artichoke farm, the Odello ranch, at the mouth of the Carmel River, in the valley just below the hills on which Carmel is sited. Developers wanted to put up more than eight hundred apartments and motel rooms on the Odello property, a hugh influx into an area with a population of fewer than ten thousand souls. Carmel succeeded in forcing the developers to reduce the density of their proposed complex to between three hundred and four hundred units and in setting aside half the Odello ranch for a state park; but so far the town has not succeeded in doing what it wants to do, which is to get the project thrown out entirely and leave the Odello ranch in artichokes.

In the meantime, the California Supreme Court, working on the perennial problem of the rights of California man, has questioned the constitutionality of zoning regulations that exclude multi-unit dwellings. *This beautiful place of suburban houses defaced with a crop of apartments.* . . . And not even the apartment dwellers, if they're ever let in, would want the kids sleeping on the beach, which isn't allowed. Is there anyone in California who doesn't think the neighborhood's going to hell?

I discovered one morning a truth about Carmel: that it was beauty without substance; that it was a rest home. I met people there who said proudly that one day they had just dropped every-thing—and "everything" was usually a *vital* job in New York—and moved to Carmel, and I wondered what sort of people could simply drop all responsibilities and move somewhere pleasant and backwater by the sea. I thought about girls I had known who spoke of Carmel with a catch in their throat—thin, neurotic girls who came out once a year on their vacations to read Hesse or Gibran or Rod McKuen or even Richard Bach (they filmed *Jonathan Livingston Seagull* in Carmel, by the way. Where else?) on the beach and reintegrate. They went back to work tempo-rarily calmed, though by the time their tans had faded, they were crying at their desks again, as if a trip to California were no more filling than a Cantonese meal. I called an elderly man who had been powerful in a large midwestern city before he retired to Car-mel. He said he didn't want to talk, he'd had three operations and did I understand? I said I did and thanked him and hung up. Slowly it dawned on me that I was on the trail of privilege and that to find privilege was to find fear. And to find fear is always to find essences—to find what people tremble to protect.

I remembered another powerful man, this one a native Californian, whom I had met on a flight to Africa, where he was going to look into mineral exploitation. When he mentioned that his offices were in a high new tower in San Francisco, I kidded him about the dangers of earthquake, but he took the subject seriously. The building in which he had his offices was earthquake-proof, he said; at most, some of the windows might go. They had enough food up there, high above the city, to last out the aftershocks, and guns to shoot looters. His eyes gleamed at that, and before long he had drunk so much champagne that he couldn't get out of his seat.

We made a swing north from Carmel to get the lay of the land, still looking for a place where civilized folk could live. A classmate of mine teaches at the University of California at Santa Cruz—a campus started in 1965 high above the faded town of Santa Cruz, at the north end of Monterey Bay, among redwoods on what used to be a cattle ranch—and we stopped there. UCSC takes top students, the next generation of California leaders, the first really numerous generation of natives. At UCSC they live apart, as at a spiritual retreat; the colleges are scattered through the trees. It would be hard to get a mob together: I wondered if the planners had that in mind when they built the place, after Berkeley, after Free Speech. My classmate said the students didn't take very well to the stylized peace and quiet. More and more of them were moving down into town.

His keenest observation, the one that interested me the most—because, having come from the Midwest and taught in the East, he was in a position to make the comparison—was that California students were remarkably different from eastern students. Not necessarily better or worse: different. Eastern students, he said, acted as if they believed the college line that they were training to be leaders. California students came to college with little interest in leadership. They trained in education and social work. They wanted to help.

In families new to wealth, the rapacious first generation gives way to second and third generations that expiate the guilt of acquisition with good works. A generation of Californians was expiating the guilt of acquisition with good works, expiating the sins of parents who had scratched their way to California for the view. Which helped explain the heat waves of suppressed rage one saw in the California air, because people don't shoulder burdens of blood attainder without rage. The older generation arrived in the land of Nod and made it theirs; the younger generation love the land and help one another. California isn't merely the land of the greedy; it is also the premier land of the guilty. If the picture of college-educated adults liberating vacant lots and bathing oil-soaked birdies isn't enough to demonstrate that guilt, only consider the magnitude and the implications of California drug abuse, alcohol specifically included. But greed and guilt together produce offspring far kinkier than either one is capable of breeding by itself. Put greed and guilt together and you get the kind of people who put sugar in your gas tank if you dare disturb the falcons on Morro Rock. Put greed and guilt together and you get the kind of people who live in fine houses on Big Sur and spend conservation money publishing elegant picture books.

Winding north along the coast above San Francisco under a perpetual fog, we stopped for lunch at Sea Ranch, that celebrated development of weekend and vacation homes for prosperous San Franciscans. Sea Ranch has received more honors than the Taj Mahal for its architecture and landscaping, but it is rather a barren place, weathered wood conferring on expensive houses a specious austerity, a place for people who get their taste from architectural magazines, people who wouldn't think of taping a child's painting to a window or shaking a mop out the back door. Sea Ranch, if the truth be told, smelled of money, the kind professionals earn, more than they know what to do with. Canny investing to save the seashore: I thought Sea Ranch rather marred the view.

Mendocino, farther up, was an assay in the other direction. It had the rough, muddy look of a frontier town, which, in a way, it is. Not many years ago, it had a population of ninety-five souls. Since then, the counterculture has discovered it, building rural communes around it that look to it for supplies as farmers look to farm towns. And some of the counterculture folk, having discovered entrepreneurship, were setting up muddy, fogbound Mendocino to be a tourist attraction. The old clapboard hotel, built in 1878 and identical to the hotel in every Western movie you've ever seen, had been painted a fresh lemon yellow and the management had cleverly made up for the absence of central heating by supplying every bed with an electric blanket. I found it, as we say, charming, but since the bathrooms were down the hall, as in former days, and there wasn't much to do in town unless you were into wave watching or macramé, my wife found it squalid and we drove on to Fort Bragg and over the coastal mountains to Willits, bulldogged by logging trucks front and rear hustling the redwoods away.

Sea Ranch and Mendocino: the third corner of the triangle was a place called Konocti Harbor Inn, a family resort of vast proportions on the western shore of Clear Lake, the largest body of fresh water completely within the state of California. A nice place: I find no fault with it: I merely want to point out that it is owned and operated, for the benefit of its membership first of all, by the joint board of labor and management of the United Association of Journeymen and Apprentices of the Plumbing and Pipe Fitting Industry, Local 238, San Francisco. And is therefore, like the two other places, like Carmel, like California itself, an enclave. California is a state of enclaves; California is an enclave state.

Let me explain: years ago, one of our more intellectual generals proposed an enclave plan as a way of solving our problems in Vietnam. According to that plan, rather than try to win the war or settle the peace, we would simply withdraw our troops into protected areas and let the rest of the country go to hell. As you know, the enclave plan was never effected. If it had been, we would be in Vietnam still, guarding acres of asphalted enclaves while the Cong lobbed in rockets. But the plan didn't die; it only got shifted from the Far East to the Far West, where Oregon, a state stolen from the English by hardy American pioneers, asks hardy latter-day American pioneers to turn their wagons around and head on home, and where California puts weekending professionals, six-gun-toting communards and sunburned plumbers and pipe fitters in separate housing. San Clemente is an enclave, as was Haight-Ashbury in mistier days, long ago. Not all enclaves are voluntary: Watts is an enclave and in valley towns in California the railroad tracks similarly divide Caucasian from Chicano. But one thing humble folk know that Californians don't, and that is that regardless of the way the top wires face, an enclave is always a prison.

And not many Americans, scrambling into enclaves right and

left though we are, would say they thought the precipitation of people into enclaves was a desirable trend in a democracy. Yet it has been a long time coming, and it is the more difficult to think about because it has its roots in the American dream.

But let's drive on down from Clear Lake to the Napa Valley before we talk of that, and tour the Charles Krug Winery, admire the huge redwood vats, smell the smells of fermentation that we love so much and that sometimes get us into trouble, stand at the bar in the tasting room and swirl the Chenin Blanc in the late-morning sun, drive over to Sonoma and stand in the square where California was briefly proclaimed a sovereign republic by an inebriated mob of misbespoken men. I am thinking about *freedom* and *comfort*, and I am thinking about the reasons Americans move around.

To begin with, I live in the Midwest, where most of the people who originally settled California and most of the people who moved there after World War II had come from. The Midwest was never quite comfortable with those emigrations. Watching their neighbors pack up and leave for the West, Midwesterners suspected the emigrants had the edge in gumption, and perhaps they did. Midwesterners suspected that the best people were moving West and wondered if that was a judgment on those who stayed behind to clean out the barn and see the cows milked.

But "best" isn't really right, is it? "Ambitious" would be more accurate, or, less elegantly, "greedy," as we have discussed. "Come on Boys," went the ad George Donner ran in the *Sangamon Journal*, of Sangamon County, Illinois, on March 26, 1846. "You can have as much land as you want without costing you anything." And besides a gout of free land, there would be the good weather, no terrible midwestern winters, and no disease, and lovely *señoritas*, and those great John Ford skies, and a chance to begin again.

Those aren't the same reasons—or, rather, those aren't the *only* reasons—we had for exploring, founding, and settling the United States of America. We also wanted to share equally in the rights of man. Without that sharing, the other reasons become reasons only of physical and psychic comfort, and in the long run, they must prove, are proving, inimicable to the rights of man. Years ago, before he moved to California, Aldous Huxley had something to say about the relentless search for comfort. "Made possible by the changes in the traditional philosophy of life," he wrote, "com-

fort is now one of the causes of its own further spread. For comfort has now become a physical habit, a fashion, an ideal to be
pursued for its own sake. The more comfort is brought into the
world, the more it is likely to be valued. To those who have
known comfort, discomfort is a real torture." And since California
by most measures—climate, per-capita income, you name it—is
the place in the United States where the scrabble for comfort has
made the greatest headway, it isn't surprising that Californians
will do almost anything to keep what they've got, including shutting the state down. California's version of saving the land is that
there isn't enough to go around, so those who have it should keep
away those who don't. Which isn't exactly the message delivered
to us in the Sermon on the Mount.

I enjoy comfort, you enjoy comfort, we all enjoy comfort; but,
as with orgasm, comfort carries you away only when it isn't
directly sought. Scrabbling for comfort is always scrabbling for an
escape from mortality, and escaping from mortality is an infant's
dream, not an adult's realistic hope. In this special way, then, to
lust for comfort as Californians have lusted is to be imprisoned in
the past, the past of childhood fantasies. To move to California in
response to a desire for greater comfort is to move in response to a
daydream, and it asks for grief.

We haven't, it seems to me, properly thought the frontier
movement through. We wanted the land filled up—it was the
only way we could be sure we owned it—and we let that obscure
our judgment. I'm not sure I want to be represented in history by
people who didn't bother to clean up their trash before they lit
out for the territories or to look back once they left. I am a writer,
and when I look to my own field of interest, I find that the one
area of the country in which the standards of writing are consistently high is the South, whose writers seldom leave home. I think
they know what ought to be obvious to all of us, that comfort is a
mirage and an excuse, that a lifetime of minute examination, a lifetime of getting to know all the trees and animals and birds and
bees, the meanders of every creek and river, the subtleties of
weather and season, the patterns of speech, the streets of cities,
the lay of the land, isn't enough to master even one place, and
that moving to another place means nothing grander than having
to start all over again from scratch.

And yet Americans move incessantly, at least once every five years, and the affluent more often yet. Move in response to opportunity, of course, move in response to climate, but move, really, in response to daydreams of pitiful grandeur: to live in a "nicer" neighborhood, to have a "nicer" house, to have a beach to dream on down at the bottom of the town, a beach they will visit once or twice a year. Move and leave their graves behind: how many Americans remember where their grandparents are buried? And having moved to a strange place in a strange season, many of the dreamers then seek out enclaves for themselves, singles complexes, suburban developments, ethnic neighborhoods, country clubs, weekend retreats. Where the wagons are circled and the Indians can't get in. Enclaves are identical to communities in every way but one, the most vital: you are born into a community or earn your place in its hodgepodge through long residence; at an enclave, you buy your way in. An enclave has a history, but it has no past, and we need a past, to lie beneath and behind us and remind us of who we are. To keep us humble. To remind us that there are things left in the world that can't be bought.

We went on down toward Los Angeles, stopping off in Santa Barbara to look up the descendants of the Reed family, the family most prominent in the Donner party after the Donners themselves, but the Reeds had moved. Bill Loud was in the phone book, not the kind of man to be modest in the face of fame. I called Joan Didion late one evening to tell her she was right, but she had an answering service and I never got through. My wife had gone home early; I took the kids and drove through Los Angeles to Anaheim, to the Disneyland Hotel. One of my brothers, a Los Angeles policeman, lives nearby.

My other brother, America's last Fabian socialist, the owner and operator of a Huntington Park welding shop, picked us up for a dinner at the policeman's house. I remember the evening as a series of snapshots; three brothers, all of them ruddy, freckled, stocky, rather awkward men, sitting somberly at the umbrella-shaded picnic table beside the modest back-yard swimming pool; the policeman proudly showing off his handmade pegged-oak bar that he hardly ever uses, because he hardly ever drinks; a pineapple stuffed with toothpick-loaded fruit; the policeman's daughter in her waitress uniform, just back from waiting on tables to earn money for college; the kids in the pool riding a giant banana; the policeman's pretty, gracious wife tearing off hunks of string cheese and passing them around; two card tables of kids, their plates loaded with food. The policeman's wife was Italian-American; the three brothers were one generation removed from an Arkansas hillbilly farm; we spent an hour talking about dogs; we agreed that good dogs make good neighbors. Didion speaks of California settlers of "the peculiar flawed strain who had cleared Virginia, Kentucky, Missouri." That was us. I think it helped that I had never left home.

The next day and night my children and I spent at Disneyland, figuring out the best rides and getting there first, before the three-hour lines began to form, beating strategic retreats to the hotel on the monorail whenever our feet got sore. It occurred to me, watching a crowd of teen-aged children milling before a rock band, that Disneyland was the ultimate enclave, a place papered with imitation history that had no past at all, a place where the only connections between people were those they brought in through the gate, and that it was the dream of a Midwesterner who went to California to seek his fortune, and found it, so they say. Not a very original thought. I felt something that was more my own at the end of the evening, after the marvelous fireworks, when a gymnast in silver lamé, lit by blinding lights, slid down a wire as Tinker Bell, poor Tinker Bell on her magic slide. "The answer to fear," J. Robert Oppenheimer once said, "cannot always lie in the dissipation of the causes of fear; sometimes it lies in courage." That was what I felt, something like that.

Easier said than done. But sometimes the real intrudes on our fantasies and requires more of us than we think we can give, and yet we give it. Before we left Carmel, we attended a ceremony dedicating a new eight-cent stamp commemorating Robinson Jeffers' life and work. Dame Judith Anderson, a long-time friend of Jeffers', was there to read from one of his poems, the highlight of the ceremony after the clang of the Fort Ord band and the mild tributes of Post Office officials shipped all the way out from Washington. Dame Judith chose a poem Jeffers had written after his wife died of cancer, when he set aside, for a time, his disdain for humanity because he found a bond with it in human grief. She read so fiercely, read with such passion and so personal a sense of loss, that all of us, strangers in a chilly room, momentarily shared what she and Jeffers felt, and so we kept our hands clenched in our laps and listened to the words of a dead man spoken and heard through tears:

The lies—the faithless hopeless unbelieved lies,
While you lay dying.
For these reasons I wish to make verse again, to drug memory,
To make it sleep for a moment. Never fear: I shall not forget you—
Until I am with you. The dead indeed forget all things.
And when I speak to you it is only play-acting
And self-indulgence: you cannot hear me, you do not exist.
Dearest. . . .

That is not greed, or fearful hauteur, that is simple grief, and it is real.

Or again: One Sunday afternoon, my wife and I had gone to an upstairs restaurant on the Monterey wharf and sat sheltered near a fireplace and ordered good wine and crab boiled and crab cioppino. Across from us, half the length of the restaurant away, sat a huge family of huge people, men and women averaging perhaps 250 pounds apiece, eight or ten of them, a row of motorcycle helmets hanging on the hatrack beyond them to indicate how they traveled if their boots and heavy sweaters did not. They had come from somewhere to eat, several generations of the same family, and they looked, from behind, like two backfields of professional football players opposing each other across a picnic table. I had noticed them and forgotten them, watching the people on the wharf below, when the room was suddenly shocked to silence by a great moan as one of the giant men slid off his chair and collapsed on the floor. I saw him grab his throat and saw his eyes roll back, and then the two backfields of his family surrounded him, shouting and arguing, and the rasping sound of desperate snoring tore the room.

I was frozen to my chair; so was my wife; I thought the man had choked on his food and I could see that his family was trying to get his mouth open while the snoring turned to the terrible silence of snoring cut off, of a wet plug smacking into place in the man's throat, while his feet kicked, drumming the floor, and I thought all at the same time that the man must be an epileptic and that I knew by the book how to perform a tracheotomy but didn't know how to dare to begin but that if I or someone didn't dare something, the man was likely to die of asphyxiation from swallowing his tongue, and I half-rose from my seat and sat down again weak at the knees and half-rose again and then, Jesus God, a black woman at another table got up and ran over and shoved the giant relatives aside and knelt down and someone stage-whispered, "She's a nurse," and she set to work to get his tongue out of his throat, and then she gave out a moaning scream once and again and once again and someone stage-whispered, "He's biting her thumb," her screams so piercing he must have all but bitten it off, and by then the manager of the restaurant had called the police and an ambulance and the fire department too, taking no chances, and sirens whooped and wailed in the distance while the black nurse popped her dented, quivering thumb out of the man's mouth and wrapped it in a bunch of napkins for safety as well as traction and bravely stuck it back in again and got the tongue turned around and pulled it forward and with great sucking sounds like a drainpipe clearing the man started breathing again, and so did we.

The fire truck was a bilious shade of yellow and the ambulance shining white and the men who piloted them were soothing and competent, and by the time the man was wheeled out to the ambulance, he had opened his eyes—the victim, we overheard someone at the next table saying, of an insulin reaction—this huge natural man from California, this huge man who had ridden in with his wife and mom and dad and brothers and sisters, all on motorcycles, artificially kept alive, when he got his dosage right, by regular injections of a drug discovered by a Canadian only fifty-two years ago, five decades ago, this huge man saved by a black nurse he'd never spoken to before, and all of us left behind in the restaurant, which was quiet now except for the nurse's hysterical giggling, waking up then to realize that our comfortable afternoon on the Monterey wharf had been forever altered into a memory of the fragility of our connection to the world, because a chicken bone might as easily have sent any one of us writhing to the floor, our entire comfortable lives caught in our throat, and if we were lucky, as the diabetic had been lucky today, there would be someone in the room who knew how to spare us, but it wasn't likely to be someone from our enclave, it was likely to be someone from our community: our pals back at the enclave hardly knew how to tie their shoes, and no more did we; privilege outfits us as badly for emergencies as it does for the long haul.

Which is most of the lesson the people of the Donner Party learned, those who survived. One of them, Virginia Reed, fourteen years old, wrote home about it afterward, wrote the last word about privilege, comfort, nature worship, golden dreams, and Pacific sunsets:

> We are all very well pleased with California. Particularly
> with the climate. Let it be ever so hot a day there is allwais cool
> nights. It is a beautiful Country. It is mostley in vallies. It aut
> to be a beautiful Country to pay us for our trubel getting there.

It is a beautiful country. It is mostly in valleys. It ought to be a beautiful country to pay us for our trouble getting there. Words that ought to be inscribed above every port and harbor and Customs in the land: two unconsciously lyric sentences followed by an outburst of dry exasperation from a girl who knew better than most men that the going can be rootless and can bring great pain.

We don't need rootlessness any more, we need roots. Thinking about that several months later, after I was back in Kansas and the winter had closed in, I remembered Oppenheimer again, something he wrote in late 1954, after his security hearing, after the witch-hunters had wrung him out, when his weaknesses and indiscretions, his strengths and loyalties alike were publicly on record and he had nothing, one way or the other, to lose:

> This is a world in which each of us, knowing his limitations,
> knowing the evils of superficiality and the terrors of fatigue, will
> have to cling to what is close to him, to what he knows, to what
> he can do, to his friends and his tradition and his love, lest he
> be dissolved in a universal confusion and know nothing and
> love nothing.

But, in fairness, you should know that Oppenheimer goes on to say that we must equally remain open to new experience. How we are to do both, the man who moved to California, the man who built the bomb, doesn't explain. Nor can I, yet, but I don't think I'd put moving to California, or laboring in California to keep the rabble out, very high on my list.

An Excursion on the Prairie

Only fools go out looking for beauty. In the worst of times, soon after my divorce was final, in late spring, I decided to drive to Oklahoma from Kansas, where I live, to see the annual dances of the Osage Indians, dances I had been told were still authentic, and to meet the aging chronicler of the Osages before he goes, a man born in 1895, part Osage, former member of the Tribal Council, an author, an elegant man, an Oxford man. I thought vaguely that a trip to the country would do me good.

Like my own predecessors, but five hundred or a thousand years earlier, the Osages came from the Ozarks, from the Ozark border. Lived in villages along Missouri's Osage River, the river they called the Place-of-the-Many-Swans. To most people the Ozarks mean outhouses, but those are not their chief distinction. They are the only mountainous country between the Appalachians and the Rockies. They exist because a swell of rock, a batholith, rose up under the region a billion years ago and rivers and creeks etched their meanders into the swell. The batholith rose up slowly, without vulcanism. The chronicler of the Osages, John Joseph Mathews, believes that the tribe postulated no Hell because it had never seen a volcano, and he is probably right. Hell is Vesuvius, or Krakatoa, or a hydrogen bomb. The Osages postulated only death and resurrection. And learned to survive the midwestern tornadoes by clinging to the sumac bush. They did not survive the encroachment of the white man, however, and eventually removed to Osage County, Oklahoma, and would have languished there, but oil was found on their tribal lands, and today pumps like earth-shattering mosquitoes suck Osage oil and deliver it to the Phillips Petroleum Company, headquartered at Bartlesville. The oil saved the Osages, people say, but we shall see. Shall see if

Previously unpublished (1974)

anyone is saved on this lickerish continent where man arrived so late and with such grandiose expectations.

The graffiti have changed in the rest stations of small Kansas towns. The walls no longer bear Neanderthal sketches of breasts and mingled genitals nor bardic verses of adolescent celebration but requests for urgent meetings: MEET ME HERE SUNDAY NITE 9 P.M. SUCK; HANDSOME COUPLE HUSBAND WELL-HUNG WANT TO MEET, etc.; and, plaintively, I'M NOT SO YOUNG ANYMORE BUT I'VE GOT, etc. Swingers in farm towns of five hundred souls seem possible but unlikely even under a harvest moon; it's more likely that the illustrators and versifiers of old have been reading the classifieds in counterculture periodicals, and in the smallest of towns kids walk the streets with hair to their shoulders and *Rolling Stone* blares from every Kwik-Shop and drugstore. The revolution is total, we're all into it now, but in southern Kansas the revolution is attenuated by distance from the urban centers of its origin to long hair and *Rolling Stone* and MEET ME HERE SUNDAY NITE and gatherings of the thin Kansas marijuana from fields left unguarded by the KBI, the Kansas Bureau of Investigation, the same that solved Capote's murders long ago. The KBI announced to the press shortly before I left for Oklahoma that it would stake out the marijuana fields as it did each summer, but that it didn't have enough men to stake out them all. The marijuana is poor, I'm told, volunteer stands left over from the days when Kansas grew hemp for the manufacture of rope. Kids still crop it, however, and the men of the KBI guard it through the moonlit summer nights like children watching over a fairy ring, waiting for the elves to come by.

In early evening I arrived in Pawhuska, the county seat of Osage County, where the Osage Indian Agency is situated high on a protective bluff, and found a motel of six rooms, the second-best in town. The girl at the desk left me in the midst of registration, slipping into the kitchen of the Taco Hut next door to fill an urgent order. The smell of burning corn blew back, corn the Indians devised. We call them Indians; they almost always called themselves the People; the Osages called themselves the Little Ones, hoping the gods of the universe would thus overlook their arrogance. The Osages and dozens of other tribes were concentrated by government fiat long ago in Oklahoma: the old maps, the maps of Oklahoma before the Oklahoma Run, before the territory became a state, show a patchwork of reservations. The Indians felt crowded, blasted; we felt them confined and thanked God. That was not exactly a standoff. The arguments continue about what we did. We thought the Indians another and most dangerous species of animal and we cleared the land: that is what we did. The Indians, the People, being human, thought otherwise. They thought we took their birthright away.

That is not exactly what the Osages thought. Deeply religious, they feared their faith had failed them. Feared that Wah-Kon-Tah, the Eternal Mysteries, despising their lack of faith, had turned away. Once the Osages commanded Missouri, Arkansas, Oklahoma and Kansas, pushing back the Caddos and the Apaches to the south and west, holding in thrall the smaller tribes to the north and east. They found in the creatures of the Ozarks and the prairie the qualities to which they aspired, the qualities that made them powerful: in the beaver, the fresh-water mussel, the white pelican, the brown bear, the wapiti, the deer, the owl and most of all the buffalo wisdom, virtue, industriousness, courage, long life. They divided into clans, each clan taking its sacred tradition from one of the creatures, sparing only the buffalo, so important to their economy that the nearest they could approach its sacredness was the Buffalo Face clan—only its face, not the animal whole. They were a fierce people, and because they lived on an ecotone, an interface between forest and prairie, and could crop the best of both worlds, they found the protein to make them strong and tall, averaging six feet or more in their best warriors at a time when white Europe averaged a little over five, able to walk seventy miles in a day, adept at horses when horses came, adept at guns, fusils, when fusils came upriver with the people they called the Heavy Eyebrows, the French trappers of pre-Revolutionary America.

So long as Spain and France contested their territory, they were courted, a valued border guard between two nations extended on overlong lines of supply, but when the English came, the people they named the Long Knives for the swords they wore, and even more when the Americans came, they began to lose ground, because the Spanish and the French only traveled through, but the Anglo-Saxons stopped and settled, parceled out the earth that the Osages thought belonged to Wah-Kon-Tah. Lesser chiefs and Nobodies traded the land away, signed treaty after treaty, and the Cherokees in top hats and cutaways pressed in, adept at the ways of Washington. The Osages never lost their land in battle, as other tribes did, and they were paid for their treaties more than most, but the land fell away nonetheless, and became, they said, like a shriveled old woman, and eventually, in the late nineteenth century, they removed reluctantly to Oklahoma, suffered the embarrassment of buying land in the Cherokee Strip that once had belonged to them by right of conquest, and settled in. They had been overwhelmed by bodies, white bodies like a horde of maggots that took up occupancy on their lands and could not be dislodged no matter how much neolithic frenzy they displayed, no matter what fierce and false masks they painted on their faces, no matter how many scalps they took. Scalps brought the Long Knives, and more treaties, and more pittances to replace the bounty they had once enjoyed. They never knew starvation, but they knew want, and if they went undefeated in battle, they learned defeat in council, because the more their ways failed them the more they increased their worship and the more Osage they became. When other tribes dressed for council cannily in white men's clothes, the Osages still swaggered in their buckskins, gorgets of shell at their necks to symbolize Grandfather the Sun shining at noon, roaches of deer hair or softened porcupine quills on their heads, cascades of bone or necklaces of eagle or bear claws over their chests, and the whites thought them unregenerate savages, and the Anglicized Indians of the other tribes thought them a shame, though a dangerous shame, not to be trifled with. The Osages were never a tribe to be trifled with. They had an essential arrogance, Mathews says, and though he denies he means the word pejoratively, I have my doubts. They had the arrogance of a people who never had to fight on their home ground. They were most American in that: neither have we, except with each other.

I found John Joseph Mathews, at the cocktail hour of my arrival, in the room he shared with his wife at the better motel. They had lived there most of a year, ever since a serious operation brought her into town from the stone house Mathews had built with his own hands long ago on his ranch on the prairie, too far from town for safe convalescence. Mathews was drinking Wild Turkey, and I joined him, his wife preferring rum and orange juice, the juice on doctor's orders for the potassium it contained. The man reclined on his bed on one elbow, beneath the elbow a folded blanket, in exactly the posture of the old Osage chiefs in the faded photographs taken long ago by the Bureau of Ethnology. He is a tall man, a big man, was dressed in a blue jumpsuit, his forehead Shakespearean and capped with fine white hair, his voice firm and commanding, with a touch of Oxford at the edges. Fifty years ago he failed to appear at Oxford until months past the beginning of term. The hunting had been good in Wyoming that year. His Oklahoma sponsors were scandalized, but the dons at Oxford understood: a chap doesn't come away to term when the hunting is good. Mathews was navigator of an aircraft in World War I, and after Oxford he hunted his way through Switzerland and down to North Africa. In North Africa one evening, making camp, he was suddenly surrounded by burnoosed Arabs on horseback firing their rifles into the air. He asked his guide if they were safe. "Joy-shooting," his guide said, and invited the Arabs to supper, but Mathews, young Mathews then, remembered another day, when he was a boy in Osage country and a crowd of Osage braves found him out on the prairie and surrounded him on horseback and fired their rifles into the air, and the two rounds of joy-shooting came together in his mind and he asked himself what he was doing in North Africa when he ought to be at home.

He went back to Oklahoma then and began his work of chronicling the history of the people among whom he had grown up. The old men of the tribe sought him out as they never would have done in an earlier time, young as he was. They were afraid, Mathews said, that their oral histories, histories passed down verbatim through hundreds of years, would be lost, and with the loss of their tribal memory, the record of their collective lines. So they allowed Mathews to take notes, and later to tape-record the histories they had learned from their fathers, and their fathers from their fathers before them, preserving every gesture and inflection as they had been taught, so that, for example, Mathews could still pull at his collar contemptuously when he described how badly the first white men the Osages had seen, nearly four hundred years ago, stank, an affliction the Osages attributed to the strange cut of their clothes.

An early novel set among the Osages was a Book-of-the-Month Club selection in the 1930s, and later came a Guggenheim and other fellowships, and in 1961, after two decades at least of work ("I had been working on that book all my life," Mathews said), he published a detailed history of the tribe, exhaustive and exhausting and touched with a sense of irony so subtle that at times it can take your breath away. *The Osages: Children of the Middle Waters* was nothing less than a history of America from the Indian point of view, without bitterness but spring-loaded with the kind of humor that is still an Osage trademark, humor that finds its finest expression in the spectacle of proud men and proud nations making fools of themselves, though there is, for the Osages, a double irony in that.

Here is a contingent of Osages visiting Paris in 1827:

It was reported that at Saint Cloud, Little Chief's face was painted with blue and red when they met the King, and after paying their respects to the Dauphin and the Dauphiness, they had breakfast with the Captain of the Guards. They were invited everywhere, and were taken to the theater so often that they became bored, even with all the glasses in the theater on them continually. . . . Certainly they would have given no sign of boredom. On the Neosho and formerly at the Place-of-the-Many Swans, one had to sit for hours listening to the chieftain and the warriors of many *o-do'n,* and to the long medicine talk of the missioners, where one sat passively with closed eyes, behind which one could escape to thrilling personal experiences. Here at the theater in Paris it was not unlike the medicine talk of the Black Robes saying mass. They did not close their eyes.

And a little later in the same visit:

The French women seemed to have been fascinated by the warriors, and Big Soldier said that he had been "married" three times while in France.

Finding this man in a small Oklahoma motel room was like finding Gibbon or Herodotus there, and Mrs. Mathews was no less remarkable, her voice lilting and her face still beautiful, surrounded by abundant gray hair. The elderly in America seldom carry such a freight of dignity and courtliness and pride. Halfway through my life, I stored the Mathewses away somewhere, knowing how much I might need their memory at a later time.

The Osages hold three separate rounds of dancing each summer, the first at Grayhorse, a village a day's walk southwest of Pawhuska that was once an Indian subagency, the second at Pawhuska, the third at the small town of Hominy. I planned to go to the Grayhorse dances the following evening, but in the meantime I drove to the Pawhuska cemetery, north of the Agency, to walk that stone record of the Osage past. The cemetery spread across the east side of a treeless hill, a mausoleum rising above it as Lee's mansion rises above Arlington. It looked raw and new, perhaps because so few trees grew among the graves or because it lacked a fence, but in fact it was old, and I soon found stones that dated from the late nineteenth century. I also found stones cut from Ozark granite in the shape of arrowheads, small stones of dead children, stones with oval ceramic plaques glued to their faces carrying photographs of the deceased in full dance dress, the photographs protected under a clear glaze. I found a long row of Mathewses and stones with Osage names I couldn't pronounce.

The biggest stones marked the period of the Osages' greatest prosperity; in the third decade of the twentieth century, full-blooded Osages received as much as thirteen thousand dollars a year in oil royalties. Oil is the one fact about the Osages that most Americans know. I had visited Phillips Petroleum a few months earlier, and each of the men I talked to there told me the same story, apparently the only story about the Osages they knew, that with his oil money in hand an Osage would buy a Cadillac without bothering to learn to drive, would smash it up on the way home and leave the shards lying and stumble to town to buy another Cadillac and eventually learn by doing and make it back to his ranch. It was a famous story, and perhaps it was true, but it put the oil money and the white feelings about the oil money in perspective. The oil money was conscience money, after all, and lo, the poor Indian, he didn't know how to spend it very well. In fact, the Osages accepted the oil money as their due, thanking God and Wah-Kon-Tah both that they had had the good sense to hold their mineral rights in community rather than allot them out to individuals as other tribes had done, but they hardly thought it compensation for Missouri and Arkansas and Oklahoma and Kansas, for the disappearance of the buffalo and their removal from the Place-of-the-Many-Swans. And the thing to do with money

was to spend it, because a man showed his greatness in these latter days not by counting coup but by the value of the things he
could give away. That would not make sense to a corporation executive: it would make sense to a Rockefeller, however, and the
Osages in their pride were hardly less arrogant than the Rocke-
fellers. The oil money comes to far less now, but the energy crisis
has encouraged new interest in the Osage fields, and engineers are
coming in to open up old wells and explore for new ones. The Little Ones in their white men's graves would not know or care
about that, dreaming of the sweet careen of their Cadillacs and
the ripping of metal that laid them low—though in truth most of
them died in their beds in honored old age.

"Budded on Earth to Blossom in Heaven," read an inscription
on a baby's grave, and farther down the row was buried a descendant of Daniel Boone. Whites and Indians lay buried side by side
in the cemetery, and Christian and Osage symbols and words
marked the graves, votive lights next to arrowheads, names in
English and names in Osage, the macaronic of change the Osages
were powerless to stop but had attempted to slow by incorpo-
ration. They were never "good Indians," but they were willing, to
a point, to adapt, in the pragmatic belief that power was power
and ought to be borrowed whenever it worked. An earlier generation had prayed to God and Wah-Kon-Tah both, had faced their
dead to the east of Christianity rather than to the west of Wah-
Kon-Tah, reasoning that so long as the dead warrior was painted
correctly he could not lose the way to heaven. So the headstones
in the cemetery faced west and the graves east, silent on the side
of the bare prairie hill, and I could read the inscriptions without
walking on the dead.

The Grayhorse dances were scheduled to begin at eight the
next evening, and I drove out from Pawhuska under a blowing,
overcast sky through mile upon mile of native prairie, fenced
along the roadside and marked with oil pumps and Hereford cows
and calves but otherwise undisturbed, crowded with wildflowers
blooming opportunistically before the big bluestem grew to waist
high and overtopped them. At the intersection with the road to
Grayhorse the highway enlarged to four lanes divided, one of
those major interchanges Oklahoma builds in the midst of nowhere to prove that it too receives a share of federal highway
funds. There I turned south, drove through a small town, then

turned east on a country road across one-lane bridges and railroad tracks, past the old stone subagency building to the sacred arbor. It was a tin-roofed pavilion with open sides and a dirt floor. Mathews had told me to find the Whip Man, and after asking around I did. He was not yet in dance costume; stocky, handsome, with gray in his hair, he wore expensive western clothes—hand-tooled boots, gray pants, an embroidered gray shirt, a massive turquoise-and-silver buckle on his belt.

The dances had become important to the Osages again, the Whip Man said. People had lost interest in them a few years ago, but now they were being revived. There were white hobbyists now who came to the dances from all over the United States, and so long as they danced authentically they were allowed to dance along with the Indians. I started at that; I had expected the dances to be confined to the Osages themselves. We can't do that, said the Whip Man; we're so intermarried now that we'd have to keep our own kin out if we didn't let any whites in. Intermarriage had changed things, he said; he was intermarried himself, and more and more Osages were intermarrying as time went on. Pretty soon you won't be able to tell the Indians from the whites, he said. Women were allowed to dance now, too, though he wasn't sure he liked them on the dance out of costume, in shorts and halters sometimes.

You won't see any feather-dancing here, though, said the Whip Man; the Osage dances were quiet and sober, no applause, no showing off for the crowd. The difference between the dances was subtle, the songs were different but you'd have to know Osage to tell the difference. The Whip Man said he had a different costume for each night, including one of purple satin made for him by a woman in California that he was saving for Saturday night. He pointed to a woman on the other side of the pavilion. She kept the sacred drum, he said, and spent maybe four thousand dollars a year to feed all the people who came to the dances and to give them beef and groceries and blankets at the Sunday-afternoon Giveaway. The expense was too much for her, and she was having to give up the drum. The Whip Man excused himself to go speak with her, and I took a seat in the bleachers at the west end of the pavilion.

The dances were scheduled to start at eight, but they didn't start until after nine: Grayhorse was running on Osage time now.

The west and east stands filled with visitors; the Osages had benches—church pews, their family names painted on the backs— to the north and south of the dance floor, a dirt floor that had been raked smooth and sprinkled with water to keep down any dust that might be kicked up by the dancers, though dust wasn't likely after the storms that had blown through that day, and the sky was black now above the arbor with new storms coming. The railings outside the pavilion were lined with cars, and many of the Indians, Osage or visiting kin, would stay inside their cars throughout the evening, watching the dances through windshields beaded with rain. And when I looked back from the row of cars to the dance floor the sacred drum was in place in the center, surrounded by middle-aged men and a few boys, the drummers and their apprentices. They wore no costumes, only cowboy hats and windbreakers and jeans. They were not even Osage, I learned later, but Pawnee, professional musicians with voice and drums.

The Whip Man stepped onto the dance floor a little after nine. He was dressed now in moccasins, black pants, a long, square-cut black shirt, with sashes down his back and front and at his sides, with a fine porcupine roach on his head tied under his chin and held in place by a headband. He carried a riding crop and an eagle-feather fan, and he was accompanied by an elderly Osage in buckskins wearing a brimless beaver hat, a pillbox. The Osage who would lead the dancers, a representative of the Tribal Council, came in on the other side from the Whip Man with a younger man in full costume but wearing glasses; the younger man looked like a Tulsa executive, which he probably was. Then the dancers filed in, most of them in their teens and early twenties, all of them in brightly colored costume pants and shirts—blue, red, purple, even flowered prints—and elaborately sashed. A few of the youngest wore sneakers instead of moccasins.

With no obvious signal from the Whip Man, the dances began, the drummers singing falsetto, *Hi, ya, hi ya ya ya, hi, ya, ya ya ya,* setting up a simple rhythm on the drum. The Whip Man stepped out and the man from the Tribal Council on the opposite side and then the dancers circled the drum counterclockwise, standing upright, making no fancy twists and twirls, the only obvious variation in their walk around the drum the pattern of their steps. The young men danced with more vigor than the old, but the old men knew the steps and the songs and would dance every dance

throughout the evening, not sweating like the young, only stepping unblinking around the drum. The songs changed from dance
to dance, and the rhythms of the drum, but the changes weren't
even obvious, and despite the singers and the beating drum we
might have been watching a troup of mimes. At the end of each
dance, an ending that also went unmarked, no tonic beat of the
drum to signal it, the dancers returned to their benches and then
the tail dancers added a coda, three young men dancing out from
the benches to the drum, arriving at the drum on the last beat and
walking slowly back as the next dance began. The dances seemed
to come in sets, two or three at a time, and between sets water
boys carried white enameled buckets down the line and the
dancers drank from a common dipper, sharing that too.

An elderly woman sat in the center of the dance floor next to
the circle of drummers, and halfway through the evening I saw
her silently weeping, for the Osages or for her clan song: the dance
songs were accounts of clan honors, the Whip Man had said, accounts of the great deeds of each clan. A boy no more than six or
seven years old was presented with his first roach by the man from
the Tribal Council and then seated on a new blanket below me in
the stands, and his father, who was blond, took pictures of him
with a flashing strobe. The old man in the beaver pillbox carried a
wooden flute, and during one dance he began playing it, raising it
above his head and lowering it to his chest, dancing with high
steps like Pan, making bird whistles with a wooden flute, playing
it for one dance only and then subsiding into the plain step he
had danced before, the flute silent through the rest of the evening. No one applauded, as I had been told they would not, no
more than they would applaud in church, but the storms that
blew over pounded the tin roof of the arbor with rain and the rain
sounded like the applause of a multitude, sounded like the applause of a crowd of Osage ghosts coming down from the sky, and
the roof leaked the driving rain, making puddles on the dance
floor that the dancers avoided without seeming to see them. As
the dances beat on, a few women and girls draped with shawls or
blankets danced in a wider circle outside the main body of male
dancers, and some of them wept. A small, gray woman who had
been seated in a place of honor below me at the edge of the dance
floor—she had given away a hog to the young dancers, the man
from the Tribal Council announced in English at one point in

the evening—stood and danced in place, her tiny feet moving up and down.

I saw no hobbyists, though I might not have known what they looked like. The dancers were all dark and all had black hair except for one man's dancing children, a red-haired boy and a blond girl in full costume. A young woman, a beautiful young woman, danced with her baby, which could not have been more than two weeks old; she was the wife of the best of the tail dancers, the dancers who perform a coda at the end of each set, and she showed him the baby after the dance with obvious pride, as if it had been inoculated, as if the rhythms of the dance had been buried in its bones.

The dances ended as abruptly as they had begun and the dancers filed out and the drummers took away the drum. Having played Indian once in the Boy Scouts, having danced with dyed chicken feathers on my tail, I sat through the evening in a daze. The Osage dances grew from another dimension, somber, dignified, giving no quarter to the audience, dances danced not for pay or prize or for condescending crowds at the rodeo but simply to keep the line open to what was left of Wah-Kon-Tah. They had the rigidity and the density of the Roman Catholic mass before it went modern, and so they also had the glory. The Cherokee Trail of Tears extended from Tennessee out to the Panhandle, but the Osage trail of tears went around a dirt dance floor in the middle of the Oklahoma prairie under a pounding line storm. There was as much pain in the one as in the other, and as much memory. Mathews had only hinted at the depth of that memory in his book. I wondered that night, and I wonder now, what will become of it, what we do with memories, painful and glorious, when they no longer serve, as my own no longer served, as the Osages' hardly any longer served, had been reduced to a book and three rounds of dances and the lingering tales of the elderly. "Part of the melancholy of the past," Lionel Trilling once wrote, "comes from our knowledge that the huge, unrecorded hum of implication was once there and left no trace—we feel that because it is evanescent it is especially human." Human, and vulnerable, and as fragile as the bodies in which it is lodged.

I saw what would become of the memory of the American Indian the next day. I drove to a place near Bartlesville called Woolaroc, a game ranch and country estate and museum and organizational center built years ago by the late Frank Phillips, who founded Phillips Petroleum. Woolaroc means WOOds, LAkes and ROCks. It is a gaudy Oklahoma San Simeon, though its gaudiness is more of the spirit, so to speak, than of the flesh. Tourists who come to northeastern Oklahoma do not come to see the Osage dances. They come to see Woolaroc, on the rolling prairie hills south of Bartlesville.

Frank Phillips was a collector, on a scale commensurate with his wealth. He collected travel junk, Indian artifacts, bad paintings and bad sculpture, awards. He collected animals. Once inside the gate at Woolaroc I was required to stay in my car until I reached the museum, acres away, as if on safari through a Kenyan game park, because the ranch was stocked with free-roaming animals: buffalo, first of all, and Scotch Highlands cattle shaggy as musk oxen, antelope, odd Himalayan climbers, bighorn sheep, llamas, deer, grazers and browsers all and not a predator in sight larger than the hawks that circled overhead. The bighorn sheep stand sentry on ten-foot outcroppings of Oklahoma limestone and must wonder why the summers get so hot. Spotted less than discreetly among the groves of trees along the way were full-sized imitation tepees that looked from a distance as if they might be made of Portland cement.

The museum, in the center of the ranch on a prominent hill, was a large building made of native limestone, entirely devoid of windows, its massive metal doors decorated in Art Deco and surrounded by mosaics of Indians in battle dress. Inside, past the central foyer dominated by a life-sized bronze of Phillips himself standing under changing colored lights, the building housed an excellent, if somewhat eclectic, collection of Indian art and artifacts that Phillips had assembled through the years: flexed mummies, flakes and points and scrapers from pre-Columbian times, extraordinary Navaho blankets hung from the walls, a photographic essay on Phillips' archaeological adventures—he was a trim man with a big nose and he excavated some of Oklahoma's larger mounds in jodhpurs and English riding boots, and paid for a good job and got it—and farther into the museum a birch-bark canoe, pottery, reed baskets so finely woven that they took years to make, the bead-and-bonework of the Plains Indians, the turquoise-and-silverwork of the Navaho. Mixed among the Indian artifacts were artifacts from a comic Byzantium: the head of an

African elephant, wall after wall of bad paintings of cowboys and Indians, bad bronzes of the noble pioneers who settled the West, including one pioneer woman whose dress the wind and the sculptor had so revealingly fitted to her body that her mons and her navel and her nipples all stood boldly in view, Oklahoma pornography in the name of Western art.

But down in the basement of the museum I found the mother lode, the dream museum of a self-made man, an airplane in one room that flew transcontinental back in the 1930s, wingspan a good twenty or thirty feet, with Phillips' name on the side, and surrounding the plane in the cases that lined the walls the odds and ends of a wealthy man's travels: Jivaro shrunken heads; a complete collection of bodhisattvas in cheap brass turned out in some Calcutta factory, bad porcelain from China, bad ivory from Japan, netsukes, pots; and down one long wall a tribute to man's inhumanity to man, a collection of knives and swords and shillelaghs and machine guns and rifles and pistols and what have you, from the primitive to the modern—the primitive and the modern, as the collection made clear, never having been far apart in the war department, all of us capable of a neolithic frenzy now and then. The ultimate room was the last room in the basement of the museum, which displayed awards, citations, keys to cities, plaques and certificates given to Frank Phillips over the years, including a selection of the presents he received on his sixty-sixth birthday (it was Phillips 66, remember?); including, embalmed under a bell jar, a blackened piece of birthday cake.

However lurid his taste, it seemed to me after touring his museum that Frank Phillips felt some affinity for the Indians whose oil had made him wealthy. What his successors have done with that personal tradition is another question. Across the road from the museum I found a modern building with a two-story stained-glass window in its north wall. The window depicted the two paths the boys of America might take, the high road of virtue or the low road of excess and vice, and an Indian chief picked out in lead and glass stood at the fork pointing the way. The building is national headquarters for a program called the Y-Indian Guides, a program that is the chief recipient of funds from the Phillips Foundation. Inside the building I listened to a tape that explained how the program came about: the director of the YMCA thought it up while attending one of the Y's annual father-son banquets. He liked the way those banquets brought fathers and sons together, he said, liked the closeness they engendered and the enthusiasm they evoked, but it seemed to him that once a year wasn't enough, that if the Y could do anything it could find a way to build relationships between fathers and sons that would last all the year through.

The pretentiousness of the notion seemed to have escaped the director of the YMCA, and the insult to the American Indian seemed to have escaped him as well. A display in the middle of the headquarters caught the tone of the program: a rotating model of an Indian dance, little carved Indians tripped and twirled by wires poking up from under the turntable. The girl at the novelty counter near the front door turned it on whenever visitors went by, and ten wooden Indians danced.

A patio with a food counter and a row of vending machines extended beyond the back door of the building. I went out to find lunch, and when the woman behind the food counter saw me coming she turned on a recorder and a reedy version of "Home on the Range" began to play from a hidden speaker. The food counter sold only one item, barbecued buffalo burgers, and since I had never tasted buffalo before, I ordered a buffalo burger and got a can of Coke from a vending machine and settled down on a rock to eat. Two swans waddled toward me from a pond beyond the patio, but the woman behind the food counter came sweeping out with broom in hand and they retreated sullenly to the water's edge. I finished my lunch—the buffalo meat tasted strangely sweet, though that may have been barbecue sauce—and looked for a trash bin, and from around the corner of the food counter a tape came on that I hadn't heard before. I followed the sound. It came from a stuffed buffalo that stood behind a low picket fence speaking in a rollicking Western voice, a John Wayne voice. "Hi," it said, "I'm Buffo. People call me a buffalo, but I'm really a bison. Buffo likes to keep America clean, so feed me all your papers and pop cans. I can eat everything you give me. Just put your paper and your cans in Buffo's mouth and he'll eat them up." Buffo went on to describe the history of the buffalo in America, casually mentioning that all the buffalo, all sixty million of them, had been killed by the second half of the nineteenth century because they were so useful to men for food, for hides, for leather and robes, for smoked tongues and tenderloins, and even more casually mentioning that the Indians had also found the buffalo useful, but failing to mention that the Indians had somehow contrived not to kill off all but a handful of America's largest native animal in the process of using it.

I fed my papers and my pop can to Buffo, through his black plaster mouth. He sucked them up eagerly and they clanked back through his body and disappeared. Buffo was threaded with a pneumatic tube that ingested trash. I wondered where the junk went after it popped down his throat, so I walked along Buffo's flank to where his hind quarters butted against the wall of the shed, and found my answer. Walt Disney would have contrived to pop the pop cans out Buffo's hoof or along an unseen inner thigh, but the people who ran the Y-Indian Guides were more forthright: Buffo had a black plastic tube projecting from his anus through the back wall. In that unnatural natural way he rid himself of the detritus of white civilization, shitting trash and pop cans into the bin beyond the wall.

I remembered then a story that Mathews had told me. Frank Phillips, it seemed, aware in his later years of how much fame and glory money can buy, decided to make himself available for physical resurrection, and in the mausoleum at Woolaroc where he is entombed he caused a handle to be placed on the *inside* of the door, and had a telephone installed, in case he should wake up and need to use it. Mathews remembered taking picnics to Woolaroc and sitting on top of Phillips' mausoleum eating lunch, hoping the phone would ring. I remembered that, and I remembered the heavy cement grave covers over some of the Osage graves at Pawhuska, and I thought about Buffo and the Y-Indian Guides, about the dimming Osage dances now filling up with white hobbyists, about the loss of memory which is upon us all, the loss of memory that is also the loss of a usable past, and it seemed to me that the Osages who covered their graves with cement to keep themselves permanently buried, to make sure they would not again be removed to some more blasted place, had the right idea, though it wasn't much help to the living. I drove back to Kansas that night. Through the glass wall of my apartment I can see the prairie sky.

II
THE ENERGIES OF MEN

J. Robert Oppenheimer, Shatterer of Worlds

In the life of J. Robert Oppenheimer—the American physicist and scientist-statesman who directed the building of the first atomic bombs at Los Alamos, New Mexico, during World War II; whose government, discerning "fundamental defects" in his character, denied him security clearance in 1954; who died of throat cancer in 1967—some have professed to see embodied the moral ambiguities of twentieth-century science, science charging breakneck over human institutions, scientists waking sacerdotal from Faustian dreams. Oppenheimer was not much of this, for these are tabloid notions, but he lived at the center of the century's most disturbing contradictions, and struggled with them, and suffered for them, and if he is often taken as their protagonist, it is partly because he was a man of disturbing contradictions himself.

He was an authentic genius, the brightest of his generation, who never earned a Nobel Prize and to whose name no seminal scientific contributions today attach; a man of fierce, lively energy who brooded endlessly on death; a man of great personal warmth and devotion whose colleagues say they never knew him well; a man of gentleness who frequently lashed out with contemptuous sarcasm to cause others pain; a man of integrity who voluntarily sacrificed many of his students and friends to the Torquemadan mercies of Army Counter-Intelligence and the FBI; a loyal patriot who was subjected to public humiliation at McCarthyesque hearings and whose security clearance, once denied, was never, to the end of his life, restored; a man dedicated more profoundly than most men to peace who helped inflict on the world its most terrifying instruments of war. Some of these contradictions have been, or can be, resolved. Others may never be, because he reserved his privacy as rigorously as did Thomas Jefferson, whose reach of mind his own resembled. But like all men—like Jefferson too—J. Robert Oppenheimer left behind his tantalizing clues.

He was born to prosperity working up to wealth in New York City on April 22, 1904. Three Van Goghs, a Picasso, a Renoir would decorate the living room of his family's spacious apartment by the time he left for Harvard. According to his birth certificate, he was christened Julius Robert; he carried through life only the initial, insisting it stood for nothing at all, but Julius was his father's name. Julius Oppenheimer, a vigorous and idealistic man, had emigrated from Germany in 1887 to join his uncle's textile-importing firm and at thirty, in 1900, became a partner. He married Ella Friedman in 1903.

Robert Oppenheimer's mother was beautiful and a painter. She had studied the technique of the impressionists in Paris and taught from her own studio in New York. She wore long sleeves always, and a chamois glove; her right hand was congenitally unformed. She was loving but rigid, a descendant of dignified Baltimore; she engendered in her son, by the time he grew to be a man, a courtliness that even Europeans sometimes found extravagant; in her presence no one presumed to raise his voice. "I was an unctuous, repulsively good little boy," Oppenheimer said later. "My childhood did not prepare me for the fact that the world is full of cruel and bitter things. It gave me no normal, healthy way to be a bastard."

The Oppenheimers' second child, Lewis, born in Robert's infancy, died soon after birth, and horrified of germs and perhaps in retreat from that bereavement, they guarded Robert from companions and the street. He was a frail child, frequently ill, extending to sensitivity in the reservation of adults.

When Robert was five, Julius took him to Germany to visit his Grandfather Ben; Ben declared Julius a royal merchant and gave his blue-eyed grandson a rock collection. It was Robert's first recorded glimpse of science: science at its most modest, classifying, and science at its most inanimate, rocks. He carried his rock collection home and enlarged it, his father indulgently supplying funds, until specimens lined the apartment halls. And that early in the involution of his aesthetics, or in his extreme isolation, he barricaded himself behind essences. He chose to specialize in crystals, atomic signatures cleaved to immutable geometries, certainties of rock that without genealogy, uncreatured, are born and perfect themselves and reproduce. He specialized so fervently that the curator of crystals at the American Museum of Natural History took him as a pupil. A professional microscope that he tuned to the enormities of minutiae was his other childhood toy.

Once he learned to read, he lived in books, precociously encountering his peers. When he was old enough for classrooms he attended New York's Ethical Culture School, the fine pedagogic extension of Felix Adler's Society for Ethical Culture to which Julius Oppenheimer belonged, which declared that "man must assume responsibility for the direction of his life and destiny": man, as opposed to God. Robert did: did laboratory experiments in the third grade, began keeping scientific notebooks in the fourth, began studying physics in the fifth, lectured to the surprised and then delighted members of the New York Mineralogical Club when he was twelve.

At fourteen, to get him out of doors and perhaps to help him find friends, his parents sent him to camp. He walked the trails of Camp Koenig looking for rocks and discoursing with the only friend he found on George Eliot, emboldened by Eliot's conviction that cause and effect ruled human affairs. The other boys, casuistic boys, labeled him "Cutie," and bullying no response they hauled him off one night to the camp icehouse, stripped him bare, beat him up—"tortured him," his friend said—and painted his genitals and buttocks green. Responsibly he stuck it out until camp ended, never went back, never mentioned the place or the humiliation again. But told a teacher at Ethical that fall, not yet fifteen, "I'm the loneliest man in the world."

The loneliest man in the world graduated as Ethical's valedictorian in February 1921. In late April, waiting for his younger brother Frank, born in 1912, to finish school so that the Oppenheimer family could summer in Europe, he underwent surgery for appendicitis. Recovered from that, rock-hunting in the Harz Mountains, he contracted severe colitis. It laid him up for months, too ill to enter Harvard with his class; determined to toughen him, his father sent him off shortly after Christmas with a sturdy Ethical English teacher for a tour of the West. At the Los Pinos dude ranch, in the Sangre de Cristo Mountains northeast of Santa Fe, he chowed down, chopped wood, learned to ride horses and live in rain and weather.

Like eastern semi-invalids in frontier days, Oppenheimer's encounter with wilderness, freeing him from civilized restraints, was decisive, a healing of faith. In the years to come he would lease a ranch in the Sangre de Cristos up near ten thousand feet, and he and Frank would ride a thousand miles on horseback in a summer, sometimes ranging as far away as Colorado, living on raisin chocolate and whiskey and Vienna sausages and cheese. "My two great loves," he wrote a friend in 1929, "are physics and the desert. It's a pity they can't be combined." Eventually he contrived to combine them, siting the bomb laboratory, the ethical Erewhon, across the Rio Grande from the mountains on Los Alamos, a desert mesa extended from below the rim of an ancient and exemplary caldera, a narrow, canyon-cut plateau eroded from the throe of the most violent extinct volcano in the world.

He came back tanned to Harvard, he said, like a Goth coming into Rome, and ravished it. He carried six courses at a time—the requirement was five—and audited for credit four more. He read *The Waste Land*, just published, and saw himself reflected, and began to seek the stern consolation of Hindu mysticism; in his later years he would list Eliot's poem along with the *Bhagavad-Gita* among the ten books that had shaped his philosophy of life. He realized during his sophomore year, 1923—looking to essences again—that in chemistry he had chosen the wrong major, submitted himself to the distinguished physicist Percy Bridgman and switched to physics. Alfred North Whitehead arrived at Harvard the same year, and Oppenheimer submitted also to him. Nobel laureate Hans Bethe, who reported to Oppenheimer at Los Alamos and admired him warmly, exhumed the connection. Oppenheimer "worked at physics," Bethe told a biographer, "mainly because he found physics the best way to do philosophy." He graduated in three years, *summa cum laude* and first in his class, with the highest grade average Harvard ever recorded, but not yet, in his own severe judgment, a human being. Harvard, he would say, was "the most exciting time I've ever had in my life. I really had a chance to learn. I loved it. I almost came alive." Noting the prodigious intake, Bridgman warned him not to consider himself a physicist until he'd done original work. He faced that sentence next.

At the Cavendish, Cambridge University's celebrated laboratory, he struggled for the first time to do physics originally and alone. Before he succeeded, the self-doubt the effort evulsed almost destroyed him. "My feeling about myself," he said of this period, "was always one of extreme discontent." A Cambridge friend remembered finding him groaning, rolling on the floor. He went into treatment with a London psychiatrist. "I was on the point of bumping myself off. This was chronic." The psychiatrist diagnosed *dementia praecox*—schizophrenia—and warned him to stay away. Oppenheimer went off to Corsica on spring holiday with friends, to whom he announced that his ideal man would be widely talented but would look at the world with a "tear-stained countenance."

Something happened on Corsica to change his mind, something he would later reveal only in hints: he met a woman, probably a married woman, and learned the certification of love. He returned to Corsica for the summer. "A great thing in my life," he told biographer Nuel Pharr Davis, "a great and lasting part of it. . . . You can't dig it out. What you need to know is that it was not a mere love affair, not a love affair at all, but love." Love affair or love, it formed no more perfect union. During the Corsica summer, Oppenheimer read Proust's *Remembrance of Things Past* in its entirety, and mingling the two Corsica experiences in memory a decade later, he told his Berkeley friend Haakon Chevalier that reading Proust had been "one of the great experiences in his life." To Chevalier he quoted from Proust a telling passage:

> Perhaps she would not have considered evil to be so rare . . .
> had she been able to discern in herself, as in everyone, that
> indifference to the sufferings one causes, an indifference which,
> whatever other names one may give it, is the terrible and
> permanent form of cruelty.

The woman may have been unknowingly indifferent to his sufferings, but something in the relationship set Oppenheimer's "*dementia praecox*" healing, and entrained for doctoral study at the University of Göttingen in the autumn of 1926, two of his papers accepted for publication in the *Proceedings of the Cambridge Philosophical Society*, he had at last begun to come alive as a physicist and a man.

Göttingen, the ancient German university where the most advanced physics of the day, quantum mechanics, took form—a cathedral of sorts, the work of many hands—was triumph again, not apprenticeship this time but solid achievement. Oppenheimer's special contribution, appropriate to the sweep of his mind, was to extend quantum theory beyond its narrow initial ground. The titles of his Göttingen-inspired papers give the sense: "Quantum Theory of the Auto-Electric Field Currents." "Quantum Theory of the Ramsauer Effect." "Three Notes on the Quantum Theory of Aperiodic Effects." "On the Quantum Theory of the Capture of Electrons." "On the Quantum Theory of Electronic Impacts." His early work "showed power and facility," his former student Robert Serber would write upon his death.

Oppenheimer's Ph.D. thesis, "On the Quantum Theory of Continuous Spectra," composed in German, appeared in the *Zeitschrift für Physik* in 1927. Max Born, his teacher, marked it "with distinction," and added to the sixteen papers Oppenheimer published between 1926 and 1929, it established for him an international reputation. He came home to lecture at Harvard and Caltech—shouting "Quantize it! Quantize it!" to startled students—then returned to Europe to study with Paul Ehrenfest and Wolfgang Pauli at Leiden and Zurich. At Göttingen he had learned Italian well enough in one month's study to read Dante; at Leiden he lectured in Dutch six weeks after he arrived. Pauli found his thinking slack—"Pauli once remarked to me," writes physicist I. I. Rabi, a Nobel laureate and Oppenheimer's staunch defender at the 1954 security hearings, "that Oppenheimer seemed to treat physics as an avocation and psychoanalysis as a vocation"—and fiercely tightened him up. The price of the mental thumbscrewing was tuberculosis, which Oppenheimer dried out that summer, 1929, at Perro Caliente, his hot-dog New Mexican ranch. Returning to Berkeley in the fall, he was prepared to found there and at Caltech a school of theoretical physics whose international reputation would eventually rival Göttingen's.

After 1929 and through the decade of the 1930s, a decade marked by his mother's and father's deaths—another lading of grief, another accounting of manhood—Oppenheimer dug harder for originality. He formulated the Dirac theory, an extension of quantum mechanics to include the theory of relativity, as a field theory, and was the first to predict the antiproton (this paper, like most of his later papers, was coauthored). He formulated the tunnel effect, the principle upon which the tunnel diode of recent electronics is based. He enlarged theoretical understanding of cosmic rays. Modeling the imploding collapse of dying suns, he predicted the neutron star—the pulsar, discovered in the 1960s, is one such structure—and the black hole. He was primarily interested in particle physics—"I never found nuclear physics so beautiful," he said—but working with Ernest O. Lawrence and his cyclotrons at Berkeley, he became an expert on nuclear physics as well. By 1945 he had published a total of sixty-six papers; after the war, particle physics would dominate American physical studies, a lasting tribute to his influence on the American school.

Without question, Oppenheimer's intelligence exceeded that of any of his peers—"I was never in the same class with him," I. I. Rabi remarked—but despite the breadth of his contribution, he reined back from work historically unique. Writing for the 1967 Oppenheimer Memorial Session of the American Physical Society, Rabi attempted to explain the hesitation:

> Oppenheimer understood the whole structure of physics with extraordinary clarity, and not only the structure, but the interaction between the different elements. Hardly any branch of physics was foreign to him. As well as theoretical physics, he also had a vast knowledge of experimental results and methods at his fingertips and would continually amaze experimenters by his great knowledge of their own subject—in some respects exceeding their own, especially in fields of great current interest. . . .
>
> One often wonders why men of Oppenheimer's gifts do not discover everything worth discovering. . . . [I]t seems to me that in some respects Oppenheimer was overeducated in those fields which lie outside the scientific tradition, such as his interest in religion, in the Hindu religion in particular, which resulted in a feeling for the mystery of the universe that surrounded him almost like a fog. He saw physics clearly, looking toward what had already been done, but at the border he tended to feel that there was much more of the mysterious and novel than there actually was. . . . Some may call it a lack of faith, but in my opinion it was more a turning away from the hard, crude methods of theoretical physics into a mystical realm of broad intuition.

And closing his tribute, Rabi netted the essential man in a qualified benediction. "In Oppenheimer," he wrote, "the element of earthiness was feeble."

Haakon Chevalier, Oppenheimer's Berkeley pal in the later years of the Depression, a professor of French and dallier with communism whose relations with Oppenheimer would be ground to Paris green at security-hearing time, inhaled the fog of sanctification and supplied the most concise physical description the record contains:

> [Oppenheimer] was tall, nervous and intent, and he moved with an odd gait, a kind of jog, with a great deal of swinging of his limbs, his head always a little to one side, one shoulder higher than the other. But it was the head that was most striking: the halo of whispy black curly hair, the fine, sharp nose, and especially the eyes, surprisingly blue, having a strange depth and intensity, and yet expressive of a candor that was altogether disarming. He looked like a young Einstein, and at the same time like an overgrown choir boy.

Oppenheimer's students, in those infatuate prewar days, idolized him even to aping his mannerisms, moving with odd gaits all over Berkeley. Chevalier idolized him too, and so fails to mention the self-inflicted stigmata: the forced insomnia, the ravaged teeth, the extreme emaciation (Oppenheimer, six feet tall, never in his life weighed more than 130 pounds and in times of exceptional stress would tighten to a cadaverous 113), the caustic martinis thrown into a tender stomach, the chains of smoke wheezed through tubercular lungs.

These were the years of the left-wing movement in America, when communism was openly discussed and openly avowed on college campuses everywhere. Walking with Oppenheimer in San Francisco one day in 1930, Ernest Lawrence discovered he hadn't yet heard of the Wall Street crash. The benevolent mentor who shared with his students the coauthorship of signal papers and supplemented their diets at the best restaurants in town learned to his indignation that all his influence couldn't lever them into nonexistent teaching jobs, and apprehending that, quick study that he was, he apprehended the revolutionary forces the Depression set loose.

The plight of his students exposed Oppenheimer to social injustice, peeled back the insulation of his wealth; the desperation of his German aunt and cousins to escape to America from the eugenic hallucinations of the Nazis, an escape that in 1937 he underwrote, alerted him to fascism. Both intercessions moved him leftward, but the private reason he joined the fringes of the communist movement in Berkeley was probably emotional adaptation to the rebellious standards of a woman he loved and hoped to salvage, Jean Tatlock, the lithe, chiaroscuro daughter of an anti-Semite Berkeley medievalist and an infectious carrier of the dangerous pale-green card. Though he never, like her, joined the Party, finding its dialectics less rigorous than his taste, he espoused her cause, read Engels and Feuerbach and all of Marx, attended meetings, tithed. What he earned in return from Jean Tatlock—as, more obscurely, from the woman in Corsica before— was passionate acceptance, and with that acceptance a bolder emotional commitment to humanity, including his own. The woman he married for life in 1940, Katherine Puening, Kitty, who had lost a heroic Communist husband, a Dartmouth man, on the practice battlefields of revolutionary Spain, who dedicated herself to nurturing and supporting him, sealed that commitment.

Oppenheimer pilgrimaged to the women in his life afflicted with more than diffidence, afflicted with something worse than the stylish Harvard *Weltschmerz* his detractors thought they saw (his enemies caught its hot scent, though they inverted it and imagined him Machiavellian at least, if not actually diabolic): afflicted with a pathological disgust with himself and a nearly pathological horror of the world. Only once, on the record, did he emerge from stoic privacy to reveal the depth of that disgust— after marital devotion into age had sweetened it, and for an important cause. "Up to now, and even more in the days of my almost infinitely prolonged adolescence," he told a group of culturally distinguished peers he'd assembled to discuss the possibility of peace, "I hardly took an action, hardly did anything, or failed to do anything, whether it was a paper on physics, or a lecture, or how I read a book, how I talked to a friend, how I loved, that did not arouse in me a very great sense of revulsion and of wrong." Which is more to say than that his standards were impossibly high: which is to say that he perceived himself worse than a failure, perceived himself a thing loathsome before the world. To his survival, if not his salvation, the women in his life saw him otherwise:

> It turned out to be impossible . . . for me to live with anybody else, without understanding that what I saw was only one part of the truth . . . and in an attempt to break out and be a reasonable man, I had to realize that my own worries about what I did were valid and were important, but that they were not the whole story, that there must be a complementary way of looking at them, because other people did not see them as I did. And I needed what they saw, needed them.

He proffered his thanks subtly, but in scale with his gratitude. In the final days of the Manhattan Project, with Jean Tatlock recently dead by her own hand, he restored himself rereading John Donne's *Holy Sonnets*. When an assistant requested a code name for the first bomb test, to be conducted on a ghastly stretch of southern New Mexican desert the *conquistadores* had named the Jornada del Muerto, the Journey of Death, he anagrammatized the rapt sonnet that begins, "Batter my heart, three-personed God," and coded the test "Trinity." He had more than one Trinity in mind, but one, an important one, was almost certainly Corsica, Jean Tatlock and Kitty Oppenheimer. His trinity of women had given him a bearable life on earth; he gave them, in return, the first crude man-made star, a weapon so terrifying that he hoped it might, in time, force peace upon the world.

The hope of peace in terror was one of the reasons he agreed to direct the building of the bomb. Its potential for monumental effect had caught his attention from the beginning. When Niels Bohr, the great Danish physicist who among all others may have been the man he most deeply admired, brought the news of nuclear fission to America, on January 26, 1939, Oppenheimer's response must have seemed incongruous to those who couldn't fathom his contrarieties: "On the very day he received the news of fission," writes biographer Denise Royal, "Oppenheimer started making rough calculations on the critical mass necessary to bring about an explosion." He refined his calculations with Edward Teller, Robert Serber and Hans Bethe, among others, at Berkeley, through 1941. A critical mass of U-235, they decided, would form an eight-inch sphere; they also decided that the odds of that mass starting a fusion reaction in the air's nitrogen or the ocean's deuterium and burning up the earth were no more than three in a million, long odds but heady eschatology for physicists then obscure.

Appointed Coordinator of Rapid Rupture, a title that delighted him, by the bomb committee that Franklin Roosevelt had established to shepherd nuclear weapons research, Oppenheimer surveyed the work of bomb design being conducted at small laboratories scattered across the United States, none of them allowed to talk to each other, and proposed that the separate projects be assembled in one place under one director. Whoever would be that director would have to deal with Brigadier General Leslie R. Groves, the overweight Corps of Engineers talent who had built the Pentagon in record time and now was head of the Manhattan Project, a blustering, difficult man. Oppenheimer was not the obvious choice. Groves and others believed the director should be a Nobel laureate; Army Counter-Intelligence was adamant that he should be politically safe; Oppenheimer was neither. In 1942, despite his lack of administrative qualification, Oppenheimer won Groves's nod—"by default," he said later, but also by coaching Groves on physics; by serving, as biographer Nuel Pharr Davis puts it, as an "idiot savant"; and by sparing the general's ego when he asked stupid questions, as Oppenheimer never spared his students'. To appoint Oppenheimer, Groves had to override his security staff's objections; he did, and he said later he never doubted that Oppenheimer was loyal, however pink his past. Groves's staff had no such confidence, and shadowed, bugged, and interrogated the bomb director throughout the war. It was during those wartime interrogations that Oppenheimer reported—painfully or gratuitously, the fading transcripts do not indicate which—on the political activities of some of his friends.

Oppenheimer located the bomb lab in his beloved New Mexico, across the Rio Grande from Perro Caliente, on a 7,200-foot mesa, commandeering a rugged boys' school for the base of established buildings it supplied. He led the lab, Los Alamos, with a skill so dazzling—inspiring and co-ordinating the work of a thousand men and women from a dozen different countries, many of whom were prima donnas, lone wolves, iconoclasts—that its story is worn to legend now. "Here at Los Alamos," one hardheaded British physicist said afterward, "I found the spirit of Athens, of

Plato, of an ideal Republic." Others called those years of back-
breaking labor on a remote mesa—years spent locked behind high
barbed-wire fences living in flimsy barracks modified to apartments with pasteboard partitions and filthy coal-burning stoves,
years deflected to technology while creative physics stalled—"the
best years of our lives." All but a few of those who lived them
agreed that Oppenheimer—"Oppie," they called him, resurrecting
the affectionate diminutive Leiden had bestowed—made them so.
Oppie's whistle blew at seven in the morning and they came out
cheering to work eighteen-hour days building weapons of mass destruction. "I believe," said Enrico Fermi incredulously, come
down one day from atomic-pile building in Chicago, "your people
actually *want* to make a bomb." They did, because Oppie did.

Why he did he never directly explained. It is perhaps his
deepest mystery. Certainly he despised the Nazis for what they
had done to physics and physicists and to political and intellectual
freedom; from his aunt and cousins he knew the Nazi pogroms at
close second hand. George F. Kennan, his neighbor in Princeton
during the postwar years, when Oppenheimer directed the Institute for Advanced Study, perceived another level of it. He saw in
Oppenheimer, he told journalist Philip M. Stern,

. . . a deep yearning for . . . friendship, for companionship, for
the warmth and richness of human communication. The
arrogance which to many appeared to be a part of his
personality masked in reality an overpowering desire to bestow
and to receive affection. Neither circumstances nor at times the
asperities of his own temperament permitted the gratification of
this need in a measure remotely approaching its intensity; and
in this too lay a portion of that strong element of tragedy which
all who knew him sensed . . . in his situation.

Humanly enough, Oppenheimer wanted desperately to be liked,
admired, adulated, even loved, and building the ultimate weapon,
serving his country at the extreme limit of his special talent for
physics and for the charismatic direction of difficult, talented
men, was a way to achieve that acclaim, particularly since he already understood that at thirty-eight his best years as a theoretical
physicist were behind him and had left him first rate but not first
rank in the scientific annals of the age.

Niels Bohr helped him see at Los Alamos what the highest officials of the United States Government failed at first to comprehend: that nuclear weapons would make world war suicidal and therefore obsolete. "First of all," Oppenheimer wrote in 1964, "[Bohr] was clear that if it worked, this development would bring an enormous change in the situation of the world, and of war. . . . When he came to Los Alamos, his first serious question was, 'Is it really big enough?' I do not know whether it was; it did finally get to be." And, further:

> Bohr at Los Alamos was marvelous. He took a very lively technical interest. But his real function, I think for almost all of us, was not the technical one. He made the enterprise seem hopeful, when many were not free of misgiving. Bohr spoke with contempt of Hitler, who with a few hundred tanks and planes had tried to enslave Europe for a millennium. His own high hope that the outcome would be good, that the objectivity, the cooperation of the sciences would play a helpful part, we all wanted to believe.

Oppenheimer carried these considerations into his interior depths, measuring them against the only moral technical manual he seriously credited, the *Bhagavad-Gita*. "It is the most beautiful philosophical song existing in any known tongue," he said once of the seven-hundred-stanza devotional poem interpolated into the great Aryan epic *Mahabharata* at about the same time that Greece was declining from its golden age. He had discovered it at Harvard; at Berkeley he had learned Sanskrit from the scholar Arthur Ryder to set himself closer to the original text; a worn pink copy of the *Gita* thereafter occupied an honored place on the bookshelf closest to his desk, for the same reason divers keep a decompression table near at hand.

There are meanings enough for a lifetime in the *Gita*, dramatized as a dialogue between a warrior prince named Arjuna and Krishna, the principal avatar of Vishnu (and Vishnu the third member of the Hindu godhead with Brahma and Shiva—a trinity again). In the moments before a major battle, seeing his teachers and kinsmen and friends opposed to him on the battlefield, Arjuna refuses to fight. Through dialogue, Krishna justifies the battle to the prince. He has a duty to his class, Krishna argues; discipline will free him from guilt in the spirit of sacrifice; and anyway, the Supreme Lord is everywhere, in the slayer and the slain:

> *Today behold the whole world*
> *All things that move or do not move*
> *And whatever else you wish to see.*
> *They stand as one within my body.*

Perverted, that argument would justify Charles Manson in casual, random murder, but though Oppenheimer personally bore his share of guilt—"Mr. President," he told an impatient Harry Truman in 1945, "I feel I have blood on my hands"—he had something else, something far less insanely subjective, in mind: the inevitability of discovery, the certainty that having found fission, and after it fusion, some nation somewhere would put it to terrible use. "It is a profound and necessary truth," he told a Canadian audience in 1962, "that the deep things in science are not found because they are useful; they are found because it was possible to find them." He wanted the United States to find them first, because he believed—who can say erroneously?—that it was the one country capable of building nuclear weapons that might in the fullness of time arrange to forestall their use.

But first he wanted the bombs used, to force the changes Bohr anticipated. The record leaves no doubt that he acquiesced to the bombing of Japanese cities. He attended the meetings where the recommendation to use the bombs against Japanese civilians was formulated; he was the most qualified technical adviser there; and in that vital capacity he argued against a bloodless demonstration on the specious technical grounds that the bomb used in such a demonstration might be a dud, though he knew to virtual certainty that it would not. He would soon send the uranium bomb, Little Boy, ahead untested to Tinian for the Hiroshima drop, and he tested Fat Man at Trinity and knew its lethal twin would work. He was forthright enough after the war. "I am very glad that the bomb was not kept secret," he said in one of his lectures. The understatement is typical, is even mocking: Oppenheimer meant he was glad the bomb was used, its destructive force horribly and indelibly demonstrated. "I am glad," he went on, "that all of us knew, as a few of us already did, what was up and what readjustments in human life and in political institutions would be called for."

And so, in that first man-made dawn, when the nest of Chinese boxes that was not Thor or Jesu or The Liberator but Fat Man, the plutonium bomb—spheres within spheres contained within a black duralumin shell studded with detonators—collapsed into itself like a dying sun and blew Oppenheimer's serenely elegant physics out to plague the world, he understood through the visionary extremity of his exhaustion that Krishna had once again made his point. He thought, he said later, of a stanza and a line from the *Gita* that described the twin and complementary qualities of the godhead that was the bomb, of the bomb that was less than, but part of, the godhead:

> *If the radiance of a thousand suns*
> *were to burst into the sky,*
> *that would be like*
> *the splendor of the Mighty One. . . .*

And as the thunder rolled east and west across the Jornada del Muerto, echoing from the fastness of mountains:

> *I am become Death, the shatterer of worlds.*

Krishna; the fiery universe of stars and neutron stars and black holes and cosmic rays; the particles that were also waves and the waves that were also particles, but never, to the possibility of human measurement, both at once; the $\overline{mc^2}$ that is also E: these were death, and worlds were shattered; $\overline{\text{these}}$ were $\text{splen}\overline{\text{dor}}$, and worlds radiated light; and these were men and women contending below, these were the truth that must inevitably be found because it was possible to find it, and these were as well the hope of no more wars. Between death and splendor, one suspects, he thought the contest no better than an even match.

He did his best, in the years after the war, to transmute the threat of shattering nuclear annihilation into a radiant cause for peace. It was, paradoxically, that effort—there are reversals in Oppenheimer's life as dramatic as any in *Oedipus*—that led to his public humiliation, that led President Eisenhower to throw up a "blank wall" between him and the official secrets that he carried in his head, that led the Eisenhower government, pushed by men like Joseph McCarthy and the imperious Lewis Strauss, men like Richard Nixon (he was there too, giving "assurances" to the McCarthy crowd that "the Oppenheimer case" "would be gone into in detail"), to convene a prosecutorial hearing and deprive him of his security clearance on the grounds, in his case the absurd grounds, that his character was dangerously marred by "fundamental defects." That story is legend too, but documents declassified within the past year have chiseled some of its ambiguities away.

With Niels Bohr's proposals much in mind, Oppenheimer worked with a government committee that included David Lilienthal and Dean Acheson to formulate the Baruch Plan of 1946 that proposed to internationalize atomic energy. Whether or not it was offered in good faith—Oppenheimer and others vehemently insisted it was—the Soviet Union rejected it, refusing to give up secrecy for mutual protection from nuclear war, and Oppenheimer consigned the Soviet Union to the same midden he reserved in his mind for the Third Reich. But in 1949 he and the other members of the Atomic Energy Commission's General Advisory Committee—tough men like Enrico Fermi, I. I. Rabi, James B. Conant—saw another opportunity, one they rated at no better than even odds: that if the United States held off building fusion weapons, thermonuclear weapons, hydrogen bombs, then so might the Soviets.

Stated so baldly, the idea sounds ridiculously naïve, but the GAC was anything but naïve. The hydrogen bomb that in 1949 the members of that committee, all scientists, thought they might, within five years, be able to build—they called it the "Super"—would not have been Edward Teller's and Stanislaw Ulam's later true thermonuclear weapon, the weapon Oppenheimer would call "technically sweet," but a booster device, a very large fission bomb with a small thermonuclear component. It would not generate an explosive force equivalent to the combined force of a number of fission bombs containing the same amount of plutonium. Oppenheimer, among others, feared that an all-out push for the Super would therefore be cheap and dangerous defense, and believed the United States would be better off enlarging and diversifying its fission arsenal with the limited uranium and plutonium then being produced.

Some of the members of the GAC believed that building the Super was morally wrong, because it was entirely a strategic weapon, intended to fry civilians a city at a time; but all the members of the GAC believed that building it was militarily wrong, that diversification of the fission arsenal was the better defense. Military men, and most notably the generals of the Strategic Air Command, who had a monopoly on nuclear weapons at that point and wanted to keep it, angrily disagreed. But the most conservative scenario that anyone has since been able to devise— the most recent reconstruction is Herbert York's in *Scientific American,* founded on the GAC's newly declassified minutes—indicates that Oppenheimer and the GAC were right, that even if the United States hadn't built the hydrogen bomb first, even if it had waited until after the Soviets tested theirs, the balance of terror would not have been shifted by so much as an inch, because the United States would have had, in fission weapons, more than an equivalency, and could quickly have added thermonuclear weapons to its arsenal.

Despite the GAC's considered recommendation, President Truman, on January 31, 1950, ordered a crash program to build hydrogen bombs. If he underestimated Soviet science—he told Oppenheimer, before the first Soviet nuclear test in 1949, that the Russians could never make the bomb—he understood politics, and knew that no government that unilaterally restrained itself from reaching for military superiority would long survive.

The other GAC members accepted the inevitable. Oppenheimer did not. He continued to battle for nuclear diversification, and for good measure he threw in continental defense, which the Air Force thought impossible. And as, with Bohr, he had anticipated the revolutionary changes in the nature of war that atomic weapons would bring, so also he anticipated the nuclear stalemate. And announcing that paradox, declaring the futility of the arms race, was viewed as more than error: it was nothing less than heresy.

"The answer to fear," Oppenheimer told Eleanor Roosevelt on her national radio program twelve days after Truman bluntly overruled the GAC, "cannot always lie in the dissipation of the causes of fear; sometimes it lies in courage." Courageously, in 1953, he took his argument to the makers of government policy and then to the open world, delivering to the Council on Foreign

Affairs and then publishing in *Foreign Affairs* a statement that is distinguished from all his other published statements by its passion, its anger, and its cold contempt for those who behind walls of secrecy would drag the United States into military danger and the world into an arms race that no nation could conceivably win. It was this statement that condemned him. Its essence is distilled in one ironic central paragraph:

> The very least we can say is that, looking ten years ahead, it is likely to be small comfort that the Soviet Union is four years behind us [it was less than nine months], and small comfort that they are only about half as big [industrially] as we are. The very least we can conclude is that our twenty-thousandth bomb, useful as it may be in filling the vast munitions pipelines of a great war, will not in any deep strategic sense offset their two-thousandth.

And further to clinch the argument:

> We may anticipate a state of affairs in which two Great Powers will each be in a position to put an end to the civilization and life of the other, though not without risking its own. We may be likened to two scorpions in a bottle, each capable of killing the other, but only at the risk of his own life.

And finally, indignantly and properly contemptuous of militarists so glory-bound that they couldn't distinguish between glory and nuclear holocaust:

> We need to be clear that there will not be many great atomic wars for us, nor for our institutions. It is important that there not be one.

The vivid desert metaphor, the scorpions in a bottle, applied to the reality of nuclear stalemate within Oppenheimer's lifetime, and the policies he espoused of tactical and strategic flexibility, of early warning and continental defense, of phased disarmament, are official policy now.

But "massive retaliation" was official policy under John Foster Dulles and Dwight Eisenhower, a bigger bang for the buck, and in 1954 Oppenheimer was summoned, and scourged, and thrown down from government and the gates locked behind. Atomic Energy Commission Chairman Lewis Strauss, a man whom Oppenheimer had publicly ridiculed at congressional hearings on atomic secrecy a few years before, was immediately responsible for the security review, "In the Matter of J. Robert Oppenheimer," convened in a jerry-built World War II building in Washington in March and April of 1954. But behind him were more shadowy figures, the enraged and vengeful generals of the Strategic Air Command first of all.

The security hearing was not a hearing at all but a purge, a trial conducted without the protection of courtroom procedures and in violation of all the usual rules of evidence. The AEC had cleared Oppenheimer of his left-wing escapades and his single wartime indiscretion—temporarily refusing to give Army Counter-Intelligence the name of a man who reported to him a Soviet spying probe (the man was his friend Haakon Chevalier)—in 1947. All the old charges were raked up again, and countered by a parade of distinguished witnesses who testified to Oppenheimer's loyalty, men such as I. I. Rabi, Hans Bethe, Vannevar Bush, James B. Conant, and even, though more ambiguously, General Leslie R. Groves. But most of the interminable spring days were devoted to Oppenheimer's opposition to the H-bomb, an opposition the entire GAC had shared, and the witnesses who condemned that opposition, Edward Teller the star among them, were unsparing in voicing their suspicions of him. Oppenheimer defended himself numbly and inadequately, shaken by the viciousness of the attack. When the hearings were finished, not even Lewis Strauss could find solid evidence of security violations. He lifted Oppenheimer's top-secret "Q" clearance just the same.

No one who objectively studies the record today, two decades later, can come away with any doubt of Oppenheimer's innocence from wrongdoing except the political wrongdoing of disagreeing on government policy. For that disagreement, in a nation constitutionally pledged to freedom of speech, he was officially destroyed. "Oppenheimer's life," writes Nuel Pharr Davis angrily, "can stand inspection down to the last senseless detail. One must, finally, put all this damned nonsense, to use Oppenheimer's term for the hearings, into its proper, dismally small perspective in order to gain any comprehension of Oppenheimer as a scientist, American, or human being."

The "damned nonsense" was dismally small, but its effects were not. Oppenheimer came back to Princeton visibly aged. He had turned fifty during the hearings; a former student who saw him afterward in Princeton remarked that he had always looked younger than his years, but now looker older. "Much of his previous spirit and liveliness had left him," Hans Bethe sadly confirmed. He never complained of it, no more than he complained of the incident at Camp Koenig thirty-six years before. "I think of this as a major accident," he told an interviewer, "much like a train wreck or the collapse of a building. It has no relation or connection with my life. I just happened to be there." It may have been a major accident for the United States as well, because it deprived the nation of the experience, the intelligence and the prescience of one of its most able sons.

He lived the last decade of his life in a lonely isolation that he also never complained of and that the honors that came to him did not alleviate. He had been appointed director of the Institute for Advanced Study in 1946; he kept the position until a year before his death, and also assumed Einstein's old post as senior professor of physics. He was called to speak to the world from Paris, from South America, from England and Japan and finally from within the United States. John Kennedy invited him to dine at the White House with forty-nine Nobel laureates in 1961, and planned to award him the Enrico Fermi Award, the AEC's highest honor, on December 2, 1963; Lyndon Johnson, in a time of mourning, made the presentation to Oppenheimer in the White House Cabinet Room—a medal, and fifty thousand dollars to take home, from an agency that still denied him clearance as a security risk.

He retired from the Institute in 1966, when illness weakened him. On his last visit to the Institute, writes the physicist Abraham Pais, "He came to participate in a discussion on the selection of the young physicists who would be members of the Institute during the coming academic year. He knew he would not be there to greet them."

Every thoughtful human being projects, somewhere within himself, a vision of utopia, a vision usually reconstructed from an imagined golden age. That golden age is frequently childhood, but Oppenheimer's spare childhood wouldn't serve; instead he found his golden age at Göttingen, and constructed his utopia from the materials there at hand. Because Göttingen was a community of scientists, Oppenheimer's utopia is more convoluted, and more tragic, than most. It considers not only the possibility of peace and communion among men but also the certainty that the larger universe is fatally inanimate, in basic ways opaque, and ultimately destructive of all human pretension, even the necessary pretension of hope.

Despite the baleful finalities, his vision was guardedly optimistic and far from Faustian. He thought that the community of scientists throughout the world, a community protected from too grievous error by the necessary and inherent openness of its work, might serve as a modest model for a peaceful, open world. Proposing such a model, he cautioned humility:

> This is a world in which each of us, knowing his limitations, knowing the evils of superficiality and the terrors of fatigue, will have to cling to what is close to him, to what he knows, to what he can do, to his friends and his tradition and his love, lest he be dissolved in a universal confusion and know nothing and love nothing. It is at the same time a world in which none of us can find hieratic prescription or general sanction for any ignorance, any insensitivity, any indifference. When a friend tells us of a new discovery we may not understand, we may not be able to listen without jeopardizing the work that is ours and closer to us; but we cannot find in a book or canon—and we should not seek—grounds for hallowing our ignorance. If a man tells us that he sees differently than we, or that he finds beautiful what we find ugly, we may have to leave the room, from fatigue or trouble; but that is our weakness and our default. If we must live with a perpetual sense that the world and the men in it are greater than we and too much for us, let it be the measure of our virtue that we know this and seek no comfort. Above all, let us not proclaim that the limits of our powers correspond to some special wisdom in our choice of life, of learning, or of beauty.

Yet he knew the futility of words to change the world. He believed in Bohr's principle of complementarity; he believed there are manifold ways of observation and manifold forms of action; he did not content himself with words. Out of physics, in concert with others from that community of scientists that was his model for utopia, he drew a simple and fundamental fact, that matter is only another form of energy and may be converted back to energy at will: that $E=mc^2$. With that incontrovertible certainty, cruder than any words, before which no man could hallow his ignorance, he made his argument secure. And assembled the bomb for us as a puzzle, a puzzle as Gordian and tangled as he was himself, knowing, this mystical man, that we would either learn in time to unravel it or explosively abrogate our claim to mastery of the earth.

J. Robert Oppenheimer died of cancer of the throat on February 18, 1967, at the age of sixty-two. His ashes were scattered on the ocean off the Virgin Islands—the ocean with its vast reserves of fuel, for energy or for bombs, the ocean with its depths. Among his last published words were these: "Science is not everything, but science is very beautiful." And, the child and the man within the scientist: "No one should say there is no hope."

Since he was buried in the sea, no epitaph marks his grave. A stanza from the *Bhagavad-Gita* might serve, though he would be the first to say it is not the whole story, is only one of several complementary and mutually exclusive points of view. He deserves it, if anyone among those who devised the machinery of nuclear holocaust does, in mitigation of the guilt he carried to his death for serving as loyally and as intelligently as he knew:

> But he who is without thought of 'I'
> Whose understanding is pure
> Even though he should slay whole worlds
> He does not slay, nor is he bound.

The Last Kennedy

The cab sweeps you through Washington, past the Capitol with its braced wall and wide, empty porch, past the National Gallery where the chalk faces of the primitive dead stare from gilded frames, past the Washington Monument marble and blank and the White House twice occupied now by other men and across the bridge into the cemetery where up a hill a wooden guardhouse stands and there the driver lets you out and makes small talk with the guard and waits for you. Lee's serene mansion glows on the hillside in the afternoon sun. You head down a road cut between the Victorian stones of dead officers and their families. Two men and a woman dressed in black pass you as they return from whatever grave they have visited and a leaf-raking machine, red and yellow, mulches red and yellow leaves and spews them into flower beds. Around a bend in the road you come up a ramp of gray granite and turn into it and follow a sign directing you to the right of the grave. It is covered with flags of rough fieldstone and roped off with cords. At its head burns the eternal flame, gusting yellow and orange, blackening its fieldstone base. A bronze plaque records the President's name and the years of his birth and death, and at the foot of the fieldstone cover two smaller plaques mark the graves of two of his children, one of them unnamed. It comes to this, this grouping of granite ramps and flat stones, this unpretentious memorial, nearly flush with the hillside, recessed into the ground, hardly a memorial, a notable grave. Some of the words he spoke are carved on a low wall nearby. You circle the grave cover and read the words. They are freshly cut and seem mundane. You turn back to the grave and watch the flame. Its soot has shaped no pattern on the stone. The walk has not weathered. The bronze has not aged. The honor guard talks to a tourist, quick motions of gloved hands. The cab is waiting. The guard is talking and you would like to be alone. There is someone here you knew. Or the grave might be your own. You have been here before. Or you read it in a book. It did not come to what you thought it would come to. *Yet the lilac with mastering odor holds me.* It should have come to more.

You descend the ramp on the south side. They are turning the earth for the President's brother's memorial, more granite ramps, more fieldstone, more words. Around and away march tongues of white marble, row upon row of our military dead, most of them killed in this ultimate century of American power. It should have come to more.

White is the color of Federal Washington. Its buildings of marble and limestone, its Mall and monuments glow with a classical light, muted and yet shadowless, a light that denies the movement of the sun across the sky and the days across the year, and inside the buildings workers and statesmen teem like crickets in new tombs. Cars flash by and tourists walk the streets, but they do little to disturb the stillness. The Renaissance invented the still classicism Federal Washington imitates, the white silent buildings and the shadowless light, disregarding the shales of colored paint that still clung to the marble of the old temples, the priapic poles danced across the stages, the soldiers' mutinies quelled by eclipses of the moon, the portents of peace and war expelled from the mouth of a hag sweating in the smoke of a cave at Delphi. The Renaissance, aggrandizing man, the mind of man, conveyed the classical stinks offstage through underground pipes, and Washington's white temples similarly deny the broil and clash of the nation's life. No city in America is more isolated from the secret movements of flesh and spirit that animate the nation. The columns, the walls, the marble covers echo only footsteps on the tomb—whose footsteps, the crickets inside do not know.

A nation may need such deliberate serenity in its capital city, where its sovereignties are chosen and judged and guarded, if it would hold together at all. But lately it has not held together, and serenity has come to dead end. We have other sources of unity. From time to time we evoke them to call us back to another kind of order, an order of generations. They remind us of what we sacrifice to live together in this wild land: coffins and funeral trains; caissons; skirling bagpipes and muffled drums; riderless

horses; candles burning in muddy night; grief and benediction.
Cards from an American tarot pack prophesying our past, declaring Lincoln and the Civil War, black crepe over a blackened land,
a past that more than the Revolution made us what we are,
bequeathed us a legacy of determination and violent death in the
name of union—legs gone, arms gone, eyes gone, the seed of generations spilled upon the ground. These, drawn somberly through
the classical city, do not mock its temples but enliven them, as
memory of the living struggle enlivens the dead historical text. We
do not grieve for marble but for flesh and bone. We do not find
benediction in marble but in flesh and bone, if we find it anywhere, if we are not benumbed. We have never quite thought
ourselves a race, as the English or the French do, but at times of
national celebration, national crisis, and especially of national
grief we have sensed what an American race might be, sensed its
potential for compassion, sensed that it would be as wild and as
strong as the land it has not yet conquered, the last wilderness
of the world that was once Europe's green fuse and is still
our hope though nearly our despair. Have our dreams destroyed us? What else could have brought us together and enabled us to act, for a time, like people bound in common cause?
But how soon over, how soon forgotten, how soon and so narrowly entombed. We are told that what we saw was not what we
saw. We are told the dead were the cause of our woes. The survivors recant, purging themselves for new religions. That is not
news. The living advance and the dead err. That is not news.

The memorial in Arlington is also a family grave. The two men
and the two dead children lie among soldiers' remains facing the
white city. It was as a family that they presented themselves to us, or
demanded that they be taken. Having few other choices, and
never having had that choice before, we did. The founding father,
and perhaps even more the founding mother, conceived it that
way. The lesson of Irish politics was part of it, and the old rule of
clan, and plain canniness, and virtue carved from necessity for a
family so precipitously risen to wealth and so clamorous for its
trappings. They could not have done otherwise. Family was the
abiding metaphor of their lives, their reference point, their pool of
knowledge, their place of retreat, their source of strength. They
said: We have all this, who can dream what we might do with it?

They made it a metaphor of nationhood. They spoke of a new generation. They said we can work together. They said we should love one another. "I had a member of my family killed"—that simple sentence stopped a riot, if only for one night.

Most men build alone. The family built together, worked to make the parental dream match the commonwealth's ambition, so that family and commonwealth both might go to glory, and succeeded all too well. The nation was swept away despite every kind of hate and prejudice and distrust and honest disagreement with what the family stood for and what it seemed to want. "Swept away" not politically, for our politics have deeper roots than awe, but swept away emotionally, in life and even more in death. The nation saw the family dream more clearly than it saw the willingness to serve, to serve responsibly, which the family understood was the nation's honest due, and responded to the dream. And one in Dallas whose wife told him he was not a man, and one in Los Angeles whose employer called him *boy*, knowing little of family themselves, also responded.

Today, some of those who fancied the dream while the men of the family were alive descry meanness in it now that the men, all but one of them, are dead. And at the same time the ordinary people of America, who need such a dream but need also its practical results, seem to trust it more than ever. In schools, in ghetto storefronts, in the homes of the old and the poor and the black, you are likely to find photographs of them, the men and their wives, clipped from magazines and framed and hung on the wall, and three of the women occupied last year's list of the ten most admired women in the world. These may seem small tokens, but anyone who looks around him will know they are not. The family dream abides, an idealization for many Americans of wealth, of beauty, of education and grace, of benevolent power, and—let it also be said—of the vanity of human wishes. It is an idealization the family was certainly responsible for, being no more than it imagined of itself, but it could not have imagined the extent to which the idealization would be accepted, nor the sufferings to which it would lead. Nor could it know how completely the dream would obscure the character of the men who would lead, one of whom waits now in the wings.

"Death ruins a man," E. M. Forster once wrote, "but the idea of death saves him." John F. Kennedy was haunted by the idea of death, and it saved him until he died. Death was his familiar. It led him to run when other men walk, to seek what other men dream of, to achieve what other men only covet. His illnesses and physical weaknesses make a catalogue of nightmare: diphtheria, scarlet fever, appendicitis, severe and nearly fatal infections; a damaged back, repeated operations; jaundice, malaria, adrenal insufficiency, stomach trouble, impaired vision, impaired hearing. Bedfast for long months, he became a bookish child, shy and unsure, a compulsive reader who rode and ruled with heroes. He studied how things work, convinced that at the heart of every system he might find the secret key, the mechanism the doctors and the priests and the engineers had overlooked that could heal the illness or save the soul or activate the machine. He learned the death of kings. Out of bed, his older brother Joe worked him over, taunted him, and his father made no effort to hold the tormentor back.

In adolescence he discovered rebellion, neglected his lessons to perfect the practical joke and the wisecrack that surrounded him with a pack of friends that owed no allegiance to his family. His father decided the boy was more Rose's child than his own. The boy's headmaster at Choate saw the conflict with different and prescient eyes. "I would be willing to bet anything," he wrote the father, "that within two years you will be as proud of Jack as you are now of Joe. . . . A more conventional mind and a more plodding and mature point of view would help him a lot more right now; but we have to allow, my dear Mr. Kennedy, with boys like Jack, for a period of adjustment. All that natural cleverness Jack has to learn how to use in his life and work, even how to cover it up at times, how to subordinate it and all the rest. I never yet saw a clever, witty boy who at some stage in his early development was not considered fresh. It is only because he hasn't learned how to use his natural gift." At Harvard he learned the uses of history, and published a best seller, with a little help from his friends, when he was barely old enough to vote.

He found himself in war. His fascination with how things work, his preoccupation with heroism and leadership, his need to be free of his older brother—all came together. He had prepared himself to be an Alexander: Alexander would command a PT boat in the Solomon Islands and there find and cut his Gordian knot. His experience of shipwreck might not have meant so much to him had illness not prepared him to be sensitive to the proximity of death and the potential for heroism that shadows it. His back damaged, he towed one of his crew by his teeth to an island. They were fifteen hours in the water—this the rich man's son from Harvard. They rested briefly, then he took a life jacket, tied his shoes to it, and with a heavy lantern swam out to Ferguson Passage, which the PT boats had used on other nights as their channel to action. He floated in the passage for half the night, remembering— remembering more than once, he told John Hersey later—the remark of one of his men that "barracuda will come up under a swimming man and eat his testicles." He lost strength in the chill water, weakened, stopped swimming and floated in a current that seemed to be sweeping him out to sea. He cast off his shoes but held onto the lantern. Hersey writes: "Now he only wanted to get back to the little island he had left that night, but he didn't try to get there; he just wanted to. His mind seemed to float away from his body. Darkness and time took the place of a mind in his skull. For a long time he slept, or was crazy, or floated in a chill trance." Hersey talked to him at the hospital soon after the shipwreck; we can assume the impressions are Kennedy's.

Coincidence, accident, the unexpected, something that reason could not count on, saved him, and he was mindful ever afterward of the place of the irrational in the lives of men: the current that seemed to be taking him out to sea carried him unconscious around the island, and he woke in the morning to find himself floating where he had floated the night before. Thus spared, he found strength to swim back to the island, where he passed out. Later he caused his own rescue and the rescue of his men.

"The poignancy of men dying young haunted him," his wife said later. We are haunted by our secret fears. He saw action as the only possible counterthrust to death's daily imminence, but he saw it consciously, as a deliberate rebellion against an event he knew to be both inevitable and beyond the reach of reason. Thus he put distance between himself and the world. If his PT-boat experience were not enough, his older brother's death added the final touches to his fatalism, for Joe had flown more than a hundred missions before his last, daredevil mission killed him—Joe who thought himself immortal. John, studying the old heroes, had never thought himself immortal. The man who could quote T. S. Eliot with understanding chose as his favorite poem Alan Seeger's sentimental "I Have a Rendezvous with Death." The man who survived shipwreck wore like a St. Christopher medal a tie clasp in the shape of a PT boat, and with private irony gave out copies of the clasp to those of his staff who lived through less difficult times with him. He liked to coin medals for his men, and after the Cuban missile crisis, awarded the comrades of that fortnight a silver calendar with thirteen days marked off. It was a *memento mori*, like all battle decorations.

He entered politics not because his father told him to, though no doubt the patriarch did, but because he had known too many men who had died. "When I think," he wrote a friend soon after World War II, "of how much this war has cost us, of the deaths of Cy and Peter and Orv and Gil and Demi and Joe and Billy and all of those thousands and millions who have died with them— when I think of all those gallant acts that I have seen or anyone has seen who has been to the war—it would be a very easy thing to feel disappointed and somewhat betrayed." He knew men needed leaders and he must have tentatively, unsurely, imagined that he might be one. His state of mind then remained his state of mind until the end of his life. "Politics," writes Arthur Schlesinger, Jr., "perhaps attracted him less as a means of saving this world than of keeping it from getting worse." "All this will not be finished," the young President said at his inaugural. "A long twilight struggle," he predicted. Some wondered at his gloom. He had, he knew, knew we all had, a rendezvous with death, and he knew that meeting place well.

On the night of his election to the presidency, when America clung to its television sets to see the outcome of the closest campaign in modern history, Evelyn Lincoln, his secretary, saw him in his room quietly reading a book. He won, and would walk around the White House in sheer delight at having lived to make it his home.

He learned the job as he went along, often too rational, often touched by the old hesitancy when faced with aggressive counsel. He capitulated to the military at the Bay of Pigs, allowed them to convince him, as they later convinced Lyndon Johnson, that any but a military course was unmanly. Perhaps he heard in them his father's barking voice. He cursed the decision afterward. He might have done more than he did for the causes of the people who elected him. His fatalism got in the way. He would have done more had he lived. He was best in crisis: crisis he had learned to command. For the Cuban missile crisis, he and his associates constructed a scenario out of Herman Kahn. The blockade, Robert McNamara said later, was a letter, a method of communication, but the President could not be sure the Soviets would read his letter as he wanted them to. At the height of the crisis, as the Soviet ships approached the blockade, he reverted for a moment to his old despair at the force of the irrational in the lives of men. Robert Kennedy describes the moment in *Thirteen Days:*

> I think these few minutes were the time of gravest concern for the President. Was the world on the brink of a holocaust? Was it our error? A mistake? Was there something further that should have been done? Or not done? His hand went up to his face and covered his mouth. He opened and closed his fists. His face seemed drawn, his eyes pained, almost gray. We stared at each other across the table. For a few fleeting seconds, it was almost as though no one else was there and he was no longer the President.
>
> Inexplicably, I thought of when he was ill and almost died; when he had lost his child; when we learned that our oldest brother had been killed; of personal times of strain and hurt.

The President turned back immediately to action, asking if some way could be found to avoid confronting a Soviet ship first. A way was found. The letter was sent and received.

But not before he had considered again the poignancy of men dying young. He knew how much was at stake if he lost—a whole world—but he confided his feelings to several of his associates in terms of young people. Schlesinger describes them this way: "This was the cruel question—the young people who, if things went wrong, would never have the chance to learn, to love, to fulfill themselves and serve their countries." The assured President thus remembered the sickly young boy within. He had recently read Barbara Tuchman's *The Guns of August,* and the dialogue there between the leaders of Germany and Austria at the beginning of World War I pained him: "How did this happen?" "Oh, my God, if only we knew, if only we knew." He wanted to make sure no one could ask that question of World War III. Reason was his last resource.

He was a complicated and paradoxical figure, shaped for crisis, determined to command, increasingly confident of his abilities, yet aware at ultimate moments that events reach beyond the power of men to change them; that death is the only certainty. Thus he trusted reason while trusting it not at all. And lived alone within himself, a private man. He is memorialized today not so much for what he did as for what he was. He became the young man of his favorite poem, and a quotation he saved in a notebook might stand as his epitaph: "He loved his youth, and his youth has become eternal." That is why he, alone among Presidents, is buried in Arlington, with our other young men. He cannot have wanted it that way. He was reaching beyond his youth when he was cut off.

If John Kennedy was first and last a private man, Robert Kennedy defined himself through an act of empathy. Physically small, he became a tough guy. Emotionally driven, he became a husband and a father who could release his emotions within the circle of his own family. His relationship with his wife was more than a conventional romance. It was a mutual delight, which his children learned to share, in play and in spontaneous affection. He would do his work, and she would do hers, and then they would play, hard play that filled every spare moment, as if childhood had been denied them. They traveled the world to find it, skiing, boating, riding, skating, swimming, throwing parties, climbing a mountain, visiting the veldt.

While his brother lived, he had no ambition to become President. He was willing to assist, the first of the brothers to accept that role. He had designed it for himself after law school, the role of getting things done for other men as efficiently and even as toughly as possible. His extended adolescence revealed itself as a crusading fervor; shadowed by his older brother, he had no need to grow up, and he kept his rigidly moral ideology until his brother was assassinated, only afterward moving it aside to show the compassion it masked.

The President's assassination moved Robert Kennedy to maturity. What the older brother, primed by childhood illness, learned in one long night, Robert brooded over for months. It came to the same sense of fatality, but John's had been nurtured on heroes, while Robert's was shaped by Greek tragedy. Two questions obsessed him: what his place should be in the tragedy of his family's life, and why anyone so obscure as Lee Harvey Oswald would want to kill his brother. He could not move, those months, until he answered the questions. It was the harder to think when every attempt at thought brought back the horror, and when the horror came he would fall into a numb stare and could not think at all. He could not bear to imagine himself taking over his dead brother's position; the very thought of it seemed blasphemous. He could not bear to continue doing what he had done, since he now had no brother to work for. "Public life," he once said, "seemed really an extension of family life," and he did not think himself worthy to take his brother's place as head of the family or the nation. Even afterward, when he had made his decision, he would turn aside in embarrassment to ask someone if he or she liked him for himself, or he would hear a crowd's cheering and imagine it was intended for his brother.

And so he could not resolve the first question by itself. He resolved it by answering the second question, why anyone would want to kill his brother. The man who saw life in rigidly moral terms discovered a social conscience. He found bloated bellies in Mississippi, suicidal Indians on western reservations, children with rat-scarred faces in Harlem, as if they had not been there all along for anyone with eyes to see. Child and father first, he could understand these outrages and he could understand that Lee Oswald was one product of them. Oswald, he must have come to believe, killed his brother because he had been, since earliest childhood, systematically deprived of his humanity. And Robert Kennedy must then have decided that if he could do anything, he could serve as witness to human deprivation. He could be—see the enormity of the decision, and the arrogance, and the redeeming naïveté—he could be brother to the poor and the neglected of his land. He suspected by then that he would be assassinated in his turn, but he had ceased to care about that, having discovered the irrational. That was his brother's discovery; he adopted it, but more passionately, as his own. And as if inviting the irrational to feast with him he threw himself into crowds, joking, kidding, playing games, singing spontaneous songs, wrestling, holding hands.

His speeches signaled a profound change in the way he looked at the world. His were the best words of any the Kennedys spoke. The distance between the Nixon-Kennedy debates and the later speeches of Robert Kennedy is the distance between a belief in issues orderly disposed and a belief in men passionately engaged. "Many of the world's great movements of thought and action," he said, "have flowed from the work of a single man." And he quoted Pericles to assert that Athens was more than the working out of a philosophy: " 'If Athens shall appear great to you, consider then that her glories were purchased by valiant men, and by men who learned their duty.' " It was inevitable that he would come into conflict with ideologists, as his brother had already done. It was inevitable that he would come into conflict with a man and a rival candidate who believed passion to be a disease of the flesh. But he convinced the weak and the disenfranchised, by pouring out his feelings to them, that whatever needed to be done to relieve them of their deprivation and at the same time to hold the country together he would do.

And with his discovery of a role in the life of the nation that he alone could fill came remission of his despair. On two separate and crucial occasions he explained, for those of us who could hear, the answers he had found to the two questions that paralyzed him in the months after the assassination. When Martin Luther King was killed, he told the crowd in Indianapolis: "I had a member of my family killed. He was killed by a white man. But we have to make an effort in the United States—we have to make an effort to understand."

He made that effort when he came to understand that Lee Oswald stood for human misery swollen into one terrible outbreak of rage. As he said: "We can make an effort, as Martin Luther King did, to understand and to comprehend, and to replace violence with compassion and love."

And in another context, but one that also engaged him personally, his responsibility for the war in Vietnam, he said: "Tragedy is a tool for the living to gain wisdom, not a guide by which to live."

He would not be an actor in a tragedy after all.

He returned, in the last months of his life, to a belief in what he called "the work of our own hands." He came to compassion for the weak later than many other men do, but he brought with his compassion the legacy of power which was his to command. It was the only use to which he would have been willing to put that legacy, not believing it truly his own. He would use it almost physically, for he was an intensely physical man, to help those who in the extremes of their despair might consider doing what one man had done to his brother and in a way, in that way, it would be his brother's still. "The work of our own hands," he said, "matched to reason and principle, will determine our destiny. There is pride in that, even arrogance, but there is also experience and truth. In any event, it is the only way we can live." It was not enough, and it came too late to save him from another of humanity's derelicts. But it was enough for him, because it was all he could conceive to do: to be a witness and a sponsor.

Edward Moore Kennedy. The last Kennedy. Whatever political commentators are saying these days, the legacy waits in the land for him to explore. In the summer of 1971, registered Democrats still prefer him over any other candidate. He fares better than any but Edmund Muskie among independent voters. After Billy Graham and Richard Nixon he is the most admired man in America, a test that may be no more than a test of visibility, company considered.

Yet he has remained the unknown Kennedy, the one about whom no books have been written, the one whose praises none have sung. Of all the omissions of all the books written about that Aeschylean family, none is more glaring than the omission of this fourth brother from the holy texts. In his last campaign, in Massachusetts, he stressed his bond with the old days, the Kennedy days, just as he did the first time around, and his Senate office is hung with photographs and posters showing him at his brothers' sides. It is as if the voters need to be reminded, need to be told: *I too was there.* And perhaps they do, perhaps they need to know he has a serious claim. Because hasn't he been, wasn't he always, the butt? In that family of striving siblings what stature had he? Teddy is the name of a toy bear. Who ever took it seriously until events forced them to? Joseph Alsop put it bluntly enough in *American Journey:* "Why, I must have received a dozen to my mind, supremely silly letters from outwardly perfectly intelligent people," he told the interviewer, "saying that now that Bobby's gone, the only thing we can do is run Teddy for President. It was exactly as though now that O'Neill is gone, O'Neill's son is the only possible chieftain of the clan. It is not at all the normal thing in America, let me tell you." He is not O'Neill's son but O'Neill's youngest brother, and nothing that can be said of him today is as important as the fact that he did not choose to be where he is. Did not choose the prominence, did not choose to see his brothers die. It is unheard of in modern American civilization that a man of his wealth and stature should have had two brothers murdered. In Harlem, in the Delta backwaters, in some dusty Montana canyon such things might happen, but at Boston and Washington and Cape Cod? And that is only one of the burdens he bears.

He is the last adult male in a family that once thrived on five. He is heir to a pressure of public interest and opinion under which few men twenty years his senior could long stand up. He has lived through two accidents of war, one long and lingering death, two brutal murders, and two personal accidents of great physical and mental severity, and he has had to live through them as a young man in full view of a nation hungry for heroes and critical of any lapse.

The family had already come to prominence before he was born. He was caught up in the whirl, pushed and pulled through politics and ambassadorships and then more politics, run through most of a dozen schools, before he was half grown. He heard the family name, Kennedy, Kennedy, even more insistently than we have heard it since. And such is the nature of things that the girls of that family could take on other names, could as it were take on foreign citizenship, but the boys had to make the name their own, had to attach their Christian names to the front of it, become duchies or demesnes or states with their own equivalent rights. And when they were cut down in order by age, my God, as if even their *deaths* were to occur according to rank, then only one was left and he without much notion of leading. That is not myth or imagination but simple fact. He had decided long years before to survey out an acreage of his own and manage it with lesser husbandry. He did not think he was good enough for more, did not want more, has only, in the days since what he still distantly calls "the events of 1968," gone through the motions. Will it ever end, he asks his friends, or will it just go on and on and on— the words paraphrase the words of another man who wanted less than events thrust upon him, tomorrow and tomorrow and tomorrow. What happened to his brothers was exactly what he expected of fame, having watched fame all those years with the candid eyes of a child, which is why he wanted so little of it. A desk

on the Senate floor—that was enough. A good job of legislation—
that was enough.

The tension shows. The man cannot stand still. He fingers his
tie, pulls at his hair, buttons and unbuttons his coat, grits his
teeth, moves to an aide, moves back to his desk, hikes over to con-
sult another senator, stands in the aisle, drops to a chair. His office
is piled with papers and documents and notes and supplies, the
disarray of one who forever has more to do and more he wants to
do than he can ever possibly get done even with the best of staffs
and the best of intentions, the disarray of one who no longer cares
to put up a front.

His specialty as a senator is bread and butter, the important
and unfinished legislation of the New Deal and the Fair Deal and
the New Frontier and the Great Society. He believes, it appears,
that the nation's problems can best be solved by enacting enlightened legislation, and that the clear and present duty of good men
is to stay at their desks. He was away too often in 1970, but he
was campaigning for re-election, and campaigning against a mar-
gin of victory six years earlier that not even a Kennedy could pull
off twice in a row. And he was campaigning against his own guilt,
campaigning to leave Chappaquiddick behind. Since his re-election, he has generally stuck to his desk and says that what traveling he does for the party this year will be done only "to help clear
up my brother's campaign debt." "What can I *do?*" he asked an
interviewer several years ago. "I can stand up and speak out and get
credit for that. But is there something else I can do that will really
help, that will get something done about it?" Ask him what issues
concern him in the months ahead—the New Hampshire primary
is only months away—and he will list the committees and legislation and causes he hopes to study and improve: health, old age,
judiciary reform, refugee programs, the Peace Corps, the National
Science Foundation. He believes the presidency to be the most
powerful office in government, but, impatient even with the question, he isn't thinking about that right now. He promised the people of Massachusetts that he would give them a full senatorial
term. That term would end in 1976, a presidential year once removed.

His legislative approach to the nation's problems is not likely to
inspire America's new radicals, but it has an appeal of honesty
about it. If, as many are saying these days, liberalism is dead, Sen-

ator Kennedy hasn't got the news. He is still working on that last holdover from the Roosevelt years, national health insurance. And he is right: the nation never needed it more.

But outside the Senate, people hound him. When he walks from the Senate Office Building to the Capitol—he takes to the street for the air, rather than ride the Senate subway—blacks stop their cars to let him go by, lower their windows and call to him. A woman waits for him on the steps of the Capitol to thrust a letter listing who knows what grievances into his hand. He ducks back into the Capitol to avoid her, but she follows him and awards him the letter when he returns outside. "Does that happen often?" "Every day. She's harmless. I feel sorry for her." At a congressional reception in a downtown Washington hotel, a reception flush with government celebrities, strangers crowd him, bringing up their friends to be introduced. And though he himself is said to have come to terms with assassination, no one who visits Washington can fail to wince at seeing him walking the streets or riding through the rush hour in an ordinary car. It recalls too vividly the hours of the funeral train when he appeared on the back platform to nod gravely to those who had come to show their mourning. We were talking to our television screens then, remember, telling him to get back inside where no one could shoot him. And experiences like these, and the almost daily publicity, he lives with.

For to be a senator, as he knows, has not been enough, not for the people, not for the now enormous crowd of retainers thirstily out of power, not for a family that despite its energetic pleasures has always been single-minded in its pursuit of first place. The boys who loved easy adventure and easy companions were expected to exceed each other at the hard tasks of state, each in his turn. Did that family really have the communion we thought we saw? It dissolves before your eyes. They were expected to kick each other down and then pick each other up, to strive, to exceed. Life would be a constant struggle to prove themselves men, even supermen. The youngest son early became a realist, is a bitter realist today. He had few illusions and less choice. John was cool, Robert a scrapper, the girls—who knows about the girls except that they were accorded second place and accepted it as better than their due? John, Robert, Edward, all understood the rules and how to play them or break them in order to win. But Edward broke them in self-destructive ways, broke them in order to lose. Thus the cheating at Harvard, thus the playboy reputation, thus also and most enormously Chappaquiddick. He lived, always, on the frayed edge, punishing himself for the demands others made on him that he did not think he could meet. His family thought him difficult; he amused his brothers, and their retainers only tolerated him; the Senate does its best to ignore him; and he himself escapes into play, if that is the word, from the fame he did not choose and can barely abide. Who would be Edward Moore Kennedy? Yet he is, inescapably. Columnists used to say he liked the Senate and might make a career there: who would honor him for that now? If he seeks the presidency he is an upstart and if he does not seek it he is a failure. Could you live with those odds? The entire world hangs on his every indiscretion. Could you live with those odds? He does, a nervous and harried man. And with other and worse odds. "Almost every young man," writes Edward Hoagland, "needs to bathe in blood at least once, if only his own." Certainly Kennedys do, but so much blood, so much blood? There are few conditions more terrible, as we learned from those who escaped the Nazi camps, than to be a survivor when all the others died. Such are the inversions of the demonic that life seems demeaning and death honorable. The survivors remember that everyone died and they lived and cannot imagine where they failed. They did not, but in an inverted universe they seem to themselves to have. They seem usurpers and they usually want out.

Psychology is less fashionable today than cynicism, but seen in that unfashionable way, Edward Kennedy's experience at Chappaquiddick has all the appearances of an accident unconsciously wished, an undeliberate willing for something to happen that would take away the burden of fame, the burden of the legacy we all know he bears, however much such a legacy "is not at all the normal thing in America." What happened within Edward Kennedy that night is normal, as normal as such things ever are, but since he is not, in the nation's eyes, an ordinary man, it is worth looking again at what he felt and what he did. He delayed reporting the accident, he told the inquest, because he could not bring himself to call Mrs. Kopechne or his mother and father and tell them of Mary Jo's death, and rather than face those parental calls he collapsed into a state of paralyzed disbelief: "I also had sort of a thought and the wish and desire and the hope that suddenly this whole accident would disappear." He came close to drowning not once but twice, in circumstances nightmarishly similar to the circumstances of John Kennedy's wartime shipwreck. He blacked out while still caught underwater in the car, but while without consciousness and with his lungs filling with water he struggled out a window and up to the air, and then spent twenty futile minutes trying to dive back into the car to get Mary Jo Kopechne out alive. And after he and his two friends had returned to the bridge for more attempts at rescue, he directed them to drive him to the ferry slip and there dove into the water for a second time to swim back to Edgartown and his hotel, having told his companions that they should go back to the cottage and calm the girls, that he would report the accident. And this is what he said at the inquest of his second swim:

> Now, I started to swim out into that tide and the tide suddenly became, felt an extraordinary shove and almost pulling me down again, the water pulling me down, and suddenly I realized at that time even as I failed to realize it before I dove into the water that I was in a weakened condition, although as I had looked over the distance between the ferry slip and the other side, it seemed to me an inconsequential swim; but the water got colder, the tide began to draw me out and for the second time that evening I knew I was going to drown and the strength continued to leave me. By this time I was probably fifty yards off the shore and I remember being swept down toward the direction of the Edgartown Light and well out into the darkness, and I continued to attempt to swim, tried to swim at a slower pace to be able to regain whatever kind of strength that was left in me.
>
> And sometime after, I think it was about the middle of the channel, a little further than that, the tide was much calmer, gentler, and I began to get my—make some progress, and finally I was able to reach the other shore and all the nightmares and all the tragedy and all the loss of Mary Jo's death was right before me again.

Edward Kennedy's decision in his weakened condition to dive once more into a dangerous, tide-swept channel dramatizes the extent to which he wanted to escape from an act that part of him understood to have been irrevocable, from a situation that for a long night and part of a morning he simply could not face. And the fact that he twice escaped drowning that night, as once, years before, he escaped what for most men would have been a fatal or at least a permanently crippling plane crash, dramatizes the depth of his determination to survive, at whatever cost to his self-esteem. He is a man fighting his own impulses, and that is a powerful conflict to rage within the mind of any man.

And losing his position in the Senate? Giving away, with only a token fight, the job of majority whip? It tells us that his colleagues no longer fear his name, of course, but it also tells us something about the burden of fame he does not want and how far he is willing to go to be free of it. Because since when do Kennedys lose? Kennedys don't cry and Kennedys don't lose. That is what they have been told since infancy, that is the distorted voice of conscience against which they flail. "Some who chatted with him," said the New York *Times*, chattily, "believe he is actually more relaxed since his surprise defeat as Senate Democratic whip and the elimination of that job's parliamentary responsibilities." Why, of course, because the lightning didn't strike him down. He proved something even harder to prove than the proposition that Kennedys don't lose: that they do lose, may even need to lose, as only he can know. But he proved it once again by not making a real choice, by letting events take his right to choose away, and so he proved it once again by letting himself down.

So many of his experiences point to the same conclusion, that he is a man afflicted with a divided mind, a man unable to decide for himself what course his life will take. The presidency teases him. He says that Edmund Muskie has a long lead but that a lot can happen along the way. And he says that one of his sisters who follows such things speculates that Richard Nixon won't run again, that the President has, as he wrote in *Six Crises*, worked out of crises all his life motivated by a need to come back and succeed in adversity and that now that he has succeeded he won't risk the ultimate defeat in 1972 but will withdraw. There is more than a little wishful thinking in both remarks. Yet he will not campaign, he will let his acts speak for themselves, will let others decide his virtue, as if speaking out, coming forth, declaring himself one way or the other, were too great a responsibility to assume.

It may be. What must it feel to be the only survivor of a fable, to know that your most painful experiences are common knowledge to everyone you meet, the deaths in your family, your own mistakes, the possibility of violent death from every window and the shadows of every hall? To know that almost every woman you meet would be willing to sleep with you and almost every man you meet to set up some conflict to take your measure? To know that some think you a wastrel and some even think you a murderer? To see the names of your dead brothers inscribed on parks, over school doors, on streets and stadiums and airports, and know that some believe you the hope of the world and some believe you an upstart and few know anything at all of who you really are? A nightmare, surely, as if the universe had become a giant mirror. The ultimate horror, says Northrop Frye in his study of the cycles of comedy and tragedy, the final demonic, is to lie in a desert beneath a pitiless and unblinking eye: thus Prometheus: thus Edward Kennedy, the last Kennedy, the one who wants to go his own way but does not know how, to make up his own mind but cannot. Who could envy him, or wish him anything but peace? But since he is himself divided, there is no reason to believe that peace will come. For these are *men* we poke and pry and tamper with, not Titans, and Edward Moore Kennedy, the last Kennedy, lives every day at the limit, and he lives there alone, facing alone, across the wide and sluggish river, the silent Arlington graves.

The Demons of Gerald Ford

Jerry Ford hates America. Not all of America. He keeps a xenophobic compendium of the glories he imagines it wore in an imaginary golden age—when the flag flew high over a nation of honest yeomen, when government was best because it governed least, when honest folk spurned cities because cities bred the spirochetes of sin, when virtues were plain, skins white, values Puritan and businesses Mom and Pop, when the lazy poor deservedly starved and the inferior, shuffling blacks knew their places and paradise was country-club golf on a sunny Saturday afternoon—tucked like an armored pocket Bible next to his heart, and this America, true believer that he is, he adores. But the America of conflict and diversity, of poverty and races, of promised equality and government brave and strong enough to guarantee it, of massive forces massively joined in a struggle for the future, the America that is the real and contentious and idealistic and unfinished place where we live, Jerry Ford hates, with the mechanical ferocity of a man whose deepest childhood fears have not yet, at sixty-four, been decently laid to rest.

If he has seemed otherwise, if he has seemed a genial and modest man, his voting record as a congressman and his priorities as President belie that dissimulation. Across twenty-eight years of elective and appointive office, Ford has worked unrelentingly to oppose those government programs designed to aid the weak, the disenfranchised, the poor and the disadvantaged. While promoting the largest possible defense budgets, he has maneuvered to cripple, gut or void every civil rights bill he ever saw introduced. He's against food stamps. He's against free school lunches for the children of the poor. He's against national health insurance, public housing, aid to education, rent subsidy, unemployment compensation for farm workers, increased social security, an increased minimum wage, support for mass transit from the Highway Trust, abortion on demand, busing, strip-mining regulation, gasoline rationing in times of shortage, "liberal" Supreme Court decisions, public works. He prefers unemployment to inflation. He's in favor of school prayers and the CIA.

These are the classic positions of an old-guard Republican, and it would be easy to pass them off as the automatic reflexes of a dutiful conservative. But no human being is merely an automaton; we are what we are because of choices we make among the pressures and opportunities that contend within us. "People," wrote Ralph Waldo Emerson, "seem not to see that their opinion of the world is also a confession of character." While Richard Nixon was able to believe, or pretend to believe, whatever suited his immediate needs, Jerry Ford's old-guard positions have held steady through decades of time and change, because they are deeply entrenched convictions. He has never wavered from them, and he doesn't waver from them now. They must therefore relate to his own ecological balance, so to speak, to the dynamics of his shadowy interior.

There is this about the Anglo-Saxon voice, scarred sequela of the Anglo-Saxon morality that aborted it: its quality of strain. Put to service for all its many official uses—counting cadence, propounding goals, condemning the faint of heart, exhorting ambition, praising the American way of life—it comes out thin, pitched too high, without range unless deliberately trained. And these fair, blue-eyed, broad-bottomed men, the recent masters of the world, who early train their bodies to hardness, invariably neglect its training, as if in the midst of their stylized manhood, a manhood as circumscribed by fear as a life of crime, they want to leave a desperate clue.

Gerald Rudolph Ford, aka Gerald Rudolf Ford, Jr., aka Leslie Lynch King, Jr., five-fingers bowlegged according to his sometimes tailor (and imagine him suffering those tailor fingers between his legs) and thirty-eighth President of the United States by vote of the House of Representatives, where he served as waterboy and center for twenty-five years, has such a voice. Compare Kennedy's nasal arrogance, Johnson's bully bellow, Nixon's oleaginous announcerese. Even Eisenhower, another Anglo-Saxon but hardened to confidence in the cowboy West, spoke more forcefully, though something burbled caution going by. To consider Jerry, four-square, fundamental Jerry, and overlook the pathology of his Calvinistic larynx is to misunderstand totally the forces and conflicts that made him what he is, and since he is temporarily in charge of our mutual destinies, we misunderstand him to our discomfiture if not to our immediate peril. Like all our Presidents, perhaps like all men everywhere, he lives behind a mask, but unlike most of our Presidents, he didn't design that mask himself: he doesn't swear in public, but he doesn't swear in the privacy of the Oval Office either: the God for whose judging, all-seeing eyes the craftsmen of the Middle Ages finished and decorated even the sealed interiors of chests and cathedral walls has eyes for him, and sometimes at noon, today at the pinnacle of his power as in quieter days past, with Machiavellian Mel Laird kneeling improbably at his side, Gerald Ford prays aloud for guidance, knowing that tape recorders far more sensitive than the Sonys Nixon used are running without switch or deletion high above the famous desk. The presidency is a terrible burden, or so we have been told, but more terrible by far is the burden of the true believer, and there's a live one in the White House now.

He wasn't always so. None of us were. We were children once, coming into the world trailing clouds of glory behind. Look at Jerry when he was three. He's sitting on a wicker chair beside a wicker couch on a Grand Rapids front porch, his feet in high, lace-up shoes dangling off the floor. Over his solid baby body he wears white short pants and a white blouse with crisp cuffs and a white dickey fore and aft, a sailor suit without the contrasting piping—the darling of his mother, the favored, first-born son. Braced against his lap, up on its powerful hind legs, its tongue flapped out, grinning and brave, is a Boston bull terrier, and dog and boy are matched in size and constitution, though the dog's overlarge for the breed.

The boy's head and face arrest us. His mouth open, he looks back over his right shoulder at someone outside the photograph's frame. A round head. A mouthful of sturdy teeth. Hair pale as straw cut in a Dutch-boy bob, bangs halfway down the wide brow clipped straight across the front. Below the bangs, lively eyes squinted against the afternoon sun. Health, happiness, innocence triumphant and physical force surprising in a child so young: Buster Brown.

But the photograph deceives, as all the later childhood photographs—somber when others are smiling, aggressive when others are content, wary when others are at ease—do not. Because at three, hardly out of diapers, this Buster Brown has already lost a father and a name, has been stripped of the identity awarded him at birth and forced to assume a second identity necessarily and forever less secure, has been bereaved by desertion and almost immediately thereafter inwardly shamed. If you think I make too much of this, wait and see.

He was born Leslie Lynch King, Jr., at 12:35 A.M. on July 14, 1913, in Omaha, Nebraska, the Sun conjunct Neptune in Cancer within a close orb. His mother, Dorothy Gardner King, of Grand Rapids, was nearly beautiful, plump in the manner of the day, big-breasted, and you may be sure in 1913 he nursed at those breasts and thrived. His father, his mysterious father, a wool trader from Wyoming, is as shadowy and fascinating a man as Bif's gold-mining uncle in *Death of a Salesman*, the daredevil fellow Willie Loman never was. What brought young, single, sexy Dorothy Gardner to Omaha in 1911 or 1912? Did she run away from home? Why did she marry a wanderer like Leslie King? At very least the man must have been exotic, romantic, a cowboy, and the woman, "lots of fun and very soft-hearted" in the words of her first-born son, the woman out on the wild packing-house town, would be an easy mark for that.

She never told her son why the marriage failed (and more to the point, he never seriously asked). "Things just didn't work out" is the most he remembers her ever having said. Was Leslie King a drinker? Did he beat his wife? Wyoming wool traders are capable of anything. But the likeliest answer is that he left her, not wanting the responsibility of a child. Dorothy King was divorced in 1915 and went back to Grand Rapids with two-year-old Leslie Jr. in tow, and there met and almost immediately married Gerald Rudolf Ford, fourth child and only son in a family of four, whose father died when he was young, a paint-and-varnish salesman in a city of booming furniture factories.

And then this curious and cataclysmic event, the renaming of Dorothy's son. Jerry says he knew it only later, but he lies, however unintentionally. Whatever his mother called him, little Leslie would have known his real name and his real father before the age of two, would therefore have known when his first full name was taken away. We walk by then and talk by then; we remember deeply, even searingly, by then, though later we forget deeply too; and fathers who are vain enough to name us after themselves, to put their brand on us, as Leslie King did, aren't likely to keep the fact a secret.

Erasing the first childhood name, giving the boy a new identity, was an act of generosity on Dad Ford's part, proof to Dorothy of his love: he married her and accepted the child as his own. Went beyond stepfatherhood and legally adopted the boy. But Gerald Ford *Junior?* He might have named little Leslie Tom or Dick or Jimmy, as he later did his three natural sons; Leslie wasn't his first-born son; he was the son of another marriage and another man. Greater love, then? Repair, one generation removed, of Dad Ford's own early loss? All that, certainly, to his great credit, but certainly also some flicker of shame, in the pious Middle West of the early twentieth century, at his wife's divorce. And of jealousy that another had impregnated her first. And of that malign spirit of expropriation, extending even to human flesh, that lies sealed like angina within the Anglo-Saxon heart. All these ambivalences the towheaded Buster Brown had to ravel before his feet had even touched the floor.

So this second father, Gerald Rudolf Ford. "Dad" Ford to his sons and to his wife. "I guess Dad was the strongest influence in my life," the President confesses. A good man. A public man. When he died, in 1964, Grace Episcopal Church, the church of his good works, was crowded to the aisles for the first time in Grand Rapids memory. Six feet one inch tall. Phalanxes of friends. He raised money for charity and the church. He ran a scout troop, set up recreation programs, helped found and support a summer camp for the poor. He loved the outdoors. He taught his four sons baseball, football, golf, swimming. He took them on fishing trips and hikes. He was a pillar of the community. He was hardly ever home. Dorothy Ford felt the deprivation; in her only recorded assessment of her second husband, she limned him with sweet caustic: "If Dad would give as much time to the paint business as he gives to public affairs, we'd be rich."

Philip Buchen, counselor to the President and one of Jerry Ford's oldest friends: "Dad Ford set a pattern for hard work. He was never really successful—the paint company was a small business and it didn't grow. But he had enough, and he got a lot of satisfaction out of life." Had enough, and got a lot of satisfaction out of life, but also lived with buried stress, eventually acquiring ulcers painful enough to keep him up at night. And Dorothy Ford grew overweight and was hospitalized for high blood pressure and back problems more than once in her middle years, which suggests that in the midst of all the family striving, not everything went well at home.

The paint company. Ford Paint & Varnish. Manufacturing and distribution. Established in Grand Rapids, the furniture capital of the world, in 1929, three weeks before the Wall Street crash. Dad Ford started his company and simultaneously moved his family to an expensive house in East Grand Rapids. Who starts a business and buys a high new house the same year? A cockeyed optimist, a man whose wife wants visible wealth? The Depression almost wiped them out. Dad Ford couldn't handle the mortgage on the house. He forfeited house and down payment, too, and moved to a smaller residence in a poorer section of town. Jerry—Junie, as he was called then, for Junior—had to petition the school board and ride the bus to stay at South High, with who knows what smoldering sense of indignation? He hated busing then; he hates it now. But Jerry was never afflicted internally with the family's stresses; Jerry learned to handle stress in other ways.

How did Junie grow? By being a boy, a certain kind of boy. An outdoor boy, an athletic boy, a boy with a problem. Like George Washington, Gerald "Junie" Ford had his cherry tree.

"He was a strong-willed little boy," a former neighbor recalls. "If he didn't want you to climb his cherry tree at the particular moment, no one did. He would climb up it and say, 'My tree.' There would be perhaps six or seven of us, older than he was, but he could hold his own. But Alice (the neighbor's twin sister) went up anyway, so he stepped on her hand. Actually, he *stood* on her hand, until she screamed. Then he took his foot off. A very headstrong little boy."

"My very young years," he told novelist John Hersey during the week he allowed Hersey to wander with him through the White House, "I had a terrible temper. My mother detected it and started to get me away from being upset and flying off the handle. She had a great knack of ridicule one time, and humor the next, or cajoling, to teach me that anger—visible, physical anger—was not the way to meet problems. . . . She taught me that you don't respond in a wild, uncontrolled way; you just better sit back and take a hard look and try to make the best decision without letting emotions be the controlling factor." But if not emotions, then what? Pure practical reason? Ulcers? Sensitized to overcontrol by his mother's fear of anger, ridiculed, humored, and cajoled, Jerry had to put his feelings somewhere. Where did Jerry's anger go?

Football. Ford's youthful forte, the delight of his metaphor and the school of his life. Of the three modest articles and one coauthored book that across his entire professional lifetime are the only written words to be published in his name, one, coauthored with John Underwood in *Sports Illustrated,* is titled "In Defense of the Competitive Urge," and in it the then Vice-President offers a remarkable opinion: "Broadly speaking, outside of a national character and an educated society, there are few things more important to a country's growth and well-being than competitive athletics." Since competitive athletics have had almost nothing whatsoever to do with any country's growth, least of all the United States, Ford can only be talking about himself.

So: football. Football, where aggression, anger, a very visible and socially accepted hatred of the *other*—the timid, the less able, the unlucky, the weak—carries the day. Ford put his feelings through the psychic projector and they beamed out contempt for the weak. Even if his family tradition hadn't been Republican, he would have been a sucker for the old-guard Republican philosophy of life, the philosophy of dog eat dog. The compassion of America was lost on the playing fields of Michigan and South High. The record repeats again and again: the President is warm and generous in person but hard as nails at any distance of remove.

Portrait of the President as jock hero. Where do you think he first heard the laving, loving roar of the crowd? Early, Junie dreamed of fame at baseball, but baseball doesn't make high-school heroes. South High football coach Clifford Gettings was the beginning of a line of bully father figures Ford would claim loyalty to, and unlike the later ones—men like the late Senator Arthur Vandenberg of Michigan, whom Ford claims sponsored him for Congress but whose records give no indication of anything more than the most formal of connections, men like Richard Nixon—Gettings at least claims loyalty to Jerry in return.

Because he admires force, Ford likes to remember his stepfather as a tough man, but his brothers disagree. Brother Dick recalls only one instance of physical punishment in the Ford house, when Tom came home late for dinner and got a ruler broken over his rear. But Coach Gettings was a bear of a man, a model of athletic deportment, the kind of hero who can go out on the high school practice field among the gangling teen-age children and growl curses and kick ass. You showed up on time for Gettings' practices; you got a lap to run for every minute you were late. Gettings remembers being ten minutes late himself one day, and the team made the old man run his laps too, all heart-pounding ten of them, and guess who maliciously chalked up each lap as he ran?

Thus inspired, the team kept busy after school. Writes biographer Bud Vestal: "Brother Tom said that in 1930, when avowed Socialists and Communists were painting slogans on walls of public buildings in Grand Rapids, Jerry led an after-dark foray of South High School athletes to halt it. Tom said they caught some young leftists at work and dumped their paint over their heads."

Wearing a coat and tie when his high-school classmates wore sweaters, remembered as serious and shy and entirely without interest in girls, Junie played football like a maniac, played center in an era when to center the ball was to throw a difficult, upside-down, ass-backward pass. "I must have centered the ball five hundred thousand times in high school and college," he recounts. He was a roving linebacker on defense, a sixty-minute man. He made All-City three years in a row. He played hard. He played to win. He learned to be a team player, a man among equals, a lesson he never forgot.

He was nevertheless a local hero, and it is not an exaggeration to say that his first sweet taste of local success determined his career. In the autumn of 1930, during his sparkling senior year, a Grand Rapids theater held a contest, part of a promotional scheme in fifty midwestern cities to identify the most popular high school seniors. Kids sauntered down to the old Majestic in droves and filled out their ballots and dropped them into the ballot box. All-City center Junie Ford won. The prize was a trip to Washington, D.C. To get to Washington, all you have to do is please the folks back home.

But 1930 brought another event, an event that preceded the popularity contest and must have confirmed its message beyond

inner debate: the former Leslie Lynch King, Jr., met his real father for the first (remembered) time.

Ford tells the story to all his biographers, repeating it like the
Ancient Mariner to drive its homiletic tragedy home. He told it
best to John Hersey:

"I was, I think, a junior in high school in the spring, 1930. I
worked at a restaurant across from South High called Skougis'. It
was a 1929, 1930 hamburger stand with counters—a dilapidated
place. Bill Skougis was a shrewd Greek businessman, and he hired
as waiters the outstanding football players. He paid me $2 plus my
lunch—up to 50 cents a meal—and I worked from 11:30 to 1,
through the noon-hour class periods, and one night a week from 7
to 10. [Ford makes much of his modest, even impoverished, childhood, but notice that his take for part-time work, counting the
lunches, was $4.50 a week at a time—the empty belly of the
Depression—when Dad Ford had been forced to reduce the wages
he paid the *family* men at his factory to $5.00 a week. Dad Ford
himself took home no more.] I waited on table at one of the
counters, washed the dishes and handled the cash register. My
working place was right near the entrance. . . . I was standing
there taking money, washing dishes, and . . . this man came in,
and he stood over there. And, he was a stranger. Strangers didn't
come in often. This man stood over there against the candy
counter. I was busy, yet I couldn't help but notice that he stood
there for 10 minutes. Finally he walked over to where I was working. Nobody was bothering me. 'Leslie,' he said. I didn't answer.
He said, 'I'm Leslie King, and you're Leslie King, Jr.' Well, it was
kind of shocking. He said, 'I would like to take you to lunch.' I
said, 'Well, I'm working. I've got to check with the owner.' He
said, 'I haven't seen you for a good many years. You don't know
me.' So I went to Bill Skougis, and I said, 'I've got a personal matter. Will you excuse me?' And he did. My father took me out to
his car, which was parked in the front—a brand-new Cadillac or
Lincoln—and he introduced me to his wife. So we went to lunch.
He was then living in Wyoming with his wife, and they had come
out to buy a new Cadillac or Lincoln, which was a beautiful car
for those days, and they had picked it up in Detroit and were driving back to Wyoming, and they wanted to stop in and see me.
[Hadn't even come directly to see *him*, the long-lost son, had
come all the way from Wyoming to pick up a *car* and on the way

home stopped by for lunch.] Which he did. And after he had finished lunch, he took me back to the school. I said goodbye. He said, 'Will you come out and see me in Wyoming?' I said I'd think about it."

But not think too hard. At lunch, Ford told biographer Jerald TerHorst, "I thought, here I was, earning two dollars a week and trying to get through school, my stepfather was having difficult times, yet here was my real father, obviously doing quite well if he could pick up a new Lincoln. . . ." "Ford's voice trailed off," writes TerHorst, "masking his resentment. . . . Inside Jerry Ford, the hurt was deep and bitter." Deep and bitter enough to freeze the event in his memory in minute detail for the rest of his life.

That's one of two Leslie King stories the President tells, and perhaps before we consider it you should hear the other one as well. It's briefer but even more to the point. "My junior year at Ann Arbor [Ford went to the University of Michigan after South High], which would be '33-'34, when my stepfather's business had long gone to pot, he was hanging on by his fingernails, my father—my real father—had been ordered at the time of the divorce to pay my mother child maintenance, and he never paid any. I was having a terrible time. [But consider this terrible time:] Sure, I was earning my board, and I saved some money working for my stepfather in the summer. But it wasn't enough. I wasn't able to pay my bills—the fraternity [Delta Kappa Epsilon, Deke, the jock fraternity], the room where I lived. And I wrote my father and asked him if he could help. And, as I recall, I either got no answer or, if I got an answer, he said he couldn't do it. I felt that, from what I understood, his economic circumstances were such that he could have been helpful. I had that impression. From that Lincoln or Cadillac I'd seen that he'd bought. And then after I graduated from Michigan, I went to Yale, of course. And then one time, out of the blue, I got a letter, a phone call, or something, saying that he was coming with his wife, the woman I had met, with his son by the second marriage—he was really my stepbrother. And they were trying to find a school in the East for him, and could they stop by and maybe I could give them some advice. So they stopped. I did meet the son. And I went to dinner with them and gave them some thoughts about schools in the East and never saw them again."

Do still, angry waters run deep? The antagonists of these tales are wealth, fine cars, a second, younger wife, a second, cherished son and Cinderella in the food-stained sweater of a letterman, but their secret agony is unrequited love. Part of Jerry wanted to be a King. Or at least a prince: twenty or twenty-one years old, he begs for child support. "Had King arrived now," TerHorst asks melodramatically, paraphrasing Ford, "so he could go back to Wyoming and brag about seeing his son, the football star?" The crowds loved Junie; why didn't his father, the Lincoln (or Cadillac) man? And why didn't he prove it by bailing him out?

"I'm a Ford, not a Lincoln"—how juiced with hidden significance the phrase suddenly seems. Obsessed with success, Gerald Ford has never loved money, which must seem paradoxical in a man who picks his friends (and his Vice-President) from among men of wealth, until you consider that the Dad who loved him never made much of it, and the father who abandoned him had it—in Ford's imagination at least—to burn. So Ford the congressman, in the first moments after his public nomination to the vice-presidency, expressed awe over the increased pension benefits his elevation would bring. And so Ford the President chose Nelson Rockefeller as his sidekick, followed the revelations of Rockefeller's enormous wealth with unabashed glee, and later, at campaign time, left the archetypal rich man turning slowly, slowly in the wind until he removed himself from the ticket. Money, Rocky, money don't buy love.

To a greater extent than most of us like to admit, parents make us what we are. Presidents in particular have been mother-driven men, men driven by mothers so intensely curbed in achievement themselves that they inculcate a psychohistorical hunger for fame in their sons: look at FDR's imperious Mrs. Roosevelt, Truman's grits-and-bacon Mamma, Eisenhower's serene Ida Elizabeth, Kennedy's lace-curtain Rose, Johnson's Texas-proud Rebekah Baines, Nixon's fighting-Quaker Hannah Milhous. The presidency is ultimately Oedipal, almost literally so. A man born from the vast continental land and nurtured there returns as husband to honor and enlarge its great affairs. Ford was an only child for five long years, and in that Eden might have nourished a huge and healthy egotism, but the conflicts of his paternity, conflicts his mother inadvertently introduced, embedded anger, vanity and insecurity instead.

It took him years to piece together the reasons for that confusion, the double paternity, the double Juniors, the father who abandoned him, the stepfather who took him in. He matured correspondingly late. In the curious, half-literate book that Ford coauthored with his Grand Rapids friend John R. Stiles, *Portrait of the Assassin,* a book about Lee Harvey Oswald that Stiles and the Warren Commission largely wrote, occasional sentences and paragraphs appear that clearly came from Ford's hand. One of them propounds a hypothesis so contrary to the traditional assumptions of psychology that it fairly shivers on the page. Apologizing for Marguerite Oswald's insistence that her son was a normal child, Ford writes: "As intimately as a mother feels she knows her son, what happens to a young man in the critical years seventeen to twenty-one can obscure everything in the past." One to five, certainly; twelve to fifteen, possibly; but seventeen to twenty-one? Seventeen to twenty-one: from the year Leslie King announced himself to the year he refused to acknowledge and aid his son.

At twenty-one, Gerald Ford put the pieces together and became a man, a man of comradely warmth and canine loyalty, but a man painfully withered within. He would make his way cautiously, secretly, with adamantine determination, believing that for every act of ingratiation the ingratiated must return a precise *quid pro quo*; he would find his security in the party and the team; he would feel at peace only in the middle of a friendly crowd. He would be, in short, the classic case of a man nursing a secret grudge and bitterly certain that someday he would find himself on top and pay them back for the years of pain and neglect. "I'm a determined person," he told Hersey. "And if I've got an objective, I'll make hours of sacrifice—whatever efforts are needed. Some people call it plodding. The word is somewhat downgraded, but I'd rather be a plodder and get someplace than have charisma and not make it." Hersey felt Ford's anger then, anger at a cruel early forking of the road that the emotionally privileged of the world— privileged by nurture to become more secure and generous—don't even notice as they pass.

The approbation Ford couldn't find in Wyoming he found on the football field, where crowds cheered his plays. It proved to him that he should seek vindication in public life. He sought that vindication with silent bitterness. Instead of a lover, he became an absentee husband; instead of a man of compassion, he became a man hard of heart; instead of a potential statesman, he became, in Lyndon Johnson's brilliant phrase, "one of the wooden soldiers of the status quo." He was always, would always be, a diligent worker, but he worked in the wrong direction, to the easier and more immediate end. He was a handsome, naïve, blond, blue-eyed football star, and like too many stars, he became an unwitting victim, missing the slow but solid passes that came his way, because he thought he already had the ball and was running down the field.

An incident at the University of Michigan. The captain of Michigan's winning 1933 team remembers Ford as "a player who had no fear," but off the field fear clocked its hour. One of Ford's Michigan teammates was a black named Willis Ward. Ford liked Ward and sometimes roomed with him when the team traveled, which you must understand to have been an act of some bravery in the overtly racist America of the thirties. Early in the 1934 season, Michigan was scheduled to play Georgia Tech when the word came up from Dixie that there'd be no game if Ward appeared on the field. The Michigan administration capitulated despite the efforts of the school's more liberal football coach. Jerry was agonized and considered protest: what if he refused to play? The night before the game, he called Dad Ford, but his stepfather declined the privilege of making up his twenty-year-old son's mind. Ford balanced the weakness of the team against the strength of his conscience; the team won. He was still stinging when a Georgia Tech lineman jeered "nigger" over the centered ball, and Ford and a guard blocked the lineman so viciously he had to be carried off the field. The story is cited in Ford's biographies as proof of his early dedication to liberalism. It's not. It's proof of his early dedication to scapegoating. "Thanks to my football experience," he would tell an audience years later, "I know the value of team play. It is, I believe, one of the most important lessons to be learned and practiced in our lives." The Georgia Tech game was not the last time Ford's loyalty to a team took precedence over his moral judgment.

Ford's intelligence has long been a matter of dispute. When he was nominated for the vice-presidency, there was those who recalled Lyndon Johnson's famous remark about Jerry and his missing helmet, and others who remembered Johnson scoffing, "Jerry's so dumb he can't fart and chew gum at the same time." Alice Roosevelt Longworth, Washington's aging resident wit, worked up her Ford material to nothing better than "poor, dull Jerry"; John Ehrlichman cracked, "What a jerk Jerry is!" which, considering the source, must be counted an expert opinion; and the leader Ford most idolized and deferred to, Richard Nixon, is said to have laughed hysterically at the notion that Congress would depose him in favor of Ford—"Can you see Jerry occupying this chair?" are the words usually attributed to the man who nominated him for office a heartbeat away. Ford's defenders hastened to point out that Jerry earned a good B average at every school he attended—at South High, at Michigan, at Yale Law. The curiosity of these grades—if B's at Yale Law, why not A's at Michigan or South High?—has even engaged the attention of Ford himself. Yale hired Ford, after he graduated from Michigan, to coach junior varsity football and varsity boxing. He'd decided by then to take a law degree, and the coaching job offered him the opportunity to apply at Yale. It took him three years to convince the law-school faculty that he could handle coaching and studying at the same time, but in 1939 it admitted him fully to studies and he performed respectably against one of the most distinguished Yale Law classes ever graduated. Ninety-nine out of that class of 125 were Phi Beta Kappas on admission, and among them moved such future notables as Supreme Court justices Potter Stewart and Byron White, Sargent Shriver, Congressman Peter Frelinghuysen, Senator Peter Dominick and Deputy Secretary of Defense* Cyrus Vance. "I seem to have had a capability of competing with whatever competition there was at each level," Ford told Hersey, after which observation he added a sly little turn of the screw: "And yet I could have enough outside activities to enjoy a broader spectrum of day-to-day living than some of them."

The man isn't dumb, a politically savvy Grand Rapids lady would later say of freshman congressional candidate Jerry Ford after seeing him perform in debate, he's just ignorant. There's truth to the remark, but the revealing aspect of Ford's academic performance is its careful positioning. In three different schools, under three different sets of conditions, he was careful to perform no better than he had to to get decently by. He was also smart enough, and driven enough by his conflicting needs, to divide his eggs between baskets, choosing to be known neither as full-time jock nor full-time scholar. Part of the basic training for politics, as

---

* And later Secretary of State

Garry Wills has cynically pointed out, is learning to feign mediocrity, a skill that seems to have come naturally to Ford.

Women were among the "outside activities" that Jerry enjoyed, though not many of them. His universal solvent of caution he applied to women too, and his rakish friend John R. Stiles once injudiciously blurted to an interviewer, "I think I know every girl Jerry ever slept with," implying that there have been no more than five and possibly as few as three in all Ford's sixty-four years. The President whose voice breaks when he speaks of his close and devoted family is also the congressman who regularly averaged two hundred out-of-town trips a year and left his wife at home to raise the kids, skirting alcoholism and incipient nervous breakdown in her abandonment. Ford fell head over heels for a woman only once in his life, and her name wasn't Betty Bloomer, and for all her charms, her hard credentials were precisely suited to his ambitions in the days when he was a fledgling golden boy.

Phyllis Brown was a student at Connecticut College, in New London, when Ford turned up at Yale. Everyone who knew her in those early days remembers her as a raving beauty with a sparkling personality and a mischievous wit (she "seemed to have the kind of personality that Ford admired and missed in himself," Ter-Horst writes with unintentional cruelty). Ford pursued her eagerly, and after Connecticut, when she went to the Big Apple and became a Powers model, she even persuaded him to invest one thousand dollars of his savings from his Yale coaching salary of twenty-four hundred a year in a modeling agency her friend Harry Conover was opening in New York. The one thousand dollars made him a silent partner; it also bought him a flash of limelight that his sensitized vanity could well have done without. The public learned of the Phyllis Brown-Jerry Ford courtship in a twenty-one-picture spread in *Look* magazine in March 1940, a spread Conover and Brown probably placed, a spread displaying the beautiful people cavorting through a skiing weekend at Stowe, Phyllis and Jerry schussing down the four-hundred-yard slope, Jerry rubbing Phyllis' back on a flowered couch in the lounge at the inn, Phyllis and Jerry falling asleep on the couch afterward discreetly head to foot, Jerry kissing a blanket-wrapped Phyllis good-by as the train pulled into New Haven on Monday morning. With the coyness that in 1940 passed for titillation, the photos and captions imply that Phyllis and Jerry spent their nights together as well as their days, and no doubt they did. Later they turned up on the cover of *Cosmopolitan*, Jerry in his naval uniform, to signify that beautiful people also go off to war.

Phyllis and Jerry went steady for four years, and he was obviously keen to marry her, because he took her back to Grand Rapids and up to the Ford cottage on Lake Michigan to check her out with the folks, but something soured the match along the way, and before he joined the Navy, unhappy with its profits, Jerry withdrew from the agency and presumably from Phyllis as well. "I only had one serious romance," he told Hersey, "other than the one I had with Betty"—the phrasing of the statement awards Betty a qualified second place—"but it didn't work out. So I just forgot being too much interested in marriage." Which recalls Mark Twain's story about the cat that learned its lesson too well. It got up on a hot stove one time, Twain said, and got burned, and skatted right down, and so it learned not to get up on hot stoves—but after that the danged thing wouldn't get up on cold stoves neither.

Ford spent the summer of 1940 working in New York for Wendell Willkie's presidential campaign. Like Jerry, Willkie was an isolationist in those cautious, prewar years, but his campaign seems to have attracted Jerry for reasons of strategy more than philosophy; Willkie was a midwestern Republican with boyish good looks and a hearty, energetic style who was taking on no less formidable an opponent than Franklin Delano Roosevelt, an entrenched behemoth whom all good Republicans despised who was seeking an unprecedented third term. Ford claims he wasn't seriously interested in politics until after the war, but his experience with the Willkie campaign probably confirmed his political ambitions and precipitated the split with Phyllis Brown. Ambitious for her modeling career, she wouldn't have wanted to give up New York for Grand Rapids, Jerry's logical political base, and confronted with a choice between politics and love, Jerry chose politics hands down. He watched Willkie beat Roosevelt in Michigan by seven thousand votes out of more than two million cast, and in 1941 he packed up and went home to open a Grand Rapids law office with his old friend Philip Buchen, and Phyllis Brown lost the chance she might have had, assuming she was equipped to survive the thirty-three leaden intervening years, to become the first lady of the land.

Nothing whatsoever happened to Gerald Ford during World War II. Although he served as a physical training instructor under Gene Tunney and an officer aboard the USS *Monterey*, a light aircraft carrier that saw extensive action in the South Pacific, the only tale he tells of war is a tale of accident: he was nearly washed overboard once during a typhoon. He returned from the war a reserve lieutenant commander, his service record packed with perfect ratings and enthusiastic comments from his superior officers. They cited him as an excellent leader, steady and resourceful, and averred that he was "at his best in situations dealing directly with people because he commanded the respect of all." Which, considering his later performance, means that the war was Jerry's finest hour. America lost a good navy man when he was mustered out. With orders from above to guide him, he performed flawlessly. He might have made a good astronaut. About him bulks like a moon suit the same humorless stoicism, the adaptive housing that such men perfect from years of dogged application to the obvious, when the last layers of inspiration have numbly ablated away.

Back from the war, Jerry moved immediately to enter politics. He organized an All Veterans Housing Committee to lobby for changes in local zoning laws that would allow the building of low-cost veterans' housing. By 1947 he was ready to challenge isolationist Republican Bartel J. Jonkman for Michigan's Fifth Congressional District seat. Jack Stiles ran Ford's campaign. He knew his candidate, and advised him to avoid speeches and concentrate on shaking hands. Ford did, stumping the district night and day, listening more than he talked, pitching hay and milking cows. The primary results proved Jonkman's vulnerability: Ford won the Republican nomination 26,632 to 14,341. He went on to win the general election by more than twenty-seven thousand votes. Between primary and general he married Betty Bloomer Warren, picking up a wife to take to Washington *en passant*.

So Jerry Ford became a congressman, matriculating with the freshman class of 1948. There are 435 congressmen in the House of Representatives, and on a national scale theirs are no more than the outer slums of elective and appointive office, but the House was the culmination of Jerry's ambition—he dreamed of becoming Speaker one day—and secure within its crowd, a team player first and last, he took no risks whatever with his seat or his seniority.

Ford's strategy for keeping his job was a masterwork of pure defense. Like Gaul, it was divided into three parts:

1. Please the folks back home.
2. Please fellow congressmen.
3. Vote the party line.

To please the folks back home, Ford set up one of the most efficient district-serving systems Washington had ever seen. It kept him in office through decades of political tumult and national cataclysm, even after the grateful citizens of Grand Rapids and its environs had moved far to their Pre-Cambrian congressman's political left. "The conservative record is Grand Rapids," Ford told reporters when he became Vice-President. "Forget Grand Rapids." Not so. As soon as he unglued himself from the Fifth District, its voters elected a Democrat.

Ford taught himself to be the irreplaceable first sergeant that every effective division requires: mastered the forms, explored the bureaucratic routings, learned how to get the Spam to the front lines. He ran, in effect, a Washington lobby for his constituents. He shipped out free government publications by the carload, set up a portrait Polaroid in the corner of his office so visitors could be photographed with their representative, took important guests to dinner. His staff sent congratulations for births, weddings and awards and condolences for deaths. If you wanted something from Washington, you wrote or dropped in on Congressman Ford and he done his damnedest to get it for you, influence that, like regressive taxes, works fine for the comfortable and the notable but does nothing whatsoever for the anonymous and the poor.

To please fellow congressmen, Ford did their butt-work, did them favors, campaigned on their behalf and compromised. When he became Vice-President, he could report to the White House Correspondents' Association, "I have had a lot of adversaries in my political life, but no enemies that I can remember," and while the brag is partly gullible, it is also largely true. Ford became the resident House expert on the fine print of Defense budgets, a useful assistance but hardly an example of statesmanlike watchdog-

ging, because Jerry was, and is, so bloodthirsty a champion of national defense that he is the last person likely to have led a
movement to cut the budgets he so assiduously studied, and never
did. In twenty-five years in the House, in fact, he introduced not
one piece of major legislation of any kind, a record with double
and doubly dreary significance: that he never felt the necessity or
the conviction to do so, and that he let other legislators take the
credit, earning for himself the resulting favor chits.

When Congress studied confirming him for the vice-presidency,
Ford produced gentle reminders of his virtues tailored to the
tastes of each body. "I said over in the Senate that truth is the
glue that holds governments together," he told the House Judiciary Committee. For the House's benefit he added, "Compromise
is the oil that makes governments go." Compromise, to Jerry
Ford, meant working to gut any and all Democratic legislation
that the Republican Party opposed and then voting for the more
benevolent bills in final passage. It made the House look more
responsive, and anyway, the reasoning went, if the Democrats insist on giving money away, why shouldn't the Republicans take
some credit too? Yet Ford preferred not to expend his energy
fighting Democratic legislation. He dreamed instead of making
the differences between the two parties perfectly clear and he
dreamed of Republican victory, of a decisive win for his consistently losing team, because without that victory, how could he
ever be Speaker of the House?

So in addition to butt-work, favors and compromise, Ford campaigned. He stumped tirelessly, helping party and fellow congressman and himself, speaking wherever and whenever anyone
asked him to. Stepping into a convenient phone booth and stripping back the plain blue serge, he exposed an entire speakers' bureau in the person of one ordinary man. His record was 238 trips
in one season. Vestal reports his typical schedule:

> Rise early, go to the Capitol at 7:00 A.M. or so and do
> office work, receive visitors, confer with Republican associ-
> ates, attend committee hearings. Noon: Attend convening of
> the House, stay awake during debate or confer with cronies in
> the hall on upcoming major business. At 2:30 or 3:00 P.M.,
> grab a briefcase with work papers and a speech text, a plastic
> garment bag with a change of suit and shirt, and rush to

Washington National Airport to fly to the speaking engage-
ment. Make speech. Fly home, arrive at 1:00 A.M. Take a re-
laxing swim in the pool. Sleep five or six hours, then repeat.

Which sounds like a recipe for early heart attack, but such was
Jerry's delight in travel that he thrived. From his safe congressional district, with his people-pleasing machine running
smoothly, Ford was free to barnstorm other districts and deliver
the Republican good news across the land. Nor was campaigning
for friends and party the only reason for his constant travel: the
income from his speaking trips nearly doubled his salary. One of
the pains in the vice-presidential ass was losing the extra income;
despite its elevation to the better-paying executive, the Ford family was forced to trim its budget and tighten its belt. Among other
things, Betty Ford was forced to cancel a trip to honor Martha
Graham, the dancer she has said was the most important figure in
her life; the Veep's budget couldn't afford the price of a round
trip between Washington and Detroit.

Loyalty and good fellowship had their slow rewards, extending
finally to the presidency itself. Richard Nixon alone didn't put
Jerry Ford in the White House; his confirmation also required the
complicity of the Congress in which he served. Some of us
laughed when Jerry Ford sat down at the piano, but was any man
better placed to receive the first presidential *appointment* in the
history of the United States? His "lifestyle of deference," as Representative Michael Harrington described it to the House committee, paid off slowly, but ultimately it paid off big. Ford expected it
would. "I've always believed," he told Vestal, "that you take a political job, or get one, you do it; you get another assignment, you
do it. And if the ball bounces your way or you get a break, you're
prepared for the next assignment, and in the process you've
earned the opportunity to qualify. . . . And the mere fact that it
takes a little time has never bothered me. Too many people in
politics get a little impatient." He has, wrote Charles McCollum
in *New Times*, "a precise grasp of where his limitations lie and
just exactly where he wants to go." He moves forward "one small
step at a time, never straining his resources or his totally ingratiat-
ing manner."

Well, at least that's the way it worked in the small pond of the
House. He did his bit and waited his turn, and twice around the

assignments came—grudgingly, with the heels of their modest dignity worn away. He was elected chairman of the House Republican Caucus because Republicans thought him a deserving, harmless, nice guy; he became House minority leader by the same default. "The pragmatic reason was that Ford was electable," said Representative Robert Griffin of the first occasion; "Jerry got along with all segments of the party." "It wasn't as though everybody was wildly enthusiastic about Jerry," said Representative Charles Goodell of the second; "it was just that most Republicans liked him and respected him. He didn't have enemies." "I had nothing to lose," Ford told biographer Richard Reeves. "I could have kept my House seat, and I was careful not to get anyone mad at me." Richard Nixon nominated Ford for the vice-presidency to a more nefarious purpose, knowing a nasty joke when he saw one, but Nixon's estimate of Congress' sense of humor was for once set too high. And even Congress had its doubts. Consistently, in testimony before its committees, congressional leaders expressed their embarrassed hopes that Jerry would somehow grow in office. Which implies that in their experienced opinions the man had a lot of growing to do.

"Oh, I am sure I made some mistakes," Gerald Ford told the House committee touchily near the conclusion of his testimony, when Democrat Don Edwards pushed. "I said [to the Senate] I was no saint and I will repeat it here." Meaning push me only so far. "But no serious major mistakes." Meaning push me no farther.

A new text for civics classes then: no serious major mistakes. Cover your sweet ass and lie low.

If Gerald Ford were no more than a mediocre, calculating politician in a field of similarly disfigured men, we would still have reason for revulsion. Because, good football player and eagle scout that he is, he has run his scrimmages from first to last dutifully by the playbook our officialdom prescribes. He believes himself to be, and thousands of pages of raw FBI files got up for his vice-presidential confirmation attest him, a completely honest man within the limitations of the rules. He never fudged his campaign receipts, never bought or sold inordinate influence, never took bribes, never called in the plumbers, never cheated on his taxes, never even screwed the secretaries and the political groupies that

crowds of congressmen and lines of Presidents have augered to
their fill. His conservatism, in its origins at least, is as philo-
sophically respectable as the conservatism of many other more rational men.

He seems to have learned it from Dad Ford; significantly, his
brothers are even more rabidly right wing than he is. It carries a
weight of small-town righteousness that disfigures its hallowed
premises—Ford emphasizes his modest childhood disadvantages
to help correct that righteousness of the comfortable before the
sufferings of the impoverished, to prove that any man in America,
if he has grit and wit, can truly make it on his own—but it grows
from a long historical tradition of belief. Like many other men in
American history, Thomas Jefferson included, Ford professes his
faith in the natural man and his suspicion of government. He believes in the untrammeled virtues of the profit motive. He believes
success rewards hard work. More coldly, he believes that poverty is
a mark of laziness and race a disadvantage any ambitious man can
overcome. Conservatism, Calvinism and social Darwinism all
combine to make Ford's philosophic canons, with a measure of
Horatio Algerism thrown in: it is a philosophy that congealed in
America in the years before 1920, at about the same time that the
nation was viciously disenfranchising the American Negro and
shutting off immigration of the less than lily-white populations of
southern Europe and Asia, and it has changed hardly at all in the
cataclysmic years since. Specifically, and despite his subsequent
education and experience, Ford has changed hardly at all since
childhood; the only one of his childhood canons he has given up
is isolationism, and even today he favors a cautious interna-
tionalism at best, coaxed to that by his war experience and by the
tutoring of Henry Kissinger.

Yet despite the shallow facility of his beliefs and the dutiful attention he has given to the prevailing rules, Ford is more—or less
—than just another politician. He is more sinister than Richard
Reeves's "least objectionable alternative," the unoffending manager of our continental McDonald's, the *reductio ad absurdum* of
two hundred years of American democracy's supposed entropic descent. He is also, as Representative Donald Riegle gently labels
him, an "ideologue." A fanatic, to be less gentle than Riegle can
afford to be and more precise. A true believer. Ford believes
furiously, and his reflex of belief is automatic. "Nixon," Riegle
says, "was in many respects an evil man. Ford is a kind man. But

Ford is an ideologue, and Nixon was flexible. Ford's not a problem solver. He's more of a traffic cop. He has a boxed-vision problem. He's not in touch with that huge part of American life different from what he's known."

No, the President is in touch, but the route of his contact runs down through the psychic basement, where the contraries crawl. Much as he craves its honor, its love, its obedience, its troops of friends, Gerald Ford thinks America an evil place, and to his bewilderment and frantic inner turmoil, it terrifies him.

These are painful regions to enter, deserving more of pity than of contempt. Let's descend slowly, putting the personal evidence before the general.

Betty Ford. Our tough but wounded First Lady. When her husband took the oath as Vice-President, he said, at the point of tears, in what has been described as his "typical" syntax: "For standing by my side, as she always has, there are no words to tell you, my dear wife and mother of our four wonderful children, how much their being here means to me." "*Their* being here" refers syntactically to the children and not the wife, but award the man a clumsy tongue and let it be. Try this one, a gush of worthy sentiment:

> The high office that I hold is *not* the most important thing
> in my life. This is a great responsibility and a glorious privilege.
> And I love the political life. But the most important
> accomplishment of my life, as I see it, is being the husband of
> my wife and the father of my children.

What should we make of such confession? Knowing that Jerry Ford *does* believe his high office to be the most important thing in his life? Knowing that he sacrificed his wife's health and his children's well-being to it for twenty-five years? The words are unaccountably turned around. "Love," Ford applies to "the political life"; "accomplishment," he applies to marriage and fatherhood, which are hardly accomplishments, which almost any poor mortal can arrange. Is he expressing guilty gratitude that his family stayed the long and unrewarding course, or merely politically acceptable bushwah, or is there subtler stuff here?

There is. Imagine the statement to be a dream that asks interpretation. In his dream, this ordinary man is transported without announcement or campaign to the presidency, and appearing before the cameras on the White House lawn, in the surreal Washington dreamlight, he proclaims to the world that he's glad to be President, love won him that, but his greatest achievement is to have been a husband and a father. We'll have to run that through the decoder, turn it back around. It means, among other things, that Ford can't believe he's man enough to be President, and fears we can't either. He proposes to display the credentials of his manhood, and since propriety won't allow him to flash the crowd, he moves on to credentials more socially acceptable: an adult woman once consented to marry him, and upon her he has fathered children. There, you disbelievers (and there, you soprano voice of disbelief within the dreamer, you child forlorn), how's that for proof?

This second statement may also be no more than clumsy tonguing (though we know what secrets clumsy tongues are heard to tell). Deeper, then.

Elizabeth Bloomer was born in Chicago on April 8, 1918, making her not quite five years younger than her future husband, Gerald Ford. Her father was a traveling salesman who moved his family to Grand Rapids when Betty was two. Nothing about her childhood survives in the record except the signal notice that she began studying dance when she was eight and gave it her undivided attention until she was at least twenty-five. Her father died when she was sixteen. During her adolescence she spent two summers studying dance at Bennington, met Martha Graham there, and so idolized her that she wanted to go directly to her New York dance group from high school. Martha Graham at one extreme, Betty's mother, Hortense Bloomer, at the other, were the two poles of her youth. Martha Graham meant dance, a career in New York, possible fame—at the cost, the great dancer told Betty, of giving up marriage and family. Hortense Bloomer meant the values of marriage and family, Grand Rapids security, but no professional dance, no career and no apparent fame.

Hortense convinced her daughter to detour through two years at Bennington. Betty did, but after that she went to New York and the Martha Graham Concert Group and work as a Powers model and friends in Greenwich Village and performance at Carnegie Hall. The time came to make up her mind. Her mother suggested she come back to Grand Rapids for six months and think it over. Betty did, and chose, at what cost only she knows, to forgo her career. She married a man named William Warren, a traveling salesman, as her father had been. She went to work as a fashion co-ordinator for a department store and did her dancing on the side. The marriage failed, the divorce becoming final in the autumn of 1947. She decided never to marry again. Not more than a month or two later, Jerry Ford asked her out. She liked his positive attitude and his reassurance, she said later, which might indicate that she was depressed. People usually are after a divorce. She liked his "drive to perfection," a drive she compared with Martha Graham's, "only for him it was first football, then his work." Impulsively she changed her mind about marriage. "So far as I was concerned, that first date was it." Jerry, in turn, certainly saw her as another Powers model and accomplished beauty, a replacement for Phyllis Brown who had already made the decision Phyllis Brown refused: who had come back to Grand Rapids and given up New York. Betty and Jerry were married a year later, on October 15, 1947, between Jerry's primary and general congressional elections. He waited until after the primary because he was afraid her past would become a campaign issue: she was a dancer and divorced.

What did Betty Ford expect of her second, impulsively joined marriage? She seems to have expected a marriage of convenience —not celibate but not passionate either—that might lead to position and acclaim. She didn't know, when Jerry proposed to her, that he was planning to run for Congress, but she knew he had financial promise and political ambitions, might possibly become famous someday, and she knew she was the smarter of the two. She must have noticed his reticence about women, sensed she wouldn't be dominated by him. She was "provoked" when she found out he'd kept his congressional ambitions a secret from her but delighted at the prospect nonetheless. "You won't ever have to worry about other women," brother Tom Ford's wife told her, "because Jerry is married to his work." Jack Stiles put it more bluntly: "If you can accept the idea that politics will come first and your marriage second, if you can live with that, then I think you'll have a good marriage; you'll make a good team in Washington." The advice was redundant: she already knew. Those were the terms of the emotional contract they signed. Jerry and Betty were married on a Friday afternoon. The next day, Jerry took her to a University of Michigan football game. Then they drove seventy-five miles to a Republican reception and another seventy-five miles to a Detroit hotel. On Sunday they drove all the way back to Grand Rapids, 150 miles on 1947 highways, so Jerry could resume campaigning on Monday morning. Such were their honeymoon days.

She became, of necessity, a loyal and dutiful wife, but as the years ground on without fame or fortune the arrangement rankled. The man was never home, the children were hard to handle, the Fords were unknown. She drank too much, popped tranquilizers, developed a psychosomatic pain in the neck. Too tough to collapse, she went to see a psychiatrist. What her husband couldn't win by diligence he then won by default, but the vice-presidency still left her stuck at home. "I want him to retire from one office to another," she told an interviewer during the vice-presidential days, "not even come home for lunch and bother the household." And again: "I can't see the two of us going off alone. We'd probably kill each other. We'd get so bored with each other. I wouldn't know how to act."

Finally the presidency brought reward. She turned it to good use in the historic and important cause of feminism, speaking out at last for her lost career. She also turned it to advantage with her husband, using calculated indiscretion to bend him to her views. "Clearly intrigued with a plus she never knew before," wrote Myra MacPherson in *McCall's*, "she mentions the word 'power' more than once. . . ." "If he doesn't get [the message] in the office in the day," Betty said, "he gets it in the ribs at night." She claimed credit for Carla Hills's promotion to the Cabinet; she worked on a female appointment to the Supreme Court. Knowing she is finally in a position to do him great political mischief, the First Lady flicks at the President in public interviews as a confident trainer might flick at a reluctant bear, though lately, during the presidential campaign, she has kept her opinions to herself. They sleep together, she told *McCall's*, shivering his toes, "as often as possible." If her daughter didn't save her virginity for marriage, she would understand. Ford said that one could cost him 20 million votes. She has campaigned, to his great discomfort, for the ERA and abortion on demand. In photographs we see her jumping on his lap and aggressively mussing his hair, pushing him fully clothed into the family pool, stepping in front of him when he stands to speak. She's not engaged in blackmail. She's collecting reparations for the atrocities of neglect he committed along the way.

Ford prefers to be, as Richard Reeves has characterized him, "away from the office and the papers, the family—on the road, a man among men." His wife lets him, but sends him public messages to keep him in line. She made a point of moving their bed into the White House and insisting they share the same bedroom, but it isn't the king-sized bed the press reported. It's two coequal twins pushed up side by side. Separate sheets and blankets, separate estates. She and Martha Graham finally got together again. It's refreshing; it's also a measure of Jerry's vulnerability to any open discussion of sexuality, an indication that he was and is an inhibited man. "Eating and sleeping," he likes to repeat manfully, referring to two of the most important rituals around which men and women share intimacy together, "are a waste of time." Which is a position even a missionary might find dull.

If there is comedy in the spectacle of a President so skillfully manipulated by his wife, there's no comedy at all in Ford's iron self-control. Hersey noted the trait and found it impressive, yet he was disturbed by the lack of emotional commitment it enforced and the compassion he suspected it denied. We see the energetic athlete, the genial official, the glad-handing politician, and wonder what fears his emotions generate in him that require such enormous self-control to confine. "He's worried enough about that temper," Philip Buchen remarks, "that he probably doesn't let it go as someone else whose temper wasn't a problem might." More than temper—more than anger—though anger drives the juggernaut to smash fear down beneath the crushing wheels.

It all comes out in the end. "People seem not to see that their opinion of the world is also a confession of character." Jerry's confession of character is recorded in votes and speeches and decisions, in a reflex of punitive negativism reaching across his entire political career. But once in that long career Jerry's anger came out publicly, and the caldron thus uncovered was witch's brew. The occasion was a speech delivered from the floor of the House of Representatives on April 15, 1970, calling for the impeachment of Supreme Court Justice William O. Douglas. Ford has claimed since that he was primarily offended by Douglas' moonlighting as director of a Las Vegas-based organization called the

Parvin Foundation, but his real motives he explained to Hersey in 1975. "Bill Douglas," he told Hersey, "had made some decisions, and his married life was different than most. . . . And then this famous *Evergreen* publication came out, a very ill-advised article by the Justice in a magazine that I think is pornographic by any standards. And that upset me. . . . I suspect it was the one thing that was a bit out of character." Ford meant attacking a public figure directly and being upset were out of character. His hostility toward Douglas, and what Douglas represented, was not out of character. It was consistent with his record across his entire life.

The Douglas attack has been over-reported and under-studied. Ford is usually charged with playing patsy or clever hod carrier for the Nixon administration, which was seeking revenge because the Senate refused to confirm two of its Supreme Court nominations, Judges Haynsworth and Carswell, and the charge is partly true; the Justice Department under John Mitchell fed him raw FBI files that implicated Douglas, through paranoid, thrice-removed connections, with the gambling world of Las Vegas godfathers, files that were incorporated almost verbatim into the House speech, implications that were later thoroughly discredited. But Ford's own memory demonstrates what really bothered him about Justice Douglas: Douglas' liberal Supreme Court decisions, his habit of marrying women decades younger than he, and his appearance as an author in *Avant-Garde* and *Evergreen Review*.

If these are crimes, they are crimes of a remarkably personal nature, and surely they are adequately covered by the Bill of Rights, which William O. Douglas as much as any man in the history of the Court had labored to defend. Yet they incensed Jerry to the point of throwing off, for the first and so far the only time in his long career, his mask of bonhomie. The three foundations for his attack were sex, money and corruption in the West. Do those themes recall to you something in Jerry's past? What other angry stories of a man from the West who prefers younger women and who seems to have money from mysterious transactions does Jerry tell? Liberalism, sexual or civil, enrages Jerry Ford; the Douglas attack in all its clumsy viciousness registers outwardly the inner violence of his response.

So now at last, knowing as much as we have come to know of this cleverly dull, seemingly ordinary man from Grand Rapids, this sharp undercover politician, Gerald Rudolph Ford, the President of the United States, whose White House staff numbers more than five hundred and servants eighty-nine, whose office is the highest and most powerful in the land, who is Commander in Chief of the most awesome military power on the face of the earth, we are ready to ask the central question: what does Jerry fear?

He says he fears big government. "A government big enough to give us everything we want would be big enough to take from us everything we have"—Jerry's favorite aphorism. But his votes as a congressman and his positions as President belie Jerry's concern, revealing instead a carefully divided commitment. He's not against big government. He's vehemently in favor of big government in its police and military garb. He's opposed only to government beneficence. He doesn't think government should help people out.

Ford is cautious when he speaks of the poor. He no more desires to offend them than he desires to offend anybody. "I happen to think," he told Hersey, "that we should have great opportunity for people in this country to get ahead. Hard work should be rewarded. I don't think people who have had bad breaks should be penalized, but I don't think you can reward people who don't try." Which is mild enough censure, though simple-minded. More interesting was his response at his confirmation hearing when asked how he would eradicate poverty. With the exception of "those people who are mentally and physically handicapped," he said in so many words, there are only two excuses for poverty: not enough jobs and not enough education. That some are poor because they are black or yellow or red or female, because they are victims of discrimination, because in poverty they were deprived even of the ability to learn, because they live in a despair so pervasive that whatever ambition they may once have had has withered to bitter fatalism, the man who was about to become President of all the people was unwilling to admit.

What Ford refused to say, his record says for him. He has not only voted to weaken the weak; he has also voted further to strengthen the strong. He is not merely negative: he is actively partisan. The record of this man—this man still angry that a father he imagined to be wealthy refused him unearned aid, this man raised in comfort who believes himself self-made—carries an ugly load of hatred: hatred of the poor, hatred of the weak, hatred of the disadvantaged, hatred of races other than his own.

That hatred, in turn, is a product of fear. Sustained, lifelong fear, because to despise the poor and the weak, who hardly need despising, who have burdens enough to bear, is secretly to despise what is poor and weak in oneself, which, in Jerry's case, is the forlorn and lonely and angry child he once was. The child is the very model of weakness, with big government in parental form bending over his head; parents may give the child everything he wants, but they may also take away from him everything he has; and his release from their benevolence and their domination comes through growth and independence, by standing on his own two feet, getting an education and getting a job. So, in the child, in the child within himself, Jerry found his metaphor for government: in the struggles he waged and still wages between his desire to be adult and his unresolved resentment, founded more on fantasy than on fact, that he was inadequately nurtured and inadequately loved as a child. Without this hidden catalyst, his vision otherwise makes no sense, because as even he knows, government isn't a parent and the poor aren't children, though there are many, too many, children who are poor. The welfare system that Jerry indignantly condemns and coldly works to sabotage pays the lowest 8.4 per cent of our population a grand total of thirty-five dollars per person per week. Disarming our defense budget by even one third could do wonders to improve that bare subsistence.

But the poor crowd Jerry's fences like a threatening mob. As he attributes to them the dependency of the child he once was, so also does he attribute to them the anger he once felt and still feels, and thus he conceives the need for protection. Once he kept a child from his cherry tree by brutally standing on her hand; once he found support at the center of a football team; in Congress he fussed with the minutiae of the Defense budget, as if he feared to find there one last gate left open, one last decisive weapon overlooked; always he has championed defense, violent response, overkill, and no mere firing of the uncongenial Schlesinger signals that he has defused more than to the slight degree necessary to ease further détente and make himself appear a Nixonian peacemaker. When even Lyndon Johnson tired of Vietnam, Jerry called for holy cause to Americanize and win that war, and he was the last man to give up when it failed. Today, a sport among the calmer bulls, he warily performs détente, but woe unto the nation that touches an American merchant ship: he'll trade two of our guys for one of theirs.

Since he despises a considerable portion of the American population, it isn't surprising that he is perpetually uncertain of our love. Thus his devotion to campaigning—devotion dampened hardly at all by the continuing threat of assassination—as if only by almost daily excursions to the hustings can he restore his flagging self-esteem. If an otherwise normal man broke off work to run and wash his hands fifty times a day we would understand him to be peculiar; Jerry Ford's campaigning is peculiar too. Gary Wills has called him a campaign junkie, and he is, and his fix is the smiling, cheering crowd, the same crowd that loved him back when family and father and fraternity dues all were lost. Except for sports, which absorb his anger, campaigning is apparently the only thing he enjoys. He hates to be alone; he hates to sit at a desk and work; conflict burdens him, opposition burdens him, disagreement burdens him, decisions burden him; and his idea of a meaningful dialogue with America is moving at a sharp clip down an endless line of proffered hands. He can't bear to eat, he can't bear to sleep, he can't bear to read, and apparently he can't even bear to think. When he took office as President he ordered the action memos that worked their way up to his desk to be simplified. In Nixon's time they arrived with brief lists of options. Ford requested a different scheme, two slots on the bottom line. "Approve_____," he could then check, quickly passing through, or "Disapprove_____."

Bearing such hardships, braving such internal foes, he is easily cowed and easily duped. During his congressional years, Ford was the unwitting victim of a two-bit slicker out of New York named Robert Winter-Berger, who borrowed Ford's good name to decorate various acts of slapdash chicanery and later rewarded his mark by publicly announcing that Ford took bribes, which he doesn't, except when the bribe is the presidency and the payoff is a pardon for his criminal predecessor. The House committee found the relationship between Ford and Winter-Berger disturbing, and Representative Jerome Waldie asked Ford: "If a fellow with such modest abilities as Winter-Berger can persuade you and compel you to do that which you did not want to do, what assurances can you give us that we can be comfortable that that seeming weakness won't display itself when you are representing this nation in foreign affairs with people from other countries?" Since he had no assurances to give, Ford's answer was lame, a general appeal to the record. "Well, you know, Mr. Waldie," he said, "if that is the only mistake I have made in twenty-five years, it is not a very serious one."

There are far slicker men in the White House now than Robert Winter-Berger, and to the extent that they are also competent we may be grateful. Nixon's economic advisers hang on, determined to prove that the proper life of American man is poor, nasty, brutish and short; Rockefeller runs domestic affairs, Rumsfeld runs defense, Kissinger runs the world; while in the stillness of the Oval Office, one on each shoulder, bathed in unearthly light, noble Philip Buchen whispers angelics and boozy Robert Hartmann whispers diabolics into the sturdy presidential ears.

Political scientists have sometimes proposed a divided executive for America, the sort of executive that European democracies have, with a president for ceremonials and a prime minister to stay at home and conduct the business at hand, and it seems we have such an executive today by default. Except that the men who conduct the business at hand are nearly as hard-hearted as the President who defaults. A government big enough to have compassion might be a government big enough to guide us through our trials. We don't have that government in the White House now. Whether we will get it, through an election process that has more and more to do with show and less and less to do with substance, remains to be seen. What we've learned this time around is that we won't get it through the workings of the Twenty-fifth Amendment, through the judgment of Congress: from Congress, apparently, we will get toadies: from Congress we got Jerry Ford.

He sleeps little, but sometimes while sleeping he dreams. When he was Vice-President he dreamed and cried out, and by his side Betty heard him and reported, as for reasons of her own she is wont to do. "One night I woke up," she said, "and Jerry was talking in his sleep. He kept saying 'Thank you, thank you, thank you.' He was in a receiving line." Eternally grateful, eternally unsure, numb without and angry within, Jerry Ford blows along that perpetual line in sleep and waking, stormed by childhood cares. "*I* didn't vote for him," people laugh these days at parties. We took him for little enough, we took him for a gift horse, and he is not even that. *Haven't you sometimes seen a cloud,* asked scandalous Aristophanes, *that looked like a centaur?*

III
TECHNICS

Once a Year on Labor Day

Bunny Bid, a two-year-old colt (a male, that is: a female of the same age is a filly), lost America's leading quarter-horse race this year (1970) by a neck, and with it lost a healthy share of a purse which, in all three divisions of the race, totaled $670,000. That is more purse than the four leading thoroughbred races combined. Bunny Bid did not go home impoverished. He picked up $83,817 for his owners, a group of six horse fanciers who operate out of Chillicothe, Texas. But the difference between second and first place, between a neck behind and a neck ahead, was $94,671, and that's a hell of a lot of money for a neck. Or think of it in terms of time: Bunny Bid's time was 20.9 seconds, the winning horse's time 20.5 seconds. Ninety-four thousand, six hundred seventy-one dollars for .4 second. This side of aborted Apollo missions, you don't find money like that any more. Money's not by far all of what quarter-horse racing is about, but it does give you some perspective on the form.

This is what quarter-horse racing is also about: Ruidoso Downs, a village of sixteen hundred people set sixty-nine hundred feet up among piñon pines in the Sacramento Mountains of southeastern New Mexico, inaccessible except by car or private plane, crowded now on Labor Day with fifteen thousand people, most of them Texans but some from as far away as Hawaii, baking in the ultraviolet sun, and at the edge of the village in a bowl-shaped meadow a country track, good buff-colored turf watered and raked between races to keep it fast in that inhumid air, the jammed grandstand electric blue before the finish line, ten top two-year-olds at the gate breaking together at the bell and already, in two or three strides, running full at around forty miles an hour straight down the track to a finish line a mere four hundred yards away.

And this: rows of pale cream Stetsons on tall, beefy men with pale green and blue and gray eyes and weathered, sunburned faces; women beside them with high, coiffed hair so fixed that it does not blow even in the incessant New Mexican wind, styles of hair long passed by in the East and even Middle West but still maintained here because these are women of strident and straightforward sexuality in pointed high bras whose models remain, as styles elsewhere change, the drum majorette and Miss America, women quick to anger but also quick to warm to strangers, quick to make you feel at home; the men downing bourbons in plastic cups that seem to have no effect at all except to add to the ruddiness of their faces and to tighten their intense silence as each of the day's ten races go by and the betting tickets pile higher and higher in the aisles and on the floor beneath their feet; the women in slacks and pantsuits jumping up and down and pounding their fists on the tables doubly animated because except for a collective straining forward of backs and arms muscled by life in the outdoors the men seem hardly animated at all; and then, as the day wears on and the heat mounts, the men gathering in knots across the grandstand as if conspiring some overthrow, chewing on toothpicks or cigars and talking intently from the corners of their mouths, their speech drawled, reluctant, their whole appearance, however much they have won or lost, the physical reality of the word *shrewd*; and down below in general admission plain cowpokes and harder women watching almost evilly the races on which they have gambled their spare money; and more than once from no particular corner of the grandstand a wild, old-fashioned rebel yell; and on the floor playing with tickets a boy of perhaps two years jutting lightly from an enormous pair of western boots.

And this: in a packed sale barn as luridly lit as any Moorish slave quarters the wealthy and the not-so-wealthy of Texas, Oklahoma, New Mexico, Kansas and Arizona (the wealthy rarely distinguishable from those who are not, often seedier, just folks) pull on their ears or tip their hats to drive up the bidding on yearlings that have not yet even been tried on the track to, in the case this year of Bunny Bid's half-sister Darling Bid, $58,500. Darling Bid could drop dead tomorrow. Assuming she does not, she stands a good chance of competing for the top stakes in next year's race.

The race is the All-American Futurity, an annual Labor Day weekend event at Ruidoso Downs. To get a horse into it you must buy one that has been nominated for the race. Then you have to train the horse while paying quarterly payments into the purse. That is why the purse is so enormous, because so many owners want to win the race. The All-American Futurity is the best proof around that quarter-horse racing is here to stay. It may even reach the East some day. It has already reached England. It's the newest kind of racing in America if you don't count the chariot races (with quarter horses) in Rigby, Idaho. Ironically, it's also the oldest. Our ancestors (in Carolina and Virginia, not in Massachusetts: in Massachusetts they confined themselves to racing God into church and to the pillory) matched Spanish Barbs traded from the Chickasaw Indians down the main streets of their villages for fun and profit. Chickasaw horses, they called the Indian stock, but the animals probably came through the Indians from the Spanish settlements in Florida. They originated in Arabia, nomad horses for a nomad people. We had no circle tracks in America in those days: our first horse race was probably a straight quarter mile, run by stocky horses with thick shoulders and thighs and surprisingly small feet. And after the race the planter might well ride the same horse home. Ultimately the length of the race would give the horse his name: quarter horse. The only real refinement in the race since Colonial days has been to shorten the distance to four hundred yards.

It can seem a disappointing race, especially if you are used to thoroughbred lengths. "You've got to *learn* to watch a quarter-horse race," one man told me at Ruidoso Downs. "You'll see this pack of horses coming down the track and someone next to you will be saying to his wife, 'Number 4 stumbled coming out of the gate,' and you didn't see anything at all like that, you just saw a pack of horses start." It's the kind of race where every horse has at least the chance of winning. It's the kind of race that a jockey can win only if he and his horse do everything right from start to finish, and even then he will lose if another horse is natively faster. And it's the kind of race where what seem the most minor of details—a track slightly softer than it should be, the right breeding five generations back, a race run two weeks ago that the horse hasn't quite come back from—demand major attention.

Jockey Larry Byers, who might, in his dedication and his craft, have come straight out of the pages of *Death in the Afternoon,* who wanted to hear no excuses for riding Bunny Bid into second place in a race that he has worked for years to win, nevertheless heard from well-meaning bystanders after the race that Bunny Bid changed stride (he did, but then took the lead that the winning horse, Rocket Wrangler, then took away) and that the turf was better out at Rocket Wrangler's eighth gate than at Bunny Bid's second (it was: Larry wished he had had a muddy track, because Bunny Bid is a good mudder and Rocket Wrangler, whose legs aren't the best, isn't).

But it is also a race singularly suited to the character of the Southwest, and especially of New Mexico. Drive east from Ruidoso Downs little more than a hundred miles and you will approach the edge of the Llano Estacado, the Staked Plains, among the most barren lands in all of America. It was on the Llano Estacado, in the 1890s, that a belated expedition of ranchers located the last twenty-five buffalo left in the entire United States among the six million that thronged the plains in the 1860s, when the slaughter of the buffalo for hides and tongues began in earnest. Only in the forbidding wilderness of the Llano Estacado could the buffalo find peace. That is the kind of state New Mexico is, barren mountains, barren plains, barren white desert, almost no natural surface water so that you cross a bridge big enough to span a major river and see below you only cracked, dry dirt. Yet New Mexicans don't care at all about the hardships of their state: they tout it to all comers as a miraculous place to live. If you like sun and a humidity that averages 15 per cent and a wind that averages twelve miles an hour year round, or if you like quarter-horse racing, it is. It is also a place where you can be invited over to a table at the restaurant where you are eating after the big race to be introduced to an attractive and wealthy young woman who lost both legs when her plane smashed into a mountain and who then invites you to dance with her and outdances you on her artificial legs and laughingly suggests afterward that you come back to watch her ski sometime. Or where a new friend, a man who thinks and looks and sounds like Will Rogers, casually mentions over a drink that he has cancer. This is the kind of state, these are the kind of people, who run a horse at top speed merely four hundred yards and hand over $670,000 for the privilege. And throw in a thoroughbred race or two for the small change.

Quarter horses really got their due in the Old West, working cattle. Watching one cut calves is like watching a cat work a mouse: he sways with the indecisive calf and when it bolts he jumps, pounces, to a new stand in front of the calf, forefeet braced and head down, mean as hell, looking to bite the calf if it makes the mistake of getting close enough, and the calf breaks again the other way and the horse is already running at full speed for the fence and he catches the calf there and begins backing the animal up until it backs into the other quarter horse behind it. And then gets roped and branded for its trouble. The horse that could cut and ride and race, the horse with the most comfortable of all gaits, the short gallop or lope, the horse fastest of all hoofed mammals in the quarter mile, was the logical horse for the West. He was ideal for cowboying and first choice for bank and stagecoach robbing. He could go places and do things that no other animal could do.

He got no stud book until 1940, when the American Quarter Horse Association was formed in Amarillo, Texas. He is only now getting any attention outside the Southwest and on the Pacific Coast. He is very much the pride of the people who raise him, race him, and go to watch him race. He is their answer to the thoroughbred with its eastern airs, running his biggest race at two years, when the thoroughbreds just get started, running faster than any thoroughbred in the quarter mile, running for bigger purses than any known to races of blood horses anywhere. And running from stock beaten out of the working brush merely thirty years ago, which may be the most important reason of all for the Southwesterner's fervor for him. Most of them didn't hang diamonds on their hands—women *and* men—much earlier than that.

The race that lasted, for the winner, 20.5 seconds and for Bunny Bid 20.9 seconds started long ago, perhaps as long ago as the day when jockey Larry Byers' grandfather watched the shootout at the O.K. Corral and wrote a letter home about it which Larry still keeps. At 119 pounds for the race, nine pounds sweated out in the last few days, Larry wears the dandy silks of the professional jockey but would look more at home in plain ranch clothes; he is of the West and of horses as naturally as a Comanche, began jockeying professionally at the age of eleven and now at thirty-two has been jockeying for twenty-one years and has reached the point where all his friends hope he will retire but he won't because he hasn't won the All-American Futurity yet and intends to keep on jockeying until he does. His dark face juts sharp as a hatchet, and his narrow, weathered eyes slant almost orientally, set back under overhanging black brows and quiet and shrewd. He says, the day before the race, that if he wins you can call his horse "Rocket Wrangler Strangler," knowing what he must beat, a horse owned by J. R. Adams of the construction business and ridden by calm, boyish Jerry Nicodemus, whom Larry has beaten once on Bunny Bid and who has once on Rocket Wrangler beaten him. Bunny Bid posted the fastest qualifying time in the Futurity trials, an incredible 19.91, and has in him the blood of one of the greatest of all quarter horses, Go Man Go, but so does Rocket Wrangler.

In two other races on the day of the All-American, Larry brings his horse from behind, once from a box in the middle of the pack, to win by a length or more, building for himself a psychology of victory that almost sees him through. Nicodemus places and shows but doesn't win his earlier races, and now that you are committed to Bunny Bid you hope that Nicodemus' psychology isn't built on holding back a little for the big race. But then a jockey is ill and Nicodemus volunteers to take his race and you begin to wonder at the man's cool. After the race you meet him and you understand about the cool, a fact of life for Nicodemus like breathing or talking to the press or catching up his little girl for a tickle while J. R. Adams nervously regards the press camera and the track manager calculates the day's handle. And you think, fine, but Larry even in loss has something else, some quality of inner tension that goes beyond cool, beyond even the obvious flirtation with death that is the essence, as Mr. Hemingway so carefully told us, of all violent sports, of bullfighting and automobile racing and ski-jumping and the others. You hear that Larry broke his back a year ago falling off a horse: "We just assumed he was dead when we saw the way he fell," a friend of his says. You hear that Larry has a jinx about Labor Days, his father died just as he was beginning a race on one Labor Day, Larry broke his leg in five places on another. That's the death thing, certainly, and Larry treats it with expected contempt.

But the other thing—his wife is the daughter of an English jockey and has other jockeys in her family, she knows all about the life, expects the problems, follows Larry to his races bringing the children too—the other thing has to do with art, with style but also with the substance of style, the impulse to shape a moment of time and a moving pulse of animal material into a recognizable but unique whole, and to do that shaping not with clay or oil or marble or even white sheets of paper but with time itself, and of time one of the smallest recognizable portions in all of sport, a quarter-horse race, a race so nearly impossible to win that not merely the weather and the horse and the track and the gate and the exact force of every hard stride must be on your side but all the gods of Olympus too, looking down over their bourbon and branch and giving you their quirky odds in token of their esteem.

And yet also not small, not unrecognizable, because if anyone took the time to break down all the things that happen in those mere twenty seconds he would have a gigantic film, a play in fifty acts, and that would be horse racing, quarter-horse racing, too: the brave WIN tickets yellow with red borders with the same rag-threaded surface as dollar bills but thicker so that they feel more permanent than government paper and yet fluctuate in value in twenty seconds more wildly than the Deutschmark fluctuated in 1921 and the timid pink black-bordered PLACE tickets and the withdrawn noncommittal pale blue black-bordered SHOW tickets clutched in hands lining the table that edges the upper grandstand, two tickets or three in most hands, dozens neatly rubber-banded together in the plump brown manicured hand of the squat Mexican gambler five places down, his thick wallet chained within a front pocket to his belt; the gates opening and the horses beginning to run, which you see not as a whole but as a glimpse through the window of a forearm next to you bent up to hold a man's binoculars; behind you men and women standing on chairs, some of them already beginning ritual chants they will repeat in rising voices throughout the race, "Hit him hard, hit him hard, hit him hard," or "Go now, go now, go on now, go on now," or "Make him go, make him go, make him go"; the horses seeming to reduce speed to slow motion because for three days you have been anticipating this race, learning not only how bets are placed and who the horses and the people are but also learning to watch,

to see more than human eyes were intended to see but not more
than the human mind can handle, no limit to that, as any good
film maker knows, the horses stretching out so that what seemed
tall and blocky seems attenuated now into a smooth brown line;
and even as you watch you remember driving past Bunny Bid's
stall last night and seeing him rocking his head from one side to
the other, rubbing his neck against the yellow plastic covering of
the chain that only formally holds him in who could kick hell out
of that weathered wooden box but refrains because he is an even-
tempered horse and because his mascot, a thievish and mischievous black nanny goat leashed to a post outside the stall, would
like him to and he isn't about to give a nanny goat that kind of
satisfaction; the horses past the furlong post now, more than halfway there, the post electric blue like the roof of the grandstand
with a comic white ball on top lacking only stripes to proclaim
the track one vast barber shop, and beyond the post an incongruous shield-shaped lake drying up in the New Mexican sun
faster than the fountain in its center can fill it out, and beyond
the lake, higher up, the silent hills that surround the track playing
with cloud shadows with entire disdain for the brief and finally
disappointing pleasures of men; and then your attention snaps
back to the race and for the first time you pick out Larry and
Bunny Bid in the lead, Larry instantly recognizable not by his
colors but by his posture, the way he sits the horse, his legs drawn
up under him closer and tighter than any of the other jockeys, his
whole body thrown far forward so that his face is almost buried in
Bunny Bid's mane as if he intended not to ride the horse to victory but to pull it there by the sheer effort of his body to get
ahead and stay ahead, and then you realize that what this race is
all about is just that, is a man doing what he cannot do, which is
to move from one place to another with no lapsed time intervening like electrons changing shells around a nucleus, instantaneous, defying all Newtonian laws, and that too would seem to
be something Larry understands who refuses to quit racing until
he has come as close to doing that impossible thing as, in his
world, it is possible to come, and in his world he can come
closest by winning the All-American; and now the horses throw
themselves across the finish line and the automatic camera makes
its impartial record while dozens, hundreds of other cameras
make their partial record, little Instamatics and huge Speed

Graphics and telephoto Pentaxes and television and movie cameras all slicing out a piece of the moment so that later you can look at what happened dozens, hundreds of different ways and remember the event with as many eyes as a bee might have who remembers the most succulent flower of his life, and if you are a horse owner or even merely a gambler you will look at those pieces of the race over and over again, come-ons really, teasing hints that something happens once a year on Labor Day that is absolutely vital to your life, a ritual event, a moment outside of other moments when you don't think of your bladder or your hunger or your desires but weld yourself to a horse, ride with a tough western jockey and feel his strain in all your muscles, become horse and jockey for a few enormous seconds.

And then it is over. The lights on the tote board blink their benediction. The head of the West Texas Florists' Association walks to the grassy ring in front of the tote board carrying a blanket shaped like an elephant's saddle bags made of green satin and covered with red roses held in place by brass pins sticking outward, a bed of nails if the jockey were to sit on it. Jerry Nicodemus rides Rocket Wrangler onto the grass, grins clownishly at the battery of cameras before him. J. R. Adams, in a blue short-sleeved shirt, appears with his attractive blond wife, who is shaking with excitement. Others—family, friends, officials, the horse's trainer—arrive to be photographed with the winners, horse and man.

I look for Larry and find him stepping onto the scale to be weighed out, his face drawn and hard, holding himself together by realizing better than anyone else on the track except perhaps Nicodemus, whose thoughts today are elsewhere, that what he has just done is absurd, has no connection with reality, an event completely artificial in its construction, in its purpose, in its conclusion, but also realizing that the absurdity dooms the event to a greater share of reality than anything real, and humanly angry with himself for having placed second, for having won for Bunny Bid's owners only $83,817 less his own 10 per cent, for having worked a day's work at a rate of something like only $420 per second or $1.5 million an hour. But even in his anger he is objective where the rest of us are not, knows that horse racing has its roots in our most ancient past, that races have run before and will run again, that among centaurs he is one of the best, and that by riding he is fulfilling a destiny within his family and within himself that binds him irrevocably to the American West of his grandfather and the British countryside of his father-in-law.

And Bunny Bid, his saddle off, is already on his way back to his stall and his nanny goat, and one of his owners has a benediction for him too. "He didn't know he lost," the man says quietly. "He's always been the kind of horse that hates to be behind, but with his blinkers on he didn't see Rocket Wrangler pull a little ahead. He didn't know he lost." Can say that, can think about the horse, when the rest of us, the visitors, the dudes, are thinking about the race and the people and the money we won or lost. And that may be the ultimate reason why horse racing, and in the Southwest quarter-horse racing, will be around a while yet, until at least the air is too thick with monoxides and particulates for man and horse to breathe, and even a little while after that.

How I Rode with Harold Lewis
on a Diesel Freight Train
Down to Gridley, Kansas, and Back

It should be a well-known fact that, all over the world, the engine-driver is the finest type of man that is grown. He is the pick of the earth. He is altogether more worthy than the soldier, and better than the men who move on the sea in ships. He is not paid too much; nor do his glories weight his brow; but for out-right performance, carried on constantly, coolly, and without ela-tion, by a temperate, honest, clear-minded man, he is the further point. And so the lone human at his station in a cab, guarding money, lives, and the honor of the road, is a beautiful sight. The whole thing is aesthetic.

STEPHEN CRANE
"The Scotch Express"

Whether his train be merely two engines and three cars, as Harold Lewis' was when I rode back with him from Gridley, Kansas, or whether it be a monster of fourteen hundred tons, a loco-motive engineer has only two controls: a throttle and a brake. Three, if you count the sander. Harold's throttle had six notches, each equivalent to approximately ten miles an hour. The brake comes in two parts, a smaller handle that controls the engine brake, a larger handle that controls the brakes on every car simul-taneously. Not quite simultaneously: the air pressure feeds back from the engine a car at a time, so that each succeeding car's brake is set automatically in sequence, a matter of nice timing for the engineer as all his train work is and must be.

Audience, March–April 1971

The sander is an anachronism. In the proud noses of railroad trains, trains run these modern days by efficient diesel engines connected directly to huge generators that convert the mechanical power of the diesels into electricity to feed electric traction motors mounted on each of the diesel's four sets of wheels, in the proud noses of such trains can be found a dusty toilet for the engineer and a fifty-gallon tank of dry sand. With a small handle next to his cab window the engineer can force sand onto the track directly in front of each of his engine wheels, increasing with homely sand the friction of the steel wheel against the steel track. Each wheel makes contact with that track across an area the size of a dime. The sand improves the wheels' purchase enough to allow the train to accelerate even uphill. The whole point of railroading is that little dime of area, because so little contact means very little friction, which means the train can carry unbelievably heavy loads and carry them fast and hard in almost any weather. The fourteen-hundred-ton train, Harold said, was pulled by only two engines. We had four—or three, if you discount the one that didn't work—to pull thirty-one cars on our outbound run and two to pull three cars on our side trip to Gridley. The needle on his amperage gauge rarely lifted above its first quadrant.

Harold Lewis is a man, a gentleman, of transportation. Tall, lean, with a weathered face and trim blond hair. My next-door neighbor in country Kansas. He plays the electric guitar. A Reorganized Latter Day Saint. A paratrooper in World War II, then a ranger. He flashed motorcycles all over Scotland, landed early on Normandy. After the war he raced motorcycles for a precarious wild living, restlessly leaving jobs when he discovered he didn't like them. His father had wanted to be a locomotive engineer and finally convinced Harold to start down that road, working in the yards, becoming a brakeman, then a fireman, finally an engineer. Working doggedly, with grit, because that is how you become an engineer, exchanging your restlessness for plain, daily, concentrated determination.* You learn, as Crane would have it, to be

---

* With the exception, in Harold's case, of a continuing interest in the farther shores of transportation that led him, six years ago, to build and fly his own experimental airplane, a single-engine one-place construction of wood and tubular steel and fiberglass which he put together on a friend's farm near Emporia, Kansas, while waiting between trains and successfully flew until he pranged one day into a tree; and a ten-speed-dérailleur racing bike on which he occasionally takes one-hundred-mile rides.

constant, cool, and without elation. Except that to be an engineer is the essence of elation, because the conductor may keep track of your cars for you and the brakemen may throw your switches, but one man, you and you alone, makes everything go on that train even if the cars stretch behind you for half a mile. With two hands and two, perhaps three controls you make it go and make it stop, ring the bell and blow the horn, calculate when to brake and when to accelerate, figure exactly where to halt before a switch, how much slack to hold between the cars, where to back up to leave a car precisely opposite the door of a shed on a siding, how much power to feed the wheels to hold the train at the many different speed limits that towns and suburbs and curves and hills and the conditions of the track require. If you are good, and Harold is very good, you spend your life learning and never do learn everything you would like to. "I try to remember what I saw the good ones do and forget what I saw the bad ones do," Harold told me as we drove to the yards.

The size, the weight, the sheer mass of the engines. Sixteen cylinders the diameter of dinner plates. An engine-block long as an automobile but cast iron, not sheet metal. Two generators big as kitchen stoves, one to feed the wheels, one to supply low-amperage electricity to light the lights and power the controls and, very occasionally, to start the engine. The wheels themselves half as tall as a man and milled steel, shiny as silver when they are new, their rims slightly angled so that they can slide across the rails around curves, one sliding to a smaller and therefore faster circumference, one to a larger and therefore slower circumference to compensate for the lesser and greater distances on the inside and outside rails. A flange, a lip, to hold them on. The Atchison, Topeka and Santa Fe freight engines are deep blue and yellow, the blue the official color of the U. S. Air Force so that to an old Air Force man like me the machines instantly seem military and I recall and can't stop recalling the trains of Hollywood war, the armored train in *Doctor Zhivago*, Burt Lancaster's train in *The Train*. In their massiveness they might seem malevolent, but every American boy over thirty and perhaps under thirty too grew up at railroad crossings, watching the engines toot by, two long blasts on the whistle (that is now the horn), one short, one long modulated by the Doppler effect of the train's speed so that your ears knew the instant the engine had stopped coming toward you and begun going away, counting then the cars, always losing count because you were nudged, then attracted, then compelled, awed by the names, Erie, Boston & Maine, Chesapeake & Ohio, MKT, New York Central, Wabash, Rock Island and Pennsylvania and Southern Pacific and Union Pacific and Great Western, a map of America and a history of America and American railroading flashing before you like giant cue cards for some ultimate final examination that loomed much larger in the mind of every country boy than any city recounting of baseball scores. And so from the age of perhaps four on if you are now over thirty and maybe if you are under thirty your secret, your cherished ambition in life, to hell with doctors and lawyers and merchant chiefs, was to be a locomotive engineer or, failing that, to ride with one.

And somehow, even then, you knew why that ambition was so important to you: because the railroads put this continent that once was wilderness together, opened it up, made it accessible to the loving and plundering human beings who laid down the tracks and then rode over them into every nook and cranny of the land, and without the railroads we would still be clinging to the continent's ocean rims and looking fearfully over our shoulders at its jungle interiors. For you and for most Americans the very towns you live in were founded because the railroad went by, were usually named by railroad men, and grow and prosper or shrivel and die because the railroad goes there more often now or has stopped going there at all. Or did, before the automobile mocked the reluctance of railroad owners to carry passengers and the truck their reluctance to compete for freight. The Santa Fe's passenger service, I should add, is a little better than the others. You can still ride a clean and pleasant Amtraked Super Chief from Kansas City to Los Angeles, but only if you are willing to board it at 2:05 in the morning.

We board Harold's engines at five in the afternoon at the Santa Fe's Argentine yards in the river bottoms west of Kansas City, and Harold checks out the four diesels as a pilot might check out his plane. The diesels are never shut off except for repairs. Sitting idle in the yards or moving down the track, they run on day and night, because they last longer that way. They even can't be shut down, because the cooling jacket around the manifold is designed to operate at high temperatures and would leak if its temperature dropped below 120 degrees and would then have to be drained,

heated and refilled. Harold pulls the oil sticks and reads the water
gauges on all four engines. He removes the control handles on the
back three, sets the two engines that face backward into reverse,
and snaps the handles into place on the front engine. Two engines are the required minimum for a working freight train, because there is no place along the way where the engines can turn
around. Instead of running backward, then, the engineer shifts
over to whichever engine is facing in the direction he wants to go.

Snapping open a panel on the wall behind his chair, Harold
turns on the power for his radio, a telephone handset mounted to
his left on the side of a row of gauges that indicate his power and
speed, a receiver horn painted neutral gray, like the interior of the
cab, mounted at the top center front of the cab. Seated in his
chair, he has these controls at hand, from left to right in a semicircle: the lever that controls the air pressure to the train brakes,
mounted on a standard the size and heft of a fire plug; the smaller
lever that controls the engine brakes, mounted on a smaller but
similar standard; behind the engine brake lever a row of recessed
switches that control various lights; directly in front of Harold the
throttle, accessible to his right hand; mounted on the right wall of
the cab a small lever like the handle of a Colonial table knife that
controls the sander; and under his left foot, to circle back now
and down, a flat steel pedal from which he may never while the
train is in motion remove his foot for more than ten seconds without actuating an alarm and for more than twenty seconds without
throwing the train violently to a halt: the deadman.

The deadman is a chilling reminder that behind Harold ride
tens or hundreds or thousands of tons of careening metal and
whatever clever or commonplace or lethal materials American ingenuity can think of to pack inside, and one man is controlling it
all, watching out for cars and people at numberless crossings along
the way, making sure its speed on curves by highways and on
overpasses over streets and houses doesn't lean it past its center of
gravity. The theory is simple: if a man dies suddenly he will probably lose his foothold on the deadman: the pedal will come up:
the train will automatically stop. Today some engines have a
different deadman, based on an even more likely theory, an electric field between the cushion of the engineer's chair and the controls. The engineer must make and break some connection every
ten seconds, touch the throttle, touch the brakes, tap the window-

sill at his side, or hear the warning buzzer or stop the train. The engine is studded with emergency devices, with levers to pull and switches to throw, but the deadman is the ultimate emergency device, because it depends, like everything else on the train, on the engineer.

We hook up our cars and ease out of the yard, moving over to one of the two main tracks that head southwest from Kansas City to Wichita. For a few miles the tracks parallel the Kansas River, brown and swollen from recent rains, then they swing south and leave all big towns behind. We pass Olathe, sere county seat of prosperous Johnson County, and quiet Gardner, and now it is night, the huge headlight in the nose of the engine making daylight before us except when Harold courteously dims it for cars passing on the highway alongside the tracks, catching then the glowing eyes of prowling possums and cats; Harold speeding up to sixty on the long open stretches, watching the speed-limit signs posted along the roadbed, one speed for passenger trains, a slower speed for freight, watching the W signs that alert him to a crossing where he must blow his horn, watching most importantly the signals—trainmen call them "boards"—that by night with lights and by day with arms announce whether or not the track ahead is clear. A earlier freight precedes us down the track, so that every other board turns up yellow and once even red: we stop for the red. "You never know what might be on the other side of a red board," Harold says. "Might be a mile away or one foot on the other side." Then speed up to sixty, the wind blowing cool into the big square windows on each side of the cab, the brakeman in front of me swinging out the windscreen to moderate the gale, calling back to Harold his response to Harold's call of the boards, the clicking rails rushing by below. At 10:30 we have parked in Ottawa and the engines purr in the yard and in the back of an electrician's pickup we ride to our hotel in town. Nothing is open in Ottawa on an autumn Sunday night; the brakeman and the conductor make their suppers on candy bars and Cokes, but Harold has prudently brought lunch, as at his instruction have I, and we eat in the quiet of our rooms and sleep to the whine of semis gearing down a hill outside.

Railroad men keep no regular hours. As they are assigned different runs they are called; they may leave the yards immediately upon arriving or three hours later, depending on the traffic;

they only know that they will not be required to work more than sixteen hours at a time and that between any two runs they will have eight hours off. Our run to Ottawa took five and a half hours and now we are off, to be called again at seven in the morning so that we can board our train at eight.

And then, that next morning, we go free, two mighty engines pulling what you and I call a caboose and what trainmen call a waycar. We are scheduled to run to Gridley, Kansas, to pick up a flatcar, an empty boxcar and a boxcar full of hay. It is not my dream of a train ride: I would have preferred a two-hundred-car behemoth. But as we switch off the main line onto an ancient trunk for a run the Santa Fe makes only once a week, I realize that this small side trip has virtues no two-hundred-car train could compass, that Harold by chance will take us on a run into the antique past of American railroading, complete with ghosts of towns that existed when Harold last made this run, twelve years before, and exist no more. Twelve years before, but Harold remembers every hill and curve and real and ghost town too.

The brakeman switches us onto the trunk and Harold slows his train to twenty miles an hour, a speed we will not exceed and will often decrease during the fifty-eight-mile journey, because the rails are old and poor. I leave the cab to sit on the catwalk in front of the engine, perhaps three feet above the rails as they roll by under us. They are rusted, light in weight compared to the heavy rails of the main line and only precariously fixed to weathered ties sunken in their age to ground level. They seem to plead for the weekly cleaning the engine's wheels bring them; they click by with a sound out of my childhood that takes some miles to place: the sound, first, of the miniature steam train at a Kansas City park to which my father, in some gentle version of a busman's holiday— for he was a railroad man too—took my brother and me on his few days off. And the sound, second, of a means of transportation that once linked the cities and suburbs of America in comfort and quiet, the electric trolley. With Harold's diesels muted by the mild demands of our light train and slow speed, the sound that drifts forward to the catwalk where I sit is the hum of electric motors accelerating and decelerating as the governors adjust our speed, and that sound was the sound of the trolleys.

We rode them as children. They gave way, as the railroads gave way, to the absurdities of the automobile, but in their time they worked magic on children, their conductors running them with a simple handle and brake pedal, their brakes long electromagnets that clamped down on their rails to slow and stop them. My father rode one to work every day for forty years. He called it the "dinky" because it was smaller than the usual trolleys; it had controls at each end so that it needed no turnaround, and as the conductor moved from one control station to the other he flipped one by one the wicker seats to face the direction in which he would now drive. Another trolley, an excursion car, was open to the air and sported a fringed top, like the surrey of the song, which for years I thought it was. It ran through town on gay summer nights, crowds of revelers aboard. You could travel out to grandmother's farm in those trolleys of long ago, traverse the city, go to the park, for a nickel or a dime. Perhaps, when the automobile has entirely failed us, we will publish some modern edition of the trolley. Heart-attack rates would go down, children give up Barbie Dolls for lollipops and elderly ladies smile again.

Harold's train flushes fat coveys of quail from the brush beside the track, four, eight, once even sixteen birds taking off in their short whirring flight, a burst like a feathered shotgun blast that forecasts their probable end. Black-eyed Susans wink yellow in the tall grass, pink Scotch thistles sway, and blue wildflowers I cannot identify glow like sample lakes reflecting the sky. Only the blast of Harold's horn at little-used dirt crossings reminds of the business of the ride; I might be on a handcar running back to the rural we have so precariously forsaken. There is irony, too, in that, because the railroad did its major share of creating cities. At the terminus of several different railroads our cities grew: at those points and near them the railroads were forced to charge competitive rates for moving freight and people, but in regions where only one line ran they could and did jack up their prices, and the effect of their robbery was to force factories and people into the terminal towns. Then the automobile and the truck replaced the railroad, and the old trunk lines withered like severed vines. This quiet trunk to Gridley must be one of them: Harold says it once moved three passenger trains a day, and now it is visited by a freightless freight train once a week, banally to move a boxcar full of hay.

Inside the cab, sitting easily at his station, his foot tirelessly on the deadman, Harold clicks the throttle up one notch, down one notch, small adjustments to hold our speed exactly at twenty, entertainment for the long run. He times himself between the mile markers to check the accuracy of his speedometer. With his horn at a crossing he gives the regulation blasts, then allows the final blast to drop to a moan. "These things are either all on or all off," he remarks. "You could really make the old whistles sit up and talk." We pass Homewood and Williamsburg, Waverly and Halls Summit, small towns and old, most with deserted stations. We pass a ghost town that once sheltered a utopia: Silkville, where an eccentric entrepreneur brought mulberry trees that still grow on the cattle ranch that has taken its place, and when the trees had matured set out trays of silkworms to feed on their leaves, hoping to start an industry in industryless Kansas in the days before the Russian Mennonites brought their modest Turkey Red wheat over and endured the scoffing of locals to put Kansas on the map. Free love, free money and silkworms would make the earth fruitful, but the scheme failed and Silkville disappeared, leaving behind an ancient schoolhouse of heavy limestone rock.

Somewhere along the way, riding through tall brush now that whips against the cab and throws a leaf or two onto the cab's floor, we ascend the highest grade on the line, then down a steep hill and around a sharp curve that would be trouble for a longer or faster train but only brings squeals of stripping rust to the wheels of ours. Harold doesn't even need the sander: the rust serves for traction. Below us the roadbed has recently been worked where over the years it had filled in, brown dirt now turned over with a plow as if a farmer planted sticks and nails that grew up ties and track, new ties too tucked in along the way where old ties had rotted. Twice we stop for road crews repairing and leveling the track who ride yellow handcars powered with engines the size of lawnmowers and precede us like couriers to sidings where they can switch out of the way.

Children wave at the crossings of small towns as they have always waved, and Harold waves back, this one of the engineer's prerogatives and obvious pleasures, the man dreaming of having been a boy, the boys dreaming of being men, the girls perhaps dreaming of the men the boys will be. He is everyone's father, the engineer, and he plays his role well, confirming the camaraderie with a wave toward schoolyards, recalling again as this country ride recalls that sense of small towns, good and ill, where everyone knew everyone and spoke easily from porches and sidewalks. At lunch, in Burlington, the largest town on our line, the pert woman who brought our leathery roast beef and heavy mashed potatoes charmed from Harold the explanation that he was making the Gridley run for another engineer who was on vacation and then requested that Harold, like the man he replaced, sound his horn at a town up the way that appears on no maps: that was where she lived, she said, and the other man always tooted as he went by. On our return trip Harold casually complied.

Finally, after lunch, we reached Gridley, a five-hour run over fifty-eight miles, and then began the process of switching. The brakeman pulled the pin on the waycar and set the brakes and we left it on the main track. Harold removed the control handles from the forward engines and we walked to the rear engine, which now became our forward engine for the trip home. We backed up to a switch. The brakeman unlocked it and moved its weighted lever from the ground to its right to the ground to its left, shifting the siding rail against the main track. Harold eased backward and the engines turned into the siding, and a hundred yards down slowly closed on the flatcar, a two-dimensional model of a docking in space, bumping the car at less than four miles an hour and throwing the couplings together like two clasping hands. Then the brakeman dropped in the pin and hooked up the air brake and we returned to the main track and on other sidings picked up the other cars. Then we backed up across open switches to retrieve the waycar and began our trip home. Lulled by the afternoon heat and the heavy lunch I fell briefly asleep; Harold drove on at an unvarying twenty miles an hour, the pitch of the engines a little higher now with the weight of three cars behind us, drove past the furrowed earth, past the flowers fading with the afternoon, past the quail bursting up and flying off the other way: *déjà vu.*

It was six in the evening by the time we reached the signal board near our turnoff outside Ottawa: it showed red, and we stopped to watch a long freight roar by from another trunk line to our left. The men's spirits were up now; they had worked ten hours and would work three more to return to the yards; they might be required to work out their full sixteen hours, but Harold thought he had heard that train crews got to go directly to the yards after making the Gridley run, especially since another crew on another local was in the area and had started work half an hour later than he. The call came over the radio to come on in to

Ottawa, and at the modern station there Harold stopped to pick up new orders and heard the dispatcher direct the other crew to some local work in Olathe. Back aboard, everyone was grinning. We took off on the right-hand side of the double tracks and the sixty-mile-an-hour speed limit added to our exhilaration. A few miles outside Ottawa, we shifted over to the left track to make room for a crack freight train bound for the Gulf Coast; it roared by us on its thirty-three-hour run loaded with piggyback trailers that would be peeled off at its destination and trucked to factories and stores—one belated way the railroads have learned to survive even though stubborn railroad men still believe it gives aid and comfort to the enemy. We are moving now, with instructions to beat the nightly passenger train, late out of Kansas City, to Gardner, where we can shunt back to the right-hand track to allow the passenger train to breeze by us on the left. We make it easily and soon roll along beside the Kansas River again.

Now it is night, the yards aglow with switches, high boards and low pots red and yellow and green, and our rails spread out from four to a dozen or more like tributaries of a silver river. Jets wink by above us; towers and overpasses shine in the moonlight; lightning cracks in the northern sky; and as Harold carefully shifts the engines across rows of rails to the siding where they will park for the night I recall another night in railroad yards, a night as a boy of four or five when my father brought me to see the roundhouse where he worked as a boilermaker on the old steam engines, a grueling job that required him to clamber into the boilers before they were cool to replace tubes and firebrick that had leaked or cracked. We rode the wicker trolley to the top of a bluff overlooking the yards—these of the Missouri Pacific—and walked down hundreds of wooden steps and across blocks of rundown houses and across rows of shining rails to the brick roundhouse, and inside from forges that towered to the top of the tall building fires flared as if in some workshop of mountain-makers, as if here were lathed and shaped and welded the landscapes of the world, the great trees and bluffs and rivers assembled, the plains worked smooth, the valleys carved out by the massive hammers that in the night dropped shrieking to shape the iron and steel of steam engines worn out pulling the goods of America from farm and factory and town. The place stank of sulfur and hot oil and I held tight to my father's strong hand when he showed me the hammer where one

night, working it, he felt his glove wet and pulled it off and discovered that he had pulled off the first two joints of the little finger
of his left hand with it, a small tribute exacted by the giant hammer that might have exacted an entire hand or an arm instead.

There is that about railroading too: the fragility of the human
body amid so much weight of iron and steel: for years after the invention of the air brake and the automatic coupling, the men who
made their millions by watering stock and neglecting repairs allowed brakemen to be crushed between cars because brakemen
were cheaper than air brakes: and men die today on the railroad
as they died before, though more often now it is ordinary citizens
in automobiles at crossings who die because they don't realize or
don't care that a long and loaded freight train requires well over a
mile to screech to a halt even with all its emergencies on: but all
men die: the beauty and the glory of men like Harold Lewis, the
lone human at his station in a cab, is that while they are working
their engines so seemingly easily and so well, you forget the danger and forget the dying, caught up in the mystery of massive
weight moved through space by the simple force of burning oil
and the skilled ministrations of two human hands.

Skywriting

In the air men shall be seen
In white, in black, and in green.

MOTHER SHIPTON

No need to believe Mother Shipton the Tudor seeress; her vision may have been the gulling of a modern London wag bent on making Bartlett's: but we dreamed of flying long before we flew. Ezekiel's wheels lifted from the earth, poor fallen Dedalus, Leonardo's tetrahedral parachutes and bat-winged men, the airy navies that rained on Tennyson's Locksley Hall, Freud's gravity-defying erection that wished us aloft: we have owned the dream since birds first crowed above our caves. And finally technology called its demand note and the prophets' and poets' visions came quaint and we flew. On bicycle wheels from the shops of bicycle mechanics. In ships we called crates because they looked that way if you squinted out their glorious white wings. Pulled by an engine so inherently unstable it should never have worked and often didn't. Yet we flew.

But the mystery never left the act, and perhaps it never will. We revered our first pilots as today we revere the astronauts—more, because they flew in style, scarves at their necks, wind in their teeth, and the astronauts have added only orbital mechanics and monosyllables to the skills the pilots long ago mastered. "Little by little," Antoine de Saint Exupéry, the priest of flight and little princes, wrote in *Wind, Sand and Stars*, "the machine will become part of humanity. Read the history of the railways in France, and doubtless elsewhere too: they had all the trouble in the world to tame the people of our villages. The locomotive was an iron monster. Time had to pass before men forgot what it was made of. Mysteriously, life began to run through it, and now it is wrinkled and old. What is it today for the villager except a humble friend who calls every evening at six? . . . Every machine will gradually take on this patina and lose its identity in its function." But perhaps not the airplane, unless the 747 and its descendants numb us. Because of the dream, the dream Norman Mailer found in Neil Armstrong's childhood nights. We have all had the dream and known its elation. Freud did it little honor to locate it below the waist, though he also did it no harm. That is another elation down there, but elations don't come in tidy packages: to allow one is to imply all.

"Young barbarians still marveling at our new toys," Saint Exupéry also wrote, "that is what we are." Enter then one of those, Virgil "Van" Noble, though he is no longer young. He was born in Muncie, Indiana, on February 22, 1900, a few miles up the road from Winchester, Indiana, where two brothers Wright had a bicycle shop. He keeps his childhood shadowy; there is no way of knowing if he made wings and jumped off barns. But in 1916, at a county fair, a woman pilot—think about that for a moment—in a Curtiss Pusher arrived to demonstrate the 1916 equivalent of a great leap for mankind, and the young barbarian, he says, "conned her into enough time at $25 for fifteen minutes to learn how to take that thing off and bring it down inside the racetrack. I guess it was natural that I just fell right into it. I had no problem." He knew how to fly before he climbed aboard, his muscles and his reflexes knew. "She couldn't even ride, she'd run along beside the plane and tell me what to do and I'd hedgehop along and then turn around and go back the other way. Finally after three days she let me take it up and go around the race track. That was my solo. That was all the instruction I've ever had." All the instruction he ever had. In his prime he could fly loops around his peers.

But he was not only a natural pilot. If he were only that, his story would be straightforward, from one plane to the next, from one war to the next, a decent pension at last from an airline. No, he had another itch. The airplane came along at the right time and he used it to scratch the itch. He is a man out of Dos Passos' U.S.A. "I've always abhorred being one of the rabble." He wasn't allowed to enlist in World War I, because he worked with mechanical engineers and that was critical employment. "I wanted to get into the damned air force, I'd already been flying, and goddamn, I couldn't even make that." It made him mad. "I saw these guys around there sitting all day long at the drawing board and they were making about $250 a month, and I coined a phrase, I said that before I spend my life doing this I'll get a tin bill and pick shit with the chickens. And I walked out."

Walked out to fly, to advertise, to study how to make the rubes look up. Operated cigar stands at hotels, made some money, made some plans. "I ran into a young Englishman who had been a fighter pilot in England and we were just sitting there hashing around and I told him I would like to take an airplane and use it in advertising. From there I went down and checked and I bought a Jenny brand new in a crate for $75, surplus." In 1921. "I built a box under the lower wing and covered it with parchment paper and put 32-volt bulbs under there in banks and blacked out all but the letters. There was a drug company in Indianapolis I sold the first deal to, Best Drugs, and I put BEST under one wing and DRUGS under the other. I'd fly at night with the cockpit loaded with automobile storage batteries to get my 32 volts, land in pastures with flares sitting on the fenceposts to mark the field, and that's the way I started in this business." He says that by the time he was twenty-two he had made a quarter of a million dollars, and he may have: imagine the astronauts selling advertising on the moon. If he did make that much money he lost it. "I was too young, I didn't know how to handle it and I spent it."

His temperament fitted advertising. He wanted to be known, to be seen, and he wanted his exhibitionism to pay off in visible returns. "When I first went out and tried to sell, I quickly learned that a pilot was a hero. I used to wear laced boots up to the knee and knickers, double-breasted cross-zipped leather jacket, silk scarf around my neck and helmet and goggles. I found out that by wearing the uniform I never had a closed door. The doors would just open." He was not an impostor: he flew, signs in the sky, and risked the engine falling out as often as any Frenchman.

He says he invented skywriting. Others may have too. It needed a smoking engine and a little imagination. "About a year after I started carrying signs I was playing around and discovered that if you had an excess amount of oil in the engine it would smoke like hell. So an idea hit me. I had to try things. I played around with it until I was getting smoke pouring out like nobody's business and I said hell, why can't you draw lines and letters in the sky with the goddamned thing? I guess the first ones I wrote I probably wrote out as you would on paper. They would have looked upside down and backward from the ground because you've got to write them upside down and backward for them to come out straight. It was a matter of trial and error." He wrote, first, in *script*, not in print, and few others have ever been able to duplicate that skill, since to write in script you must have no hesitation, you have no time to calculate how and when to bank and loop and roll, you must know your plane as a scrivener knows his pen. "I haven't been able to teach anyone the script writing. They don't seem to have the rhythm, the unconscious timing. You can figure it on the ground, I do with my pilots today, but I never had that problem. I'd know when to bend this way and that way and it always seemed to come out pretty good. I don't know what it was I had in the way of a feel and timing that I've never been able to find in anybody else. Or at least to impart to them. I've tried every way in the world. I've had two pilots in the last fifteen years that I thought might cut the mustard, but by God when you come right down to it they couldn't bend it that much at the right time. You bend it and if you don't go around enough you go skidding off or you stall out. I can transfer my knowledge to them pretty well but I can't give them that same sense of what the airplane feels like. And that's where the difference is."

And that's where Noble's real career began, a slim young man of twenty-three already working on a mustache, a natural pilot with a mechanical bent, a promoter who found a place above the rabble in the sky. After a time, he turned up in Denver for a last try at respectability, but respectability couldn't hold him. "I was working as director of public relations for the Denver telephone company and Palmer, the guy who originated the Palmer School of Chiropractic, appeared at a Lions' Club meeting. He got up in a big black hat, black coat, great big black bow tie and he made a statement. He said 'No man that ever met me ever forgets me.' I thought about that, especially with my previous experience in aviation. I thought, well, in my position I can't be too far out, so I went to the rig of a derby hat, black derby hat and black suit and a vest with white piping and black oxfords, gray spats and a cane. I was about twenty-five at the time and every place I went I dressed the same way. It wasn't long before I was a known character in Denver. I walked very stately, tipped my hat. I put on the royal act." Dos Passos, you see, but behind *U.S.A.*, behind the twenties, when even Christ, Bruce Barton wrote in *The Man Nobody Knows*, was about his Father's *business*, stretch back all those determined young men who put on the royal act to get where they were going, the stern bearded clipper captains playing Ahab at twenty-five, young Tom Jefferson in his powdered wig penning the Declaration, Jedediah Smith among the mossy mountain men scraping his face clean every morning, sickly Teddy Roosevelt charging with his polo-society friends up San Juan Hill. They have their counterparts today in our best television performers, though character lost something in the trade. They had an innocence, a knowing innocence that told them men follow appearance if appearance is backed by intelligence and a double shot of gall.

Noble kept up his skywriting in Denver, helped a friend deliver Travelairs and Waco Taperwings to oil millionaires in Texas— "We'd take off and follow the railroad tracks down into the Panhandle, the old iron compass we called it"—and got involved in operating a radio station. Radio and aircraft came together in those days, as witness the career of Bill Lear. "The guy who owned the radio station offered to let me take it over but I was still pretty young and I didn't think I could take on all that responsibility. I could have made a million right there. But I told him no and it wasn't two days before the station went into federal receivership. So I decided what the hell, I'd go on out to California and try it." California, land of the free. Off came the spats and out went the cane. "The lady at the Chamber of Commerce in L.A. recommended some apartments up on the hill in what they called the Clear Lake area. I rented one. I'd get up in the morning and go outside and the whole range of mountains stood out, beautiful, sunshine all day long. And you didn't have to have a stuffed shirt on to go to dinner and I said hell, this is paradise, what am I looking for? I've been here ever since."

In the thirties, besides his Wacos and Travelairs, Noble acquired an Autogiro, one of those aborted crosses between the helicopter and the airplane. The Autogiro had a standard engine and prop arrangement forward for power and a non-powered rotor overhead for lift. It could take off on a short runway and descend almost vertically but it was a strange plane to fly, especially at low speeds. Noble used it as a camera plane, flying for the movies, used it to carry signs, and made smoke the rest of the time with his biplanes.

World War II grounded him. He became a civilian consultant to the Army Air Corps, approving contracts for aircraft manufactured in California. It was a long slow war with no chance to fly, but afterward he came into his own, acquiring the planes he uses today. "They're Boeing Steermans, made in Wichita, Kansas. They were built back around 1940 as primary trainers for World War II. They were built like a tank and the most maneuverable airplane that was ever put together—they'll stand sixteen G's, which is more than a man could take. I used them for this reason, that you can really rack them around." He acquired six of them and fitted three out for skywriting, converting their standard 220-horsepower engines to a fierce 450 horsepower, resewing the seams on the Irish-linen wing and fuselage covers until they could take the G's he pulled without ripping off. They have radial engines up front and biwings forward of their double cockpits, which are open to the air. The forward cockpit Noble closed up, replacing it with a fifty-gallon oil tank. Running out of the engine on the right side of the plane is a five-foot exhaust pipe attached through an oil line to the oil tank inside the forward cockpit, and the oil line can be opened and closed by a solenoid valve connected electrically to the plane's stick. When the pilot hits the button on the stick, oil sprays out into the hottest part of the exhaust pipe, volatilizing in a thick cloud of smoke that billows out in a line three hundred feet in diameter—the writing line. Fifty gallons of oil make about forty letters in the sky if you write them the size Noble writes, seven eighths of a mile long, ten to fifteen thousand feet up. At forty dollars a letter, with a minimum of twenty letters.

The Steerman's cockpit, painted a military green, looks battered. It houses few of the complicated instruments you find today even on small aircraft—only an altimeter, an air-speed indicator, fuel gauges, and on a strap attached to the windshield, a stopwatch. The panel is padded with foam rubber that has blackened and pitted with sun and air until it looks as if it came out on the bad end of a dogfight. "This is a stick-and-rudder airplane," Noble says, "and you can bend it just any way you want to bend it. You have the pilotability. These planes are built up far beyond the miltary requirements because we really and truly wring them out. You could take these up to 350, 400 miles an hour without even hurting them." In an open cockpit, with the wind roaring by. A stick and two rudders. It all seems simple. It isn't. "I've had excellent pilots say, oh hell, I can skywrite, and we'd get to arguing about making a straight line and I'd say okay, go draw me a straight line. There's a tendency to want to turn left. What that is I don't know. You would think, especially with a stick, that you would want to turn right. But the torque is to the left, the engine is turning that way, and that's probably a contributing factor, that they don't compensate for the torque. I've had guys with thousands of hours get into that plane and say hell, I'll show you how to draw a straight line, and then come up there with the nicest curve you've ever seen. They have the same problem with curves, especially reverse curves like the S. They make one bigger than the other. It's surprising the precision it takes to skywrite. There are times you'll rack up to a 90-degree bank. To hang in there, especially with all the power on these planes, you've got to push a lot of air. That seat will feel a little hard under there. It's been so damned fascinating that I think it's kept me young. It's been a goal I've wanted to make."

This is skywriting: load the Steerman with gas and fifty gallons of oil in the forward tank. Put on the old-fashioned flying helmet and tie a handkerchief to the loop on top of it so that when the oil fogs your goggles as you fly through your own smoke you can reach up for the handkerchief and wipe them off. Taxi out and get clearance and watch for jetliners and take off, up to ten or fifteen thousand feet without oxygen, altitudes Noble can't fly any more because he smokes and has lost lung capacity. Calculate for wind drift. The wind will move you and the plane and the writing downwind at whatever its speed, but the smoke won't break up unless there is turbulence, just as clouds don't break up, scudding across the sky, unless there is turbulence. You have worked out your message on the ground, either on paper or, if you are Van Noble, in your head. The message is BEST BUYS and you will write it backwards and upside down, ƧɅUꓭ TƧƎꓭ so that it can be read from the ground. Noble likes to send up two planes, each taking a word, nice calculations of spacing there, because two planes writing in the sky look as if they are continually about to crash into one another and come plummeting down in that roar-

ing spin we all learned to lust for in war movies. "It makes it
more spectacular," Noble says. "I figure people are bloodthirsty.
They'll run miles to a fire or to see the results of an accident. I always said they'd go with their spoons to pick up the blood. From
the ground, you look up at two airplanes darting around and even
if they know what they're doing, people are looking to see if
they'll hit each other and come down in a heap." You are in the
airplane that is spelling out the word BUYS, S⅄∩B at fifteen
thousand feet, where the temperature on a hot California day is
below freezing and you are averaging 120 miles per hour as you
start the writing, coming in on a bank and hitting the smoke button and beginning a banked curve to make one loop of the S and
then throwing the stick the other way and making a half roll to
begin the second loop of the S, compensating for the torque of
the engine and concentrating on duplicating your first loop, which
you cannot see, all you can see is a line of smoke parallel to your
plane and when you sense you've finished the S you roll again and
come around and begin one fork of the Y, hitting the bottom of
the fork and cutting the smoke and flying at an angle to the leg of
the Y until you can bank around to pick up the leg and when you
hit the bottom of the fork again you angle right and write the second fork and cut the smoke and make a steep bank and start on
the comparatively easy U. Then a long bank over to the starting
point of the B, a tough letter to make but not the toughest, the T
is the toughest because it's a nice bit of instinct to get the left and
right branches of the crossbar equal in length with nothing more
than a stopwatch and a prayer and the seat of your pants. You
circle all the way to the middle of the B and start the upper curve
of the letter and come around in a tight bank and cut the smoke
where you think it lines up with your starting point. You are making a figure 8 but only running the smoke on one side of the 8 and
now you bank around again and start the smoke again at the same
point you started it the first time but this time you curve off the
other way, go north instead of south, and make the second loop
and again guess where to cut the smoke because the last thing you
will make is the reference line and then you do a hammerhead,
pull the Steerman straight up with four or five G's mashing you
into the foam seat and then fall off on one wing and bring the
plane around and you have no time at all to see if you're lined up
properly with the ends of the two curves, you're into the line,

straight past your first smoke stop and past the two joined smoke starts in the center and then past the second stop and you cut the smoke and go home and if you've done your job right and there's not too much turbulence or too strong a wind, your work of a few minutes will be seen that day by hundreds of thousands of people doubly transfixed: by the giant writing in the sky—always a little spooky to see words up there as if by God out of Cecil B. DeMille —and by the excitement of knowing that men in open planes wrote these words.

They can be seen, the words, to a radius of at least twenty miles, and depending on the weather they can be gone in five minutes or hang there all day. Noble remembers writing BIG NEWS CBS CHANNEL 2 at eleven o'clock one morning and finding his message still hanging there at five in the afternoon. And he remembers a time when he got the wrong weather information from the tower. The tower told him forty knots at ten thousand feet and he wanted the writing to be seen over the Los Angeles Coliseum. He flew out to the mountain pass northwest of the Coliseum and wrote his message at ten thousand feet and before he was through, words and Steerman and Noble were zipping past Torrance. "I check with the tower when I got down and they said sorry, those winds are better than 120 knots at ten thousand feet. Sorry we gave you the wrong dope."

But there is little skywriting in Los Angeles any more, little for that matter anywhere in the United States. The sky is white in Los Angeles most of the time, covered with a haze that floats up to three thousand feet, and you cannot write with white smoke against a white sky. To fight the smog, Noble experimented in the 1950s with colored smoke. "I got it past the experiment stage. I proved to myself how you do it and that you could do it. You had to *make* colored smoke. Otherwise at altitude it wouldn't hold. The Air Force teams, for example, just drop dye into the smoke as it comes out the stack and it lasts about ten seconds and then it's gone. I found a way to color the smoke, using Chinese red, magenta and green as the primary colors. It made Ripley's, but there wasn't much demand for it and I never got the equipment actually installed in the planes." But Los Angeles haze doesn't account for the almost complete disappearance of skywriting from the skies of the United States. Perhaps jet contrails, which are ice crystals frozen out of the water produced in engine combustion and which act exactly like Noble's smoke, have inured us to the excitement of writing in the sky. Or perhaps skywriting has fallen victim to our distaste for pollution or to the faddishness of advertising. The last advertising job of any scope that Noble did was a television commercial for Kool cigarettes, using his Steermans and pilots and hangar as a setting.

He has found a new market for his skills, or, more accurately, a new market has found him. He had a call one night from an urgent voice that identified itself as Mason Williams, the writer and singer and composer, and after a good deal of argument he agreed to bring himself and his wife into Beverly Hills for dinner. Williams wanted skywriting, but not words. He was staging a happening and wanted Noble to make it happen. He asked Noble if he could draw a sunflower around the sun just as it broke over a mountain peak at dawn. Noble said he could and they went back to his house and Williams and his kid sister pored over Noble's maps, they mastered the maps in about twenty minutes, and that won Noble's respect, and the skywriter pointed out a mountain near the desert that came to a nice point, Tit Mountain the pilots called it, and at the appointed time Noble's pilot took the Steerman up and Noble worked the radio on the ground and Williams directed three full camera crews to film the event. The sun broke over the mountain peak, the pilot flew the loops of the sunflower petals around the sun, the cameras turned. To no permanent record: they were shooting directly into the sun and all three crews ruined their film.

More recently, Noble has been visited by bearded and sandaled artists with money to spare, graduates of one-man showings at better galleries on the Coast, and he has guided the drawing of their drawings in the sky. If he was put off at first by their costumes and their hair, he finally decided that they were doing no more than he had done in his pilot's gear or his Denver spats. They call him from time to time with a new assignment, cash on the barrelhead, more than ten thousand dollars of it to date. He is considerably amused, considerably pleased, an energetic elderly man who swears like a trooper still, a gust of youthfulness in all that swearing. A man who has watched the crowds arrive with their thirsty spoons at the scenes of accidents doesn't mind at all being the accomplice of wealthy hippies making a splash.

It was appropriate, then, that the producers of the film *The*

Grasshopper called on him to arrange the final, hilarious scene of that movie. But let Noble tell it: "She was a nice girl, she comes down to Las Vegas and gets car trouble. She was one of these unsettled girls and a guy gets her into Las Vegas and finally she becomes a whore. Supposedly in the story she even marries a black football player and he takes her money and dumps her. Then some little punk kid, supposedly a skywriter out at the airport, gets after her, so she goes out and tells him if he'll go up and do some skywriting he'll get what he wants. We went out into the desert to do the skywriting. I've got a contract with the studio that says that under no circumstances could we write the whole message. We had to fake it. They handled it beautifully. No one in his right mind could have missed the message. I directed it from the ground. I sent my pilot up and he wrote FU and then the camera cut to a couple of actors in the back of my pickup truck eating their lunch. The one guy is drinking a Coke and he looks up and sees this goddamned thing and he just pours the Coke all down his front. They shot that scene a dozen times, used up a case of Coke. They ran out of shirts. Then we let the FU drift away and wrote LU, the pilot hesitated in there, slowed it up enough to let the L and the U blur out, and then he hit the CK and the IT, so you got the whole message, but the way they handled it, showed the guys in the control tower saying oh my God, surely he's not going to put a K on that, the build-up, the people in the streets, one old lady looking up and seeing it and fainting, I got the hugest charge out of the way they built that son of a bitch up, it was unbelievable!"

It may be every skywriter's dream. Noble remembers teams of pilots in Hollywood in the old days who performed stunts like tying the wings of three planes together with three feet of line between them and doing loops and rolls, pilots who later killed themselves in crashes or took to drink or became hermits in cabins in the mountains; he remembers others of no ability who claimed those pilots' reputations and made money off their deaths or bitter withdrawals, and perhaps that is at last what stunt flying, skywriting, racking an open-cockpit biplane around in the sky is really about, FU and LUCK IT, staying above the rabble, getting away from the earth. A doctor who has studied the derelicts who skyjack jetliners found in them one common characteristic: they invariably hijack planes soon after an Apollo flight, having been encouraged by the flight of astronauts to get away from it all. And that, in its criminal or its heroic aspect, may be the point of stunt flying, the dream working itself out in the lives of men, challenging not death or even gravity but the biology that condemns us to creep about on the surface of the earth with our peers. And when the challenge can no longer be made, when age and health ground you, you crash or drink or take to the hills, nursing thus your misanthropy. Van Noble is moving out to the Mojave Desert, building a house there. He plans to "whittle and spit," he says, and maybe to write his memoirs.

Borrowed Finery

Christmas is come, the holiday season, and with it our annual deluge of cards, whose successful dispersal across the land the Postal Service heralds to justify failing us for the rest of the year. "By God, we moved the Christmas cards!" Well, half of all the personal mail moved annually in the United States is greeting cards. Cards for Christmas but also cards for New Year's, Valentine's Day, Easter, Mother's Day, Father's Day, Independence Day and Thanksgiving and Halloween, the official holidays of the American year. And for the occasions greeting card people call "Everyday," though they are not, births and birthdays, graduations, weddings, anniversaries, showers, vacations, friendship, promotion, hello, love, thanks, good-by, and illness and bereavement, and even to have Thought O' You and for a Secret Pal. We are not a nation of letter writers but of card signers. If the personal letter is long dead, maimed by the penny post and murdered by the telephone, the mass-produced card thrives, picturing what we haven't skill to picture, saying what we haven't words to say. Cards knot the ties that bind in a land where a fourth of us change residence with every change of calendar and where grown children no longer live at home. They show us at our best, if in borrowed finery. You may buy a card made of pansies and doggerel or you may buy a card made of Da Vinci and the Sermon on the Mount. Whoever receives it will understand what you meant, and that you meant well.

The Christmas card was an English invention, but the greeting card an American. One hundred twenty-three years ago this season, an Englishman distracted by business matters failed to get his Christmas letters written. Boldly he turned an embarrassment into an opportunity, commissioned a paper tableau of Pickwickians, their glasses raised in toast, and inside each engraved and colored folio he printed a verse. His friends' reactions were not recorded. No doubt, some found the idea distastefully impersonal and lamented the decline of manners in a declining age. Others, alert for new twists, thought it charming. The sensible saw its efficiency. It met the first requirement of all mechanical inventions: it saved time.

We have taken the idea and made it ours. The English send few cards today, and Europeans fewer still. We send cards for everything, mechanizing and standardizing the complex relationships we maintain with one another, to give us time to breathe. We needn't be ashamed of our custom. Elegant mechanizing is what we do best. It is the form our national character has taken. Look at our office buildings raised on narrow pillars ten feet off the ground as if someone had dared us to float a fifty-story building in the air. Compare our white and graceful moon rockets to the Soviet Union's drab boilerplate. Look at our cards, little shuttles of sentiment weaving across the land.

Some of the old cards, the nineteenth-century cards that borrowed the Englishman's invention, were masterpieces of reproduction, printed in as many as twelve colors with verses selected in national contests with cash prizes, verses no better than they should be for all the fanfare. The Victorian age produced German cards that opened up into three-dimensional sleighing scenes of marvelous intricacy, cards with moving parts, cards fringed like a loveseat pillow with gaudy silks, cards as ornate as any gingerbreaded house. Cards, one presumes, for the wealthy, because the rest of us hadn't begun sending them in today's incredible numbers, today's fifteen or twenty *billion* cards a year. Now that we do, the special effects that subsistence handwork supplied have had to be scaled down, though the cards we send today carry their weight of handwork too, and with it their weight of amusing stories, cautionary tales of American ingenuity gone berserk. I remember a humorous card that required for its gag a small plastic sack of what it called "belly-button fuzz" stapled below its punch line. No supplier could thumb out enough of the authentic material to meet the demand, so the manufacturer turned to the clothes dryers of a nearby college town, bought up the lint franchise, sterilized the lint to meet health regulations and bagged it and stapled it on, by hand, and got the effect it was seeking and probably, college towns being college towns, got some belly-button fuzz too. "Attachments," such devices are called—plastic tears, toy scissors, miniature boxes of crayons, feathers, spring-and-paper jumping jacks, pencils, beans, the detritus of industrial civilization shrunk to card size. An attachment will sell a humorous card all by itself if it isn't stolen first, a problem for greeting-card manufacturers as surely as it is a problem for the sellers of screws and beads and hair ribbons in dime stores. Like children, we lust to get our hands on little things, finding magic in tiny representations of the lumbering world.

The business of greeting cards began in the improvisations of hungry men. There are schools of nursing and schools of nuclear physics, but there are no schools for the makers of greeting cards, only apprenticeships. When Joyce Hall of country Nebraska began his enterprise in Kansas City, Missouri, more than sixty years ago, there weren't even many kinds of cards. Christmas, Easter, birthdays and weddings were about the only occasions we announced. Hall, Fred Rust of Rustcraft and a few people like them had to teach us to send cards by making cards we wanted to send. In that work, Hall's career strikingly parallels the career of another Midwesterner, Walt Disney, for both men learned to parse our emotions and recast them in visual and verbal form. Disney, for example, took some shadowy figures from a fairy tale, clothed them in universals, and gave us the Seven Dwarfs. Hall and his people took our need to signal our degrees of social familiarity and our various notions of good taste and gave us a choice among cards.

For any given social occasion, depending on how well you know someone and what you want him to think of you, you may select a card for him that is Formal, Traditional, Humorous, Floral, Cute, Contemporary, or some other among Hallmark's many categories of mood. Two cards for a friend who is hospitalized give the flavor. One, an embossed vase of flowers, says, "Glad your Operation's Over" on the cover, and inside:

> *You're thought of so often*
> *As days come and go*
> *That this card comes to tell you,*
> *And then let you know*
> *How much you are wished*
> *A recovery that's quick—*
> *For someone like you*
> *Is too nice to be sick!*

The other card, a photograph of a cotton bunny in a flower-bedecked four-poster, opens with "Hope you'll soon be out of that *blooming* bed!" and carries the flower pun through:

> *Sure like to see you back in the* pink,
> *So just take it easy, 'cause then*
> *You'll soon be in* clover,
> *Feeling just* rosy,
> *And fresh as a* daisy *again!*

Moods and tones and levels, you see. You are not likely to send a Contemporary card to your maiden aunt or a Formal card to your spouse. The greeting-card people give you a range of choices. It may be a narrower range than you would prefer, but if you are a sender of cards at all, the choices will not be so narrow that you turn away in disgust and write a letter. You may choose frank sentiment; humor ranging from modestly ethnic (hillbillies, Indians, Dead End Kids—blacks, Italians and Eastern Europeans are out today, though they used to be a staple) to the heavily punned to the backward compliment to the gentle slap; simple statement, favored for Christmas and Sympathy cards, both occasions being to some people matters serious enough for prose; and a number of alternatives between. Visually, you may choose flowers, cartoons, arabesque gilding, photographs, even reproductions of fine art, though few enough of those because few people buy them. Or stylized little children with ink-drop eyes, or encrustations of plastic jewels, or velvet flocking, or metallic glitter. Variations in texture and surface are legion and the pride of the older generation of greeting-card men, who believed in making a quality product, who learned what would sell by selling, and who relied for their judgment on what Joyce Hall once called "the vapors of past experience."

Even if you have never given thought to such matters as categories of emotion and levels of taste, greeting-card people know you operate by them, and know how many cards to make to meet your needs. Such is the variety, of cards and of needs, that the largest of the manufacturers, Hallmark Cards, would have collapsed a decade ago if the computer hadn't come along to speed their sorting. The company claims twelve thousand products, counting each separate design a product, and the figure is certainly conservative. Twelve thousand different products in quantities of six each to perhaps twenty thousand different stores: you can do the multiplication yourself, but count in the envelopes; count in as many as ten or twenty different manufacturing operations on every card; count in all the designs being prepared for future publication, designs that pass through hundreds of hands at drawing boards and typewriters and approval committees and lithographic cameras and printing plates; count in all these different bits of information and many more besides and you arrive at a total that demands the kind of machines that track astronauts to the moon.

And count in one thing more: every display in every store is a modest computer of its own, each of its pockets filled with designs that favor the social and cultural biases of the neighborhood around the store, and among those favored designs the best sellers of the day. "Tailoring," Hallmark calls it—loading the display to favor the preferences of the young or old or black or white or Catholic or Jewish or rich or poor who regularly shop there. The salesman sets up the display with the help of the owner; after that, the computer in Kansas City keeps track. The point, of course, is to give you a maximum range of choice among the choices available. Tucked away in the stock drawer below the display, quietly humming, an IBM card meters every design.

Despite appearances, then, greeting-card manufacture is no work of hand coloring performed by elderly ladies in lace. The Hallmark plant in Kansas City occupies two city blocks, and the company doesn't even do its own printing. Times Square would fit nicely inside the distribution center Hallmark has built on a railroad spur outside of town. More than one printing firm in the United States owes its giant color presses to Hallmark orders, which is why the company gets the kind of quality it is known for —because it has the heft to stop the presses and pull a proof. It claims four hundred artists in residence, the largest art department in the world, and if you include the girls who separate out the colors of a design by hand, a procedure that still costs less for certain designs than separating the colors photographically, the claim is fair.

So many different operations go into the production of greeting cards that even a glimpse of them boggles the mind, serene and simple as the cards look when they finally reach the store. Hallmark buys paper by the boxcar, paper of every imaginable texture and weight—parchment, deckle, bond, pebble-grained, leather-grained, cloth-grained, board, brown wrapping, hard-finished, soft-finished, smooth. Special committees earnestly debate the future popularity of roses or ragamuffins. An artist conceives a group of cards that feature cartoon mice and the cards sell and the artist is rewarded with a trip to San Francisco. Down in the bowels of the building, behind a secret door, a master photographer labors as he has labored for most of a decade to perfect flat three-dimensional photography using a camera on which Hallmark owns the license, a camera that rolls around in a semicircle on model railroad tracks, its prisms awhirr. In California, a contract artist makes dolls of old socks and ships them to Kansas City to be photographed for children's cards. Market-research girls carry cards mounted on black panels to meetings of women's clubs where the ladies, at a charitable fifty cents a head, choose among various designs with the same verse, or various verses with the same design, helping Hallmark determine the very best that you might care to send. An engineer, a stack of handmade designs before him on his desk, struggles to arrange them on a lithography sheet to get the maximum number of designs per sheet so that they can be printed all at once with minimum waste of paper—"nesting," the process is called. Artists roam the streets of major cities at Christmastime, studying shop windows and the offerings of art galleries to discover new trends in visual design. A deputation of sales managers retreats to an Ozark resort for a multimedia presentation of next year's line. A mechanical genius grown old in the service of the firm remembers the tricks he has taught mere paper cards to do, walking, talking, sticking out their tongues, growling, snorting, squeaking, issuing forth perfume at the scratch of a fingernail across microscopic beads. An engineer sits down at a handwork table and conducts a motion study and designs a system and lines and lines of young girls in gray smocks follow the system to assemble a complicated card by hand, their hands making the memorized motions while they dream of boy friends or listen to the rhythm of the gluing machines interweaving fugally along the line. A master engraver puts the finishing touches on a die that will punch a dotted line around a paper puppet on a get-well card. A committee of executives meets and decides that the pink of a card isn't cheerful enough and the cartoon figure on another card not sufficiently neuter to appeal both to men and to women. A shipment of paper for a line of children's books is frozen into a harbor in Finland when it should be steaming its way to a printing plant in Singapore. A baby leopard runs loose in the photography department while an editor upstairs sorts through another shipment of amateur verse mailed in by the card lovers of America. He has not found a writer worth encouraging in three years. Greeting cards aren't simply manufactured, like soap or breakfast cereal. They are rescued from the confusing crosscurrents of American life, every one of them a difficult recovery. John Donne found the King's likeness on a coin: greeting-card manufacturers must discover Everyman's likeness and somehow fix it on paper with all its idiosyncrasies smoothed away.

Hallmark employs far fewer writers than artists, about fifteen or twenty. Unlike designs, verses enjoy a long half-life if they are adjusted for minor changes in the language along the way. These days, they are often selected—selected entire, not written—by computer from a stock of the most popular verses of the past. The writers try to think up new words, and from time to time they do. Greeting-card verse has come in for its share of ridicule, which perhaps it deserves, but before it is ridiculed its distinction ought to be explained. Most song lyrics look equally ridiculous when printed bald, because the rhetoric of a song lyric, the source of its emotional impact, is the music that accompanies it. The rhetoric of greeting-card verse is the card, the physical and visual accompaniment to the verse. A few greeting-card makers have caught onto the similarity between song lyrics and greeting-card verse and have begun to borrow effects they can use, as in this verse from one of American Greetings' new "Soft Touch" cards, cards for young people that feature soft-focus photography:

> *untold the times i've kissed you*
> *in the moments i have missed you*
> *and our love goes on forever . . .*
> *with you softly on my mind*

If that doesn't quite make sense, well, neither do most lyrics away from their music, or greeting-card verses away from their cards. A poem, a real poem, the thing itself, works no better on a greeting card or in a song, because it contains its own orchestration and goes dissonant when larded with the scrapings of Mantovani strings.

Modern young people don't like eight-line rhymed verses, preferring song words or evocative sentences. One card on my desk is captioned merely "Peace," which makes it appropriate to almost every occasion except Halloween. Finding the right words for a card is harder today than it used to be, because a generation trained on the film expects the words and images to subtly interlock. Getting new words approved by management is harder still. Like most American corporations of healthy middle age, Hallmark has discovered the benefits of redundant personnel and of a certain resistance to fad. Good ideas don't come along every morning, and they must always be weighed against the success of the old: there are only so many pockets in a greeting-card display. Joyce Hall, a tall, spare man with a W. C. Fields nose and a lifetime of practical experience, used to approve every card Hallmark made, words, music and all, and his son, Donald Hall, who is now president of the firm, still approves every Contemporary card that gets past his secretary, or did when I worked there. A friend of mine who free-lanced for Hallmark once earned that secretary's enmity with a design she thought in questionable taste. "It's nice, Bill," she told him, "but it's not Hallmark." You cannot be too careful, and who is to say she wasn't right?

If the process of selection was once a matter of subjective judgment, it is today at least outwardly scientific. For reasons that only statisticians understand, Kansas City is a superb test market. If products sell in Kansas City, they will sell to the nation, a fact that city sophisticates might soberly consider the next time they buy a card. The formula doesn't always work—the East Coast prefers the word "Pop" to the word "Dad" on its Father cards, for example—but it works often enough to keep Hallmark researchers close to home. Yet market research is often discounted at Hallmark. The vapors of past experience still blow through the halls, and men whose only business experience has been with greeting cards still ignore the information of market tests if it conflicts with the information of the gut.

Daring subjectivity was Joyce Hall's genius, and remains a legacy of sorts in the hands of less remarkable men now that he has reluctantly relinquished command. Like every successful self-made man, he has found retirement difficult. He is a man of quirks and crotchets and always was, but the enterprise he began out of a suitcase stashed under his bed at the Kansas City YMCA now ranks high on *Fortune* magazine's list of the five hundred leading privately owned American corporations. The Hall family still owns the place lock, stock and barrel. It is one of the few privately owned companies of any size left in Kansas City, where wealthy sons of fathers who sweated their way up from poverty tend to sell out to national conglomerations and pass their time at Martha's Vineyard or Harbor Point or Cannes. "You can teach your children everything but poverty," Hall once said, but he taught his son to care about the family firm, and today Hallmark thrives, branching out into gift books, stationery, party goods, calendars and albums, puzzles, candy, pens, urban redevelopment, retail stores on the Neiman-Marcus model, and whatever other enterprises it can find that fit its broad conception of its business, which it calls, modestly enough, "social expression."

I could complain against greeting cards. It isn't difficult to do in a world where more people feel pain than feel pleasure. There is even the risk that if I don't complain you will take me for a patsy. The greeting card's contribution to literacy will not be decisive, but I don't believe it does us that much harm. By definition, popular art can be defended only numerically, and to those who equate numbers with mediocrity, to the antipopulists, a numerical defense amounts to a certain conviction. Television is mediocre because it caters to popular tastes, and greeting cards too. No. If either have a glaring weakness, it is that among their plethora of choices they do not give us all the choices we might want, or need. That is the effect of the marketplace, lopping off the ends of the bell curve, but the marketplace pays our bills. And if you would like to consider an opposing view, consider Joyce Hall's, who remembers this nation when it was largely rural and uneducated, and who believed that one of Hallmark's responsibilities was the elevation of American taste, a view that might seem didactic of him, but I was a country boy too, and the first play I ever saw, chills running down my back, was *Macbeth*, on the Hallmark Hall of Fame.

Hallmark established its considerable reputation with thought and care, spending far less on advertising than most companies that make consumer products do. It sponsors television specials and between the acts simply shows its cards. Can you remember a year when the Hall of Fame didn't come in for at least one Emmy? Do you know how many Americans traipsed through art galleries they had never visited before to see the collection of paintings by Winston Churchill that Hallmark shipped around the land? No breath of public scandal has ever blown through the organization. It does not make napalm and until very recently was old-fashioned enough to pay its bills in cash. One of its best men, now retired, a German Jew named Hans Archenhold, whose printing plant was seized by the Nazis, came to Kansas City in its gangster years and found the printing industry there a sty of kickbacks and corruption. With the leverage of Hallmark printing orders, he helped to clean it up. Hall himself switched his employees from coffee to milk breaks during the Depression, reasoning, in memory of his own hungry years, that they probably ate no breakfast and might not be sure of lunch, and I doubt that many complained of paternalism. By all means rail against the size and impersonality of American corporations, your arguments will be well taken, but remember also that most are little Denmarks now, dispensing profits and medical care and life insurance and retirement funds with a cheerful hand.

Today Hallmark's brand identity, an elusive commodity in a competitive society, approaches 100 per cent. School children, asked to make cards in class, often draw a crown on the back of their productions or attempt the famous slogan, "When you care enough to send the very best," in sturdy Big Chief print. There are other greeting-card companies, American, Buzza-Cardoza, Rustcraft and Hallmark's own poor cousin, Ambassador Cards, to name only the biggest, but the one giant has come to stand for them all.

Strangely, eighty per cent of the buyers of greeting cards are women. That is why cards are tested at women's clubs. Even cards for men are designed with a woman buyer in mind, and feature scenes so romantically masculine that only the coldest feminine heart would not be touched: pipes and slippers, a red-capped hunter knocking down a brace of ducks, a fleet of galleons in harbor unaccountably full-sailed, knightly shields and lordly crests, racy automobiles, workshop tools, or smiling Dad (Pop) himself. Why do women buy most of the cards? The answer may be simpler than it seems. Men think themselves too busy running the nation to find time for the smaller amenities, but they rationalize. The truth is that they are locked into an office or on a production line all day. Running an office, doing a job, no more takes all day than housework—few of us have brains that run so uniformly by the clock—but when the housework is done the woman who does it is free to go visiting or wander through the shops, while the man must shuffle papers and watch the clock. The woman may feel uncomfortable with her freedom, may feel she buys it at too high a price. It is hers nonetheless, and she uses it, among other good works, to buy cards. The new cards, by the way, the cards for young people, don't draw such sharp distinctions between masculine and feminine roles. They are androgynous. We all are, underneath: the kids have found us out.

I suspect we send each other cards partly from guilt, believing we haven't kept our friendships in good repair. If we are gregarious, we are also shy, uneasy as only a people raised in a society straining toward egalitarianism can be. Most of us were never rich and never desperately poor. We never learned our place: we started this country so we wouldn't have to, but our mobility leaves us unsure of where our elbows belong. We are known for our humor, but not for our wit; for our ability, but not for our style; for our strength, but not for our grace. We find ourselves harried and we fumble, or think we do.

Our guilt is misplaced. Thoreau's three chairs for company and two for friendship nicely define our human limits. They are no longer limits to which we can comfortably adhere. We would hurt too many feelings if we did, the feelings of the people we work with, of our relatives and our neighbors and the neighbors we left behind. Anyone who has moved recently knows how much sheer matter we accumulate in our houses, but imagine also the long list of acquaintances we have accumulated, back to our earliest years. If we are fond of people at all, we have met thousands in our lives. Perhaps that is why so few of us read. Perhaps our culture is really oral, despite the science fiction of our media, satellites above and wires and presses below and the air itself in fervent vibration. One recalls the theory that ghetto children have difficulty in school not because of deprivation but because of excess, of overstimulation by the teeming world in which they live. It is true to some degree of us all. With China and the Soviet Union, and for much the same reasons of origin and purpose, we are a national people far more than we are local. Our traditions and our associations extend from ocean to ocean, and our burden of communication, too. The Communist nations, not having finished their first industrial revolution, turn to party meetings and rallies to stay in touch; with a more ritualized social structure, we send cards.

Making greeting cards to suit us isn't easy. Try to imagine a card that would please both your grandmother and your revolutionary son—and yet your Christmas card probably did. For reasons no one knows, green cards don't sell. Writers of greeting cards must search their verses for unintentional *double entendre,* and because of that danger, the word "it" used as a direct object is taboo. "Today's your day to get *it!"* It won't do. St. Patrick's Day cards that kid Irish drinking habits elicit indignant letters from Hibernian Societies, a sign that the Irish are ready to melt the rest of the way into the pot. A card is two years in the making: what if hemlines change? Superman cards reached the stores the day the Superman fad collapsed. And what do you say, in a card, in mere words, to a widow whose world has emptied of the life she loved?*

When I worked at Hallmark I sometimes thought of cards as pretty packages with nothing inside, but I am older now and I wonder. Perhaps, ephemeral though they are, they carry a greater weight of emotion to a greater number of people than we can bear to carry ourselves. They are tactful, discreet, they strike the right tone. Their designers sweat blood, believe me, to make them so. Even when they fail, we forgive the sender and blame the card, as we forgive a caller a bad connection on the phone. Greeting cards have inertia. Like Santa's bag, they hang a little behind. They are innately conservative because the occasions of our lives are too important for fads, of style or of spirit. Hallmark has discovered that the young people who buy its breezily pessimistic Contemporary cards return to more traditional forms when they acquire families and careers. Pessimism becomes a luxury they can no longer afford.

We grow older; the cards for our stops along the way await us in the store. They are not dangerous or subversive or mean; they espouse no causes except the old, mute causes of life itself, birth and marriage and begetting and death, and those gently. I celebrate them as E. M. Forster celebrated democracy, with a hearty two cheers. Merry Christmas.

---

* You say, in rhymed verse, that words can't express your sympathy.

A Little World Made Cunningly

These are toys, old toys, in the basement of an acquaintance's house, perhaps five thousand toys, most dating to the last four decades of the nineteenth century or the first three decades of the twentieth. Some shine in well-spaced arrangements in lighted cases, but most are simply shelved on open shelves like books, by categories: fire engines, horse-drawn carriages, Noah's arks, trains and trolleys, airplanes and much more. Their collector owns a Buick dealership and has hunted old toys his entire adult life as other men might hunt quail or the philosopher's stone. His collection is one of the best in the United States and he exhibits samplings of it in New York and elsewhere and collects the fees for a children's hospital, a nice balancing of conscience. He gets the toys and the children get the money the toys earn. That is one point about toys in the hands of adults, that they need justifying, as this fragment of a sign from an old toy store implies: "For things of use and things of sport/The gay and curious here resort." Use or sport, which? Gay or curious, which? Like us, toys come with a doubleganger, a ghost that walks beside them, and that is the ghost we will look to exorcise.

But first look at the toys, some of them, you cannot possibly see them all in one visit to that sprawling basement where the walls are heavy with toys and even the sliding compartments in the walls of the recreation room and the spaces between the books upstairs and the boxes in the corners open to reveal more toys and twelve cast-iron horses prance impaled on a number 10 wire over the workbench and tin Spirits of St. Louis crawl up the joists like summer moths and castings of fat glass children hide behind cast-iron drays loaded with barrels or trunks or feed sacks or squatted grunting pigs. Here: cap bombs of cast iron, the size and heft of glass eyes with slots in their sides to insert the cap and a plunger on their bottoms to fire it when you throw the bomb to the ground on the end of a long string. Some are simply bombs, round and rusted as Civil War cannonballs, but Admiral Dewey also frowns from one and the Liberty Bell explodes rather than peals the news of Independence and a donkey kicks and a clown bites the cap to fire and a man even fires from the seat of his pants, a bit of bawdy that has only recently returned to our visual arts and seems forever banished from our modern toys unless you count Creative Playthings' engenitaled dolls.

An Uncle Sam bank with Uncle staring out of the cast iron with the fierce expression he wore in those days of unvarnished patriotism, an expression that might have been borrowed from our tough bald eagle—Uncle could have been modeled on a New England drummer and probably was. A William Tell mechanical bank with William's crossbow converted to fling coin at his brave little son backed up against a ruined castle with a slot above his head to receive the dangerous throw. Tin darkies dancing on the roofs of tin houses with interiors stuffed with clockwork, one house bluntly labeled "Coon Jigger." Hard now with the Panthers at cocktails to recall the depravities of our country Waspishness that allowed us to laugh at dancing darkies or overpolite Frenchmen like Alphonse and Gaston who sightsee from an iron omnibus labeled SEE NEW YORK or incomprehensible Germans like Mama Katzenjammer who methodically spanks one of the kids when you pull the cart in which she rides. Miniature iron street lamps from Paris. A clown leading two dogs. A boy in a cart pulled by a fearsome wild boar. Tin butterflies as gaudily painted as the real article pushed flapping on long wooden sticks to develop little legs and delight little eyes. A tin drum, one of the millions that appear under Christmas trees to disturb the white morning. A 1911 slot racer, red, with two intent Frank Merriwell figures aboard, driven not by electricity or little puffs of air like the slot racers of today but by heavy clockwork gears of the best brass. Felix the Cat in tin and Barney Google on his faithful Spark Plug and behind a sliding door eight matched cast-iron Andy Gumps in eight matched Car 348s, a boggling repetition that shades into nightmare if you imagine a thousand, ten thousand, a hundred thousand Andy Gumps coming off an assembly line somewhere in Connecticut or New Hampshire or New Jersey, if you imagine the souls who worked that line assembling all those Andy Gumps. A cast-iron showboat with the word SHOWBOAT cast into its sides as if we didn't know and lounging iron sailors sprawling its decks. A threshing machine that works and a street-cleaning machine that works and a cream separator not four inches tall that looks as if it should work. Dirigibles like tin cigars with celluloid props on strings and biplanes of tin or wire and cloth and merry-go-rounds and iron bell carts and every kind of glorious fire engine and carriage, some with the textures of even the lap robes cast in. The big basement is jammed with the spirits of children dead or grown old, and when you remember that even in 1900 some two million children between the ages of nine and fifteen worked in factories or on farms, those at least who survived infancy, you know how intensely the spirits play, with a will.

The toy collectors used to argue about the age and productivity of the American toy industry, picking up the ardent battles of the toy manufacturers themselves against foreign imports. The industry came of age not, as many thought, in the twentieth century but soon after the Civil War, the war that inured us to readymades of every kind. Before then, most toys were locally made or, rarely, imported. Yankees looking for a sideline started the toy business in New England, Yankee carpenters and tinsmiths and iron founders. You must see the fine shivers of existential dread in the souls of these New England men who invented and manufactured and sold American toys. Here was their neighbor the Iron King or the Wicker Furniture King or the Quincy Granite King and here were they making toys. Patenting toys, casting them in sand as if they were boxcar wheels or the cylinders of steam engines, milling them, assembling them, painting them, shipping them off to the cities and towns of a nation so bent on industrial gigantism that it put millions of children to work fourteen hours a day. Making good toys, finely detailed, sometimes perfectly scaled, toys so heavy that you wonder today how any child could even have picked them up, but still "only" toys. And you can well bet these were men who had no such toys as children, who picked rocks out of New England fields or swept out the store every morning, who quit such school as they had at sixteen and by seventeen launched their first factory with casters and filers and a dozen girls not yet pubescent lined up behind paint pots each to daub on one color of paint as the cherished fire engine or hackney or surrey went by with matched geldings all aprance.

The age was a riot of invention anyway, the second half of the

nineteenth century, every man jack in America whittling or sol-
dering or sketching. Steam! Iron! Power! Mother Nature discreetly looked the other way. Why, they were going to reconstruct
the universe in iron castings with interchangeable parts. But toys?
They were not just another item of commerce, lucrative though
they could be. They came trailing clouds of glory behind. Out of
the adult world and into the child's, who was not yet allowed to
enjoy the special privilege we today routinely confer upon children, the privilege of indulging his inner world as so few adults
even today indulge their own. For long years there weren't enough
adults to go around this enormous land and so children stood in
for the missing numbers. Twelve-year-olds fought in the Revolutionary War, as they fought for Germany at the end of World
War II. If you were old enough to walk and talk, you were old
enough to do something in a factory or on a farm. Old enough to
buy penny gin too and go reeling drunk through the muddy
street. When did children become children? Certainly not until
the late nineteenth century. They were little adults before that, all
but the rich ones, which is why they could share the same room
with their parents and the same work and the same wars. Their
lives were compressed like a telescoping tin cup, rings within
rings. Born at zero and a near miracle if you survived your first
four years and out to the factory at seven or eight and if you did
well a factory of your own at seventeen and very likely marriage
and begetting and death of disease by forty. Which is why the
people of those ages seem so bizarre today, all rough edges and
half-baked notions and a frenzy of living. Childhood came and
went in the twinkling of an eye. Today we bend the other way
and begin to extend it into the twenties, the thirties, even the for-
ties of life, and when we have finished automating everything we
may well extend it all the way if the vapors don't get us first. Edward VII ordered and got a Crandall Spring Horse and no doubt
rode it too, a handsome young man. Kings and the wealthy lead
the way: we will all ride Crandall Spring Horses by and by, pursuing a childhood that lengthens before us. Compare an early New
England diarist: "I was a very naughty boy, much given to play."
He hadn't time to play. The land lay before him.

But for grown men and Yankees too to manufacture toys, the
toys must seem to have a use. Play without usefulness was hardly
the ethic of their industrious lives. One maker of steam toys went

on to become the leading manufacturer of the real thing, of steam locomotives, and that is closer to the function of toys at the time, and perhaps also explains the use of a material so unwieldy as cast iron. We were building an industry that would be the most productive in the world and building it on the backs of children and of wage earners. It took the athletic Dr. Gilbert to go all the way and invent the Erector Set, but even before that event toys came rolling out to industrialize the little time children had to play. Thoreau caught a whiff of it at a trader's shop in the Maine woods and didn't like it at all. "Here was a little of everything in a small compass to satisfy the wants and ambitions of the woods . . . but there seemed to me, as usual, a preponderance of children's toys—dogs to bark, and cats to mew, and trumpets to blow, where natives there hardly are yet. As if a child born into the Maine woods, among the pine cones and cedar berries, could not do without such a sugar-man or skipping-jack as the young Rothschild has." But children who grow up on pine cones and cedar berries cannot assemble machinery, as we discovered among ARVN helicopter mechanics in Vietnam. If you would think in gears and circuits, you had best start thinking that way early. Our toys today are less utilitarian, consumer toys rather than little trade schools, but it is no great step back from the tools of the late nineteenth century to the toys. They had real parts and were modeled on real equipment and they brought the stink of the factory to the clearing under the pine and cedar trees. It was no stink to people then, because it meant more food on the table and coin in the pocket and a sense of national destiny most called progress, but we can easily see why Thoreau, primed with Emerson's philosophy and Emerson's wit but lacking Emerson's spacious metaphysics, would think it so. He himself had invented a better pencil and his friends told him he ought to go into the pencil business, and it was that kind of well-meant advice that sent him raving to his borrowed pond, only to find a man there who had invented a mechanical ice cutter and was stripping off in uniform blocks the cloudy winter ice.

The irony of toys, all toys, old toys especially, the ghost in the miniature machines, is also the irony of childhood itself whether we give it much or little space in our lives: not that children cannot after a fashion cope as adults, for the past makes it clear that they can: but that we allow children to live in all the world, the inner and the outer, and hardly any longer allow it of ourselves. Those harsh nineteenth-century years disguised the secrets of children that old toys only grudgingly reveal: the play of fantasy in their lives. The toys are as small in relation to the child as the child is small in relation to adults, and from them he makes a world that exists around and alongside the adult world as invisibly as the air. He may kill, and if it is wartime he probably will—one recalls the Jewish children in the Warsaw Ghetto playing at Nazis and Jews—he may love, a doll or a horse or a Teddy bear, a creation that some denounced from the pulpit as a potential cause of race suicide because it could turn little girls away from maternal affection for their more human dolls, he may fly or drive or dig or railroad, and if an adult interrupts, well, it is part of the nature of play that it is interruptible, if not entirely, if no more often than dreams may be interrupted if the dreamer is to stay sane.

And what is play in the child becomes, for most adults, the work and the institutions of their lives, their jobs if they are lucky in their work, their clubs and causes whether they are lucky in their work or not. Specifically, among the old toys, the play of science stands out. It was a time of simple experiments and simple invention; there were few professional scientists in the land, and playing at science occupied the time most children, most boys at least, had. They built wings and jumped off barns, they drove their trolleys and their fire engines, they explored magnets and coils and new kinds of propulsion. It was hazardous duty for which they got no ready pay, but the pay came later. The exalted of Woodrow Wilson's war planners thought one year of abolishing Christmas by passing a law making it illegal to buy Christmas presents, and the indefatigable Dr. Gilbert assembled his fellow toymakers for an assault on Washington, dragging behind them like Santa Claus himself a bag of toys. The planners awed them and they hid the toys behind a couch in the board room until the moment seemed right and then they brought them out, and the mature and serious planners sat down to play, and Dr. Gilbert told them American boys were sure marksmen because they had grown up with BB guns and skilled mechanics because they had learned the intricacies of bolts and nuts and screws and the argument was won and America enjoyed a booming Christmas once again. Toys mean less now, less of mechanics certainly, but less too of thought: you cannot easily disassemble a plastic car, nor build dreams on an Easy-Bake Oven complete with boxes of cake mix, and perhaps that is why they tend to the grotesque, idiot-faced dolls encased in plastic spheres like replicas from a Ripley's Museum, black rubber spiders and giant green-and-red flies, bloodshot Cyclopean eyes left on the floor to be horribly chewed by the family dog, or the pretension of wooden dolls with their features sanded away in psychology labs. They are less than real and more than real, and they imply that the fantasy of play must be a fantasy of monsters or of ciphers, and children leave them disdainfully for their crayons and chalk or for the pines and cedars, the wheel having come full circle.

But here in the crowded basement you find larger dreams, a tricycle for a prince with wheels set into a carved and enameled spotted pony with a real mane and a real tail and cranks to drive the wheels where handlebars would later be, or tin angels with bells to strike hanging from a tin windmill, or four children at the corners of a wagon pulling on a swing set lightly in the wagon bed. A portion of childhood sealed in amber by men and women who collect old toys, a portion of childhood to be indulged later with the resources of adults. The owner of this collection grew up on a farm and had no toys, and hence this basementful now. The trick is to get out of that basement once you get thoroughly in, no special trick for the collector, because he must go out to collect more, searching the attics of America. He finds city toys in the city, country toys in the country, a secret code of flecked paint and bent wheels and the missing legs of harnessed horses, a trip through the looking glass into an alternate world.

Someone has remarked that it is the strangest of all indulgences in a highly industrialized society that the society allows it children to play, encourages them to play, even demands it of them as if it were their particular civilized work, but is it really so strange, seeing how dreamlike civilization itself has become, how withdrawn from the natural world into a world where water flows ceaselessly from taps and pictures fly through the air and temperatures change at the change of a dial? Was childhood more poignant when you could lose half your family in one epidemic winter or is it more poignant now when the one thing we can no longer give our children is any work truly responsible?

That would seem to be an enigma of old toys too. We called dolls "babies" in the early years of the Republic, and what a girl learned from her babies she would soon enough use on her little sisters. Bicycles preceded automobiles and cyclists first agitated for decent roads, which leaves one wishing the bicycle had never been invented.

Did the toys civilize us or did we civilize the toys? Surely it was an exchange, and at the time it seemed a worthy one, if it does not always seem so now. You snatched such childhood as you could in those days even as you are lucky to grow beyond it today, and one of the reasons why this well-lighted basement seems crowded with more than toys is the blunt mortality of a time John Donne knew well when he talked of himself but might also have been talking of toys: "I am a little world made cunningly/Of Elements, and an Angelike spright,/But black sinne hath betraid to endlesse night/My worlds both parts, and (oh) both parts must die."

That is much of it, perhaps even most of it, elements and an angel-like spirit, but we ought to be sure we know what that spirit is: the spirit of inconsequence, of murders that do not maim and loves that do not end, which is why childhood carries such a burden of sentiment and toys such a freight of pleasure. Go ahead and smash your cars together, they will only break, go ahead and crank up the darkie, he will only dance, go ahead and ring out the hook and ladder, there is no real fire. Privileges of children, which we may be sure they appreciate in a world where chairs are too large and drinking glasses too clumsy and parents too often incomprehensible: the inner world they necessarily explore is larger still, and it commands all their attention. We dream of it to the end of our lives.

Strung Out on Blast

Dynamite: the big, red, paper-wrapped sticks lying in their box ominous and yet exhilarating, fuel for fantasies of some ultimate Fourth of July, giant firecrackers packed with brown paste that looks like plastic wood—isn't plastic wood, is diatomaceous earth, but the binder that glues the diatomaceous earth is nitroglycerin. Wicked, lethal stuff, the weapon of choice of skyjackers and left-of-far-left radicals and terrorists and underworld hit men; but today two clean-cut, fresh-faced young guys in white hard hats, Mark and Doug Loizeaux, are handling it. They pull sticks out of the box and slash them with a razor blade and prime them with blasting caps, fine orange and yellow wires running out the end, and load them in holes drilled into concrete columns that support Kansas City's moribund State Hotel. And after they've loaded the dynamite, my God, they ram it into place with a sawed-off hoe handle, as if it were so much packing, and then ram some stemming turf on top to plug the hole and move on. The owners of the hotel put a contract out on it. Tomorrow morning, Sunday, Mark and Doug and their dad, Jack Loizeaux, are going to blow the place up.

They make a formidable team, though none of them looks the part of beefy demolition. Jack, fifty-seven, is slim and handsome, with trim gray hair and a small mustache; Mark, compact, poised, self-assured as someone must be who took over the business temporarily at the age of nineteen, when his dad broke his back in a car accident; Doug, tall and bearded, the younger son but already dropping buildings and bridges on his own. The Loizeauxs are a family outfit, and even Freddie Loizeaux, wife and mother, former head of the Maryland P.T.A., is a licensed blaster and travels with her husband to handle public relations with officials nervous at the thought of what will happen to them if the explosives break loose.

Playboy. February 1974

The box of dynamite sits in a pile of plaster rubble in what used to be the lobby of the hotel next to a battered blue Samsonite suitcase full of time-delay blasting caps and the Loizeaux boys move systematically from one column to the next, loading the holes spaced evenly around each column. Each hole gets the smallest possible charge of dynamite, a pound or a pound and a half; one of the qualities that have made the Loizeauxs the best demolition men in the world is their fanaticism about using the least possible amount of explosives to get the job done. They'd take down the Empire State Building with Black Cats and ladyfingers if they could figure out a way to do it, but as it is they've brought down twenty-two-story buildings with no more than a couple of hundred pounds of dynamite—which is why, in eighteen years of work, Controlled Demolition Inc., the family firm, has never had an accident or an injury. Occasionally, very occasionally, a building won't fall on the first shot, a consequence of the Loizeauxs' refusing to overload it with explosives, and then Jack has to go in and set more charges and try again. But such undercalculations have become increasingly rare as Controlled Demolition has refined its techniques. The days when it had to go to Lloyd's of London for insurance are now far behind it.

The State Hotel isn't anything special to look at, ten stories of brick, the decayed repository of tens of thousands of Kansas City weekends and Kansas City weeks, but its physical roots go back to the nineteenth century, hand-laid masonry columns down in the basement six feet square supporting a welter of columns upstairs, some of them structural steel, some of them poured concrete embedded with heavy reinforcing rods, some of them poured concrete wrapped with bands of steel like giant springs, an array right out of Rube Goldberg, every support different from the last one and every support requiring its own unique arrangement of explosives if it's to be turned, as the Loizeauxs intend turning it, into instant gravel. The concrete and masonry supports get dynamite charges. The structural-steel H beams running ten stories up the front of the hotel inside its brick facing get something special from the technology of the space age: linear shaped charges. When the stages of the Saturn 5 separated from one another in all those moon shots, linear shaped charges wrapped around the inside of the rocket's skin separated them. A linear shaped charge is an explosive device that looks like a segment of a copper picture frame, an extruded V-shaped copper tube filled with plastic explosive. When the explosive goes off, it turns to a gas and expands at twenty-seven thousand feet per second, which is fast enough to generate pressures of three million pounds per square inch. The shape of the copper tube forms the expanding gas into a jet and the jet makes a cut as thin as a sheet of paper along the line where the charge is attached, an instantaneous cut cleaner than the work of an acetylene torch straight through the three inches of structural steel.

But if the hotel is nothing much to look at, in another sense it's very special indeed, because its east side, ten stories high, rises only the width of an alley, twelve feet, away from a twenty-two-story hotel next door, a hotel still in service and filled with weekend guests. The Loizeauxs have taken down larger buildings than the State, but they've never before taken down one so tight. The least mistake and they're likely to tear up the neighboring hotel and destroy their perfect record and bring on monumental lawsuits and maybe kill somebody, and don't think they don't know it. Jack Loizeaux is a praying man who nevertheless believes the Lord helps those who help themselves, but this weekend he's praying whenever he can find the time. He's already handled three other jobs in Kansas City, a smokestack and an old packing house and a hotel, but a few months before the State job another outfit tried to take down a building a block away and botched it. They blew it up three times before the last of it fell and they broke half the windows in the central city. Jack has to sell the city fathers all over again on the virtues of explosive demolition, and the only way he knows how to do that is to put his own reputation on the line by taking on the worst job in town. The State is the worst job in the country, and if he's not actually sweating, he's certainly checking and rechecking the building and his plans, and so are his two sons, and the night before the blast he will find himself wide awake at three in the morning with diagrams and delay patterns dancing before his eyes.

Loizeaux first handled explosives back in 1938, when he was a junior at the University of Georgia in Athens. He owned a bicycle then, and an Airedale, and a cabin in the woods. He was a forestry student. The Oconee River was washing out the forestry-department nursery and the school decided to straighten the channel to bypass the nursery area. Jack worked the surveying transit and then helped the DuPont engineer load dynamite into the holes the students drilled. "When it came time to shoot," says Loizeaux, "he said, 'How would you like to shoot it?' Wow! I was just a kid. I pressed that plunger and we threw *hundreds of thousands* of tons of loam and mud and it just went skyward and when it was all over and the mud settled, the old lazy river came straight as an arrow for about two hundred yards. It just fascinated me. The tremendous power that was at my finger tips. I couldn't sleep for a week." He remembers an earlier experience with explosives that may have impressed him even more: he remembers his father blasting holes in his orchard where fruit trees would be planted. Then the father had power; now the power was his.

But Loizeaux didn't go directly from college into demolition. World War II intervened, and after the war, the memory of tremendous power perhaps quiescent, he started a tree service out of Towson, Maryland, specializing in big contracts from cities, twenty thousand trees at a time. Those were the years when the American elm died off in the East from Dutch elm disease. Loizeaux had all the work he could handle, and to get the job done he innovated. "When we had dead elms and dead sycamores, we'd cut them off low and drill holes and blast and split them and then we'd take a navy winch truck and pull out the pieces, so we had no disposal problem." Thus began his practical experience with explosives. And notice: felling a tree means figuring out how to put it exactly where you want it, using ropes and gravity to lay it in the slot, a skill that Loizeaux would later turn to good account.

Builders, hearing about a tree specialist around Baltimore who used explosives, would come over and ask Loizeaux if he'd take on a stubborn rock or a recalcitrant footing, and for one hundred bucks or so he'd do it. He began to like the money he was earning from those extra jobs and he began to learn about blasting. He hung around DuPont, studied engineering at night school, read his way through the blasting library, took chemists and engineers to lunch. The specialists at DuPont came to think of him as an expert, and one day they had a problem that matched his talents. "DuPont called me and said a colonel at Aberdeen Proving Ground thought he'd be cute and there were three smokestacks to come down and he shot one and he's broken windows for many miles, so he's in hot water. So I went out there. He'd taken three cases—fifty-pound cases, one hundred fifty pounds of explosives—and he'd had his men scaffold the stack and his engineers had lowered the cases into the stack at different elevations. Well" —this from Loizeaux deadpan—"he blew it. So I went out there with six pounds of explosives for each stack and I dumped the other two."

Loizeaux has a film showing the most outstanding of his many shots over the years, and prominent among its scenes are the ballets he and his sons perform with smokestacks. Loizeaux knows where to drop them, like trees. He leans them east, west, north, south and points between. Or he telescopes them into themselves so that they disappear before your eyes, leaving behind as they fall, suspended in the air, a ghostly column of soot. The colonel at Aberdeen can only have been chagrined. But, for Loizeaux, a chimney was just another kind of tree.

In the early fifties, Loizeaux shot nothing but stacks. Then he was called to Chile to blast out a deepwater port, one of the few foreign assignments he has accepted, not wanting to spread himself too thin, and when that job was done he was in business. He's been blowing stacks, bridges and buildings ever since, until today he has as much business as he can handle, and he's brought in his two sons, both licensed blasters and competent demolition experts in their own right, to help him keep up with demand.

Like many other self-made men, Loizeaux has looked hard for something beyond himself that might explain his success, and the search has made him an amateur mystic, in his case a Christian who usually manages to testify to his faith whenever he speaks in public, testimony that can have remarkable results at college graduations and in chamber-of-commerce halls, coming as it does from a man whose power over inert matter fascinates and awes most people who meet him. Loizeaux, whose chosen work is reducing the American past to pieces of rubble conveniently sized for loading into dump trucks, has made more than one audience weep for its lost innocence. Ask him how he does what he does and he will say that "one who knows the Lord has an advantage over others, or should have. I just say, Lord, take care, take charge." He also does his homework, however.

The Loizeauxs serve as explosives consultants to wreckers. When the Vince Bahm Wrecking Company of Topeka got the contract for the State Hotel, Bahm called in Controlled Demolition, and Jack went to Kansas City and figured out what Bahm would have to do to get the building ready. Following Loizeaux's plan, Bahm weakened the masonry columns with a jackhammer, knocked out part of a load-bearing brick wall in the back of the hotel with a wrecking ball, cleared out the partitions in the basement and on the first floor and partly cut some of the structural-steel beams. He would do as much for any demolition, but then he went on to add the special Loizeaux touch. He ran seven-eighths-inch steel cable from the columns in the back to the columns in the front and then pulled them as tight as their fifty or sixty thousand pounds of tensile strength would allow. Several floors above the first were cabled together, ready to pull the walls inward when their supports were cut. Rest beams, their points of rest severed, thus became cantilever beams, pulled over like trees. Bahm also drilled the holes that would hold the dynamite that the Loizeaux boys would later load.

Eighty-five per cent of a building, Loizeaux says, is empty space, air. The rest, the shell, is steel and cement and brick and plaster and wood. Those materials were raised into the air against the pull of gravity, and sitting there now, they retain as potential all the energy that went into their raising. Loizeaux puts small, selectively placed charges in the basement of a building, and having cabled the building together upstairs, times them to go off in a pattern and lets gravity do the work. The energy of the building's raising, released when the supports are kicked out, also brings it down, an elegant economy. Having tremendous power at his finger tips, Loizeaux uses as little of it as he possibly can. Seismographs placed in nearby buildings show more disturbance when a bus goes by.

Knowing dynamites—densities, velocities, dynamites that shatter, dynamites that gently heave—is part of Loizeaux's secret, but his delay patterns are the key to his extraordinary ability to put a building wherever the wrecker wants it. Knock out the supports on one side before you knock out the supports on the other and you tip the building over in the direction of the earlier explosions. Cable a building together, knock out first the middle and then one end and then the other and the building will fold up like the flaps on an ice-cream carton. It sounds easy. It isn't. Loizeaux also has to consider how fast each part of the building will fall. End A has to fall a certain distance before end B can fall on top of it. Falling objects, unhindered, travel at thirty-two feet per second per second, but falling sections of multistory buildings are hindered by walls and floors and lag behind. Loizeaux must also take that delay into account. He learned by doing. There's no book on the subject, though someday he may write one. In the meantime, he's passed his arcane skills on to his sons. They grew up in the business. Every big job the Loizeauxs have done in the past eighteen years has been filmed; they study the films as carefully as the coaches of the N.F.L. study the films of their past games, and they've saved the diagrams of delay patterns as well, catalogued them by type, and with every job they take them out for review.

Mark, who is twenty-five, put the Loizeaux skills to good use in 1972 on a project heavy with unintentional ironies. Back in the mid-fifties, at the height of its efforts to solve the problem of housing the nation's poor, the federal Department of Housing and Urban Development (HUD) built a thirty-six-million-dollar high-rise housing project in St. Louis called Pruitt-Igoe. Architect Minoru Yamasaki, who later designed the World Trade Center in New York, designed Pruitt-Igoe, thirty-three 11-story high-rises that at one time housed twelve thousand people—not in comfort and security, as HUD intended, but in violence and squalor. Fighting costs, Yamasaki designed elevators that stopped only at every third floor; residents then walked down galleries and stairs to their apartments. Yamasaki envisioned the galleries as places where children could play, but they became, instead, places where muggers and junkies and drunks could skulk, no man's lands. Population densities in Pruitt-Igoe were far too high for either comfort or safety. And because most of the residents were on welfare and could pay little or no rent, the project went so deeply into debt that it began draining funds from the entire St. Louis public-housing program, blocking any development of alternatives. Finally, in desperation, the housing authority decided Pruitt-Igoe needed surgery and proposed to demolish some of the high-rises and scale the others down to manageable size. That was where Controlled Demolition came in. Mark's job was to peel off one wing of a building and leave an adjoining wing intact. It was a demonstration project to prove what the Loizeauxs have been proving for nearly two decades, that explosives do the job faster and safer than jackhammers and wrecking balls. But there was symbolism, too, in the assignment: radicals had been blowing up government buildings in the name of a new and better world; at Pruitt-Igoe, a member of a conservative family from Maryland was blowing up a government building that had become an embarrassment to the liberals of America. The building came down without a hitch, and rumor has it that the residents of Pruitt-Igoe cheered. So did Mark Loizeaux: with relief that it had fallen where it was supposed to.

Sunday morning in Kansas City, unseasonably cool, the air crisp, the sky blue, a west wind having blown the smog away. Across the street from the State Hotel at the Muehlebach, downtown Kansas City's finest, the manager greeted guests at an Implosion Party he was sponsoring. The Defenders of Bataan and Corregidor, meeting that weekend in reunion, were just waking up. Notices in the elevators had warned them of the demolition so that none would be jolted out of bed imagining the Japs had descended again from the western sky.

I went early, my two young children in tow, a lifelong pyromaniac eager to see the benevolent destruction. Whatever our recent pacifism in the United States of America, who among us doesn't like explosives? At the boys' home where I grew up, on the Fourth of July, we would finish our chores and eat supper and wait impatiently for near darkness to troop up to the superintendent's house, on the hill. There, milling in the back yard, we would gleefully fire off a crateful of fireworks, taking out our hostilities on the thickening blue air. Once someone accidentally or deliberately dropped a Roman candle and all forty of us danced the Independence jig while flashing colored balls of fire rocketed through the grass. If my children are any measure, the next generation of Americans will be just as gone on fireworks as we; last summer they took out a stump behind the house with nothing more than Black Cats and persistence, little Loizeauxs at practice. Like a giant piece of punk, it smoldered for two weeks, turning slowly to fine gray ash and leaving a hole where its root system had been, deep in the ground.

The first floor of the State Hotel was boarded up when we arrived, halves of old steam boilers wired around the columns to contain any debris from the shaped charges attached there. Tons of sand hauled in from the Kansas River bottom covered the sidewalks, protecting gas mains and electrical vaults beneath. The glass windows of the Muehlebach's first-floor offices were protected by two semis parked in the street. Wires from the dozens of charges loaded inside the hotel snaked out to a cable and the cable ran southwest across the intersection of Twelfth and Baltimore to a green park where a crowd had gathered to watch. Jim Redyke, one of Controlled Demolition's new men and soon to become its western representative, connected the cable to a box the size of a storage battery that contained six flashlight cells and a condenser and two buttons, one red, one green. Both buttons would have to be pushed at once to trigger the charges. Doug Loizeaux was up on a nearby building with a Canon Scoopic 16 set to record the blast and it was ten to eight in the morning and the entire project was waiting for enough light. Vince Bahm had piled bales of straw against the wall of the hotel across the alley from the State and now sat on a high-loader ready to clean up the streets. Jack Loizeaux roamed near the building, worrying.

Police cars blocked off the streets around the hotel and a traffic-control officer parked alongside the green ordered the crowd back. The light came up and Doug called in to Redyke that he was ready. The last few stragglers moved off the street into the crowd and the police pulled back their cars and then only one man stood next to the building, Jack Loizeaux, with his radio in his hand. The siren on the traffic-control car whooped once and stopped and then a minute passed and it whooped twice and stopped and then in the silence Loizeaux's voice crackled over Redyke's radio, *Thirty seconds and counting,* and silence, and then, *Fifteen, fourteen, thirteen,* into the countdown now just like a moon shot and the police loudspeaker picked it up and boomed it out to the crowd, *nine, eight, seven, six, five*—Loizeaux running away from the building now toward the detonator, still counting—*four, three, two, one,* FIRE!, and Redyke mashed the two buttons with the heels of his hands and instantly the shaped charges went off, muffled sharp raps of sonic boom as the jets cut the H beams at twenty-seven thousand feet per second—*boom, boom, boom*—and then the dynamite delays went off in sequence—four, five, six, seven, eight, nine—and the sound merged into one rolling roar and the building began to come apart as if every brick had been pried loose from its neighbor, light and space showing between bricks and stone window frames and keystones and facings, the center of the wall falling first and then the west end and then, as a cloud of dust rolled up from the foundation like a tsunami surf, the east end fell away from the alley and the rubble disappeared in the dust.

The dust rolled toward the green and enveloped the cheering crowd and Loizeaux disappeared in the direction of the rubble and it was five minutes before the dust cleared to reveal a pile of bricks and twisted beams and shattered blocks of concrete less than one story high where before a ten-story hotel had been, and when it saw that pile, the crowd was awed again into silence, the latent image of the solid hotel, built in 1923 and a fixture of the corner for fifty years, a memory out of childhood, still imprinted on everyone's eyes.

One steel beam had broken free of the building and fallen the wrong way; leaning across the street, it had nicked a cement-block screen in front of the Muehlebach and whomped one of the semis, folding it up like a bent beer can. But the State Hotel had fallen into its own foundation and the hotel across the alley was untouched, only its lowest fire escape slightly twisted. Loizeaux was already kicking himself about the beam that fell across the street, vowing to cable higher up next time. Vince Bahm was wheeling the high-loader through the streets around the rubble, pushing it into the foundation, and the sweeping machines were hosing down the streets to wash away the thick layer of dust that now covered the streets and crowd alike. And then the crowd rushed off to hotels and coffee shops to put the world back together with drink and food.

The Loizeauxs went too, and Doug and Mark talked about their work. Their father is obsessive about safety and so are they, but for once they mentioned the other side of demolition, the side that draws the unwanted crowds, the secret kick of concentrating all your skill and hope and reputation too on one shot of juice traveling through a wire. Mark: "It's all worth it, because when that thing's down you look up there and you say, oh, man, we did that. It's like winning the Grand Prix or bagging your elephant."

Doug: "The feeling of success. It's definitely a rush. Strung out on blast."

IV
RAGES AND INVESTIGATIONS

Sex and Sin in Sheboygan

Sheboygan, Wisconsin. The name of the town is borrowed from the name of the river that winds through it. Sheboygan, an Algonquin word, means a passage connecting two bodies of water. It also means a hollow bone. When Sheboygan was a village, its inhabitants called it "the mouth." The Sheboygan River rises in the hills only a short portage away from Lake Winnebago and flows north and then bends eastward and on the shore of Lake Michigan halfway up the Wisconsin coast, at the river's mouth, lies the city of Sheboygan. It is not a picturesque city but it is situated in a picturesque place. Kettle moraines, hills with kettle-shaped holes ground out between them by the Lake Michigan glacier, mark the land westward and in the winter the river freezes like a miniature glacier to break at the shoreline jaggedly into the huge unfrozen lake. Indians fished here and steamboats docked pioneers to settle the wilderness west. Yankees came to girdle the trees and grow corn. Germans came to escape religious and political persecution and settled and started dairy farming and built exercise halls. Serbs and Croats came to work in furniture factories and mills. Yugoslavs came and Lithuanians, and Luxemburgers and Russian Jews. Fourierist utopians like those who founded New England's Brook Farm came and established a short-lived socialist colony, a *phalanx*, but their crops failed and reluctantly they moved on.

Sheboygan is possessed of two other picturesque distinctions. Its main industry today is a toilet-and-bathtub factory. And although it is a city of only 48,484 people, it annually prosecutes more adults for fornication, adultery and lewd and lascivious behavior than any other city in the United States.*

A few years ago a young man named Jim Decko came to Sheboygan. He had been an exceptional student. He was an exceptional athlete. The Sheboygan school system had hired him to direct the city's extensive public recreation program. It was a responsible job. Decko supervised more than two hundred part-time employees, and because he was outgoing and handsome and athletic, people in Sheboygan soon came to recognize him on the streets of the town. He played semipro football. He was married to a beauty queen, and had two small daughters, but the marriage wasn't going well. Decko began to look around. He met a girl and started divorce proceedings. He got a divorce.

Wisconsin winters blow long and cold. Decko shared an apartment with his girl. Stories of convictions for cohabitation turned up in the Sheboygan *Gazette* alongside stories of robberies and record snows. A police captain lived next door, and the sister of a detective down the hall. Decko moved out, but continued to visit on weekends. Someone whispered into the phone. The young director of public recreation got a call and drove to the police station downtown.

Cohabitation is a crime in Wisconsin. The crime is defined in Section 20 of Chapter 944 of the Wisconsin Criminal Code. The chapter is titled "Crimes Against Sexual Morality" and the section "Lewd and Lascivious Behavior." The law provides:

Whoever does any of the following may be fined not more than $500 or imprisoned not more than one year in county jail or both:
1. Commits an indecent act of sexual gratification with another with knowledge that they are in the presence of others; or
2. Publicly and indecently exposes a sex organ; or

* Detailed records in these matters are scarce, but all available evidence suggests the statement is true. Sheboygan police arrested 118 people in 1971 for class II sex offenses, excluding rape. In 1967, the only year for which a statistical breakdown is available, Sheboygan arrested thirty-five people for adultery, twenty-seven for lewd and lascivious behavior, eleven for fornication, ten for intercourse without consent, four for bigamy, and one for sexual perversion. In contrast, New York has prosecuted two people for adultery and none for fornication in the past fifty years; Boston in 1966 reported six arrests for fornication and seven for adultery.
Playboy, August 1972

3. Openly cohabits and associates with a person he knows is not his spouse under circumstances that imply sexual intercourse.

The first clause protects the public from swingers and live sex shows, the second from exhibitionists. The third is less precise. "Circumstances that imply sexual intercourse" is a phrase that requires of law officials an act of imagination. For example, the presence of fifteen adult males, a German Shepherd and a tin whistle in the home of a matron would not imply sexual intercourse, though the dog often barked and the whistle often blew, if the home were a licensed boarding house. The presence of a man in a woman's apartment overnight would, if they were known not to be married to one another. The statute does not forbid sexual intercourse. It forbids two people from "openly" behaving as man and wife. Wisconsin maintains the creature comforts of home and hearth under license, and treats failure to obtain that license as a crime.

To establish that Jim Decko was behaving lewdly and lasciviously, the Sheboygan Police Department observed the behavior of the lights in the apartment and the behavior of his car. On August 27, 1970, Sheboygan police officers Frederick Zittel and Howard Durow filed a report:

The area of _____ was checked periodically during the night and this blue Ford license R96-240 was parked at this location throughout the night.

On August 28, Officer Durow and Officer William Eichmann filed a similar report. Other reports chronicled times when the apartment lights were on or off. From such objective facts the Sheboygan police could draw rigorous conclusions.

In 1970, the Sheboygan Police Department apprehended four window peepers, a fact mentioned prominently in its annual report.

Two detectives interviewed Decko. They asked him if he stayed overnight at the apartment. They asked him what the sleeping arrangements were. Decko answered some of their questions and evaded others. He asked the detectives what they thought to be logical hours. He asked if he could visit the apartment at all and they said yes. He asked how late he could stay and they said, well, 12 or 1 o'clock. The exchange reminded him of college. He said after he left the station that he felt ridiculous. He felt as if he had been placed under curfew. He continued to visit the apartment, but surreptitiously, leaving his car at home. Sometimes his amused friends, galvanized by the quaintness of a challenge to young love, dropped him by. Two weeks after Decko's interview he was issued a summons and his world fell apart.

He was a talented and successful young man. He had been an all-state linebacker. His job required enthusiasm and a good measure of skill. When he was summoned by the State he should have been angry, but instead he was mortally afraid. Later, some would remember that he seemed a man inordinately concerned to please. He opened car doors for ladies and wrote I LOVE YOU in the white Wisconsin snow.

When he got his summons he called the Sheboygan chief of police, a man named Oakley Frank, and arranged to talk it over. He said, look, I've been in this town a long time. What can we do? Can we keep this out of the paper? Can we settle this out of court? Frank said he had come too late. Frank said he would like to help Decko, but the matter was no longer in his hands. He said he had the problem of the people who had encouraged him to prosecute. He said that if he didn't prosecute he would get the entire department in trouble.

Oakley Frank doesn't love the press. It hasn't done him honor. He consented to an interview reluctantly. He is a stocky man with graying hair combed back from the temples. He has a heavy face and a firm, forceful voice. That is most of what I know about him, except that his signature, printed on his glowing annual reports, is surprisingly immature for a man of his age and position, the letters round as babies' eyes and drawn without conviction leftward and vertically and leaning right. I asked Chief Frank if I could use a recorder to take notes. He said I might not have any notes to take, so I left the recorder off. One of his men entered the office then and sat beside me, a silent witness.

Chief Frank said that Sheboygan had been maligned. In 1968, *The Wall Street Journal*, in a story about renewed enforcement of archaic sex laws, possibly as a way of harassing welfare recipients and student activists, cited Sheboygan as a notorious example. A British journalist saw the story and came to Sheboygan with good cheer to set the record straight. He went home and filed a story for one of London's dailies headlined SHEBOYGAN: TOWN OF PEEPING TOMS. Chief Frank didn't like that kind of treatment, especially since he had come down to the office on a Sunday morning to give the man his interview.

In fact, said Chief Frank, his department never aggressively ferrets out consensual crimes. His police investigate only when such cases are dumped on their doorstep. The cases result from citizen complaints. His job is to enforce the law, and if such laws are not enforced elsewhere, he doesn't see how other cities avoid enforcement. He suspects that blame for Sheboygan's record, which he believes to be less exceptional than some have claimed, lies with the legal profession. He believes Sheboygan lawyers encourage their clients to bring morals charges to beef up their divorce cases. The boys down in Madison, in the state legislature, ought to change the law, Chief Frank said. There's a difference, he believes, between the kind of man he called "John Q. Lunchbox," down at the factory, who is arrested for lewd and lascivious behavior and pays his thirty-five dollar fine and goes back to the factory a hero, and a doctor or school teacher or police officer who is similarly arrested and pays his fine but has his career ruined. I don't think that's justice, said Chief Frank. I think that's injustice.

But Jim Decko flaunted his situation. The sister of a detective lived in the same building, the chief said, and a police captain lived next door. By his behavior, Decko held them up to ridicule. We told him this couldn't go on, said the chief, but it went on anyway. Chief Frank also said that Sheboygan is a good place to raise a family, and he intended to keep it that way.

Stung by Frank's refusal to negotiate, Decko submitted his resignation to the Sheboygan school board and left for the weekend. When he got back he found his picture on the front page of the newspaper under the headline

'REC' DIRECTOR

DECKO, RESIGNS

The lead said that he had been charged with a morals offense. One of the first things he did that day was shave off the mustache he had been growing and have his sideburns shortened and his hair cut.

The Sheboygan County district attorney had jurisdiction in Jim Decko's case. His name is Lance Jones, and he is an elusive man. He has been known to speak to the press, but he wouldn't speak to me. He is not yet thirty, is single, and lives at home. He is an "active" district attorney who likes police work and rides with the patrol cars whenever he can. He is believed to show promise of a considerable political future in Wisconsin. After Decko had been charged with lewd and lascivious behavior, his attorney, Peter Bjork, appealed to District Attorney Jones to consider amending or dismissing the charge to avoid destroying Decko's career. Jones responded with a formal letter to the judge who would hear the case and carboned "all county law enforcement agencies." The letter said that lewd and lascivious charges were not negotiable and would be fully prosecuted. The letter angered Bjork, and he responded in a letter to the judge that described Lance Jones sarcastically as "savior of the morals of Sheboygan County." Bjork said that henceforth he would enter a plea of not guilty for every client charged with a consensual sex crime and would insist on a jury trial. "If the District Attorney's office has nothing better to do," Bjork wrote, "than to play around with this sort of matter, it apparently has plenty of time to clog up its own office and the Court's docket by trying all cases to conclusion." In fact, in 1969, faced with a heavier than usual load of consensual sex cases, Jones had reduced most of them to charges of disorderly conduct. With the Decko case, and without giving any reason for his decision, Jones inaugurated a new and more punitive policy of full prosecution—a policy, Jones's decision made clear, that was optional and arbitrary.

Decko left town, first to Chicago and then to Los Angeles. In L.A., encouraged by Bjork, he agreed to fight the case. Bjork filed a legal brief in Sheboygan County Court that supported a motion to dismiss the Decko charges on the grounds that they were unconstitutionally vague and overbroad and violated Decko's right to privacy. Judge John G. Buchen, county judge of branch number two of the Sheboygan County Court, soon denied the motion. In his opinion, the laws in question were clear to common understanding and applied to a specific kind of behavior. He noted that the constitutional right to privacy is subject to the law, including Wisconsin's lewd-and-lascivious law. The defendants, Judge Buchen wrote, "See nothing wrong in their alleged conduct and therefore [feel] they should not be subject to any criminal penalty. If this is the position taken by these defendants and others of the younger generation their remedy is through the legislature, not the courts. It should be remembered that the legislature reenacted the lewd and lascivious statute in its present form in 1955 in the general revision of the criminal code of Wisconsin."

"The State of Wisconsin," Judge Buchen concluded, "has a legitimate interest and duty to uphold moral dignity and general welfare of its citizens, and what constitutes conduct harmful to such public interest is for state legislature to decide. . . . A state law may not be invalidated on due process grounds because [it] may be unwise, improvident, or out of harmony with a particular school of thought."

Judge Buchen's father was an attorney and a Wisconsin state senator. He studied history in college under the famous historian Frederick Jackson Turner, who revolutionized the study of American history at the turn of the century by proposing that the advancing western frontier made Americans the civilized and democratic people they are. Gustave Buchen took up Turner's implicit challenge and late in life published privately a history of Sheboygan County. He thought the county had a past "as colorful and romantic as can be found anywhere," but that today "farms, towns, schools, churches and factories . . . provide the comforts of life and the amenities of civilization where only raw and untamed nature has since the dawn of time held sway." Gustave Buchen is dead, but his face and his political name live on in his son, whose eyes shine as bright, and whose hair is cut as close above the ears.

The present Judge Buchen was Sheboygan County District Attorney during the 1950s, when the county was notorious throughout Wisconsin for its whorehouses. "There was quite a hullabaloo," Judge Buchen told me in his chambers, on the fourth floor of the county courthouse. "The League of Women Voters and other do-good organizations were getting quite irate about the number of houses of ill fame. I remember seeing an article in the Minneapolis paper pointing out that Sheboygan County was *the* place to go. I didn't run on any ticket of reform, but there was a growing feeling that Sheboygan County wasn't very proud of its reputation. Busloads of college kids used to come up from Madison. So I did start an investigation with the help of what were then called state beverage-tax agents. We raided the houses several times and finally brought padlock proceedings. From the beginning to the end it took practically a year to get rid of them. But as district attorney, other than in that area of morals, I didn't prosecute except where necessary. I'm sure the cases of adultery and fornication and lascivious conduct I did prosecute were very isolated. The increase in prosecutions came after my time. For what reasons I don't know. More and more of these cases were investigated and prosecuted. Once something like that starts, successor district attorneys can't very well stop it. I'm sure there aren't many communities where some neighbor can call up the police department and say, *I've seen his car out there night after night, I know she's separated from her husband but not divorced,* and get the police to investigate. I remember when I was district attorney, if somebody came to me with a complaint like that—usually it would be a wife who suspected her husband—came to me like that without proof, I'd say, if you don't want to live with him get a divorce, this is grounds for divorce, this is your personal problem, not a community problem. Most prosecutors take that point of view. In the first place, you've got *enough* crime that you're concerned about without ferreting out this type of thing."

Judge Buchen's belief that consensual sex crimes are relatively harmless is probably reflected in his usual fine for such crimes, thirty-five dollars and costs, about as stiff as a fine for speeding. But he was not, in the Decko case, willing to carry his belief farther and throw the law itself out of his court. "I wasn't about to declare the statute unconstitutional. I wish Pete had taken that up to the Supreme Court. If I said it was unconstitutional it wouldn't mean it was, except for the purposes of the case. If I had said so it would have resulted in the dismissal of the case. No one would have been able to bring any more cases of that kind in my court. Wouldn't prevent them from going to some other court. We have three county courts and a circuit court that have almost identical jurisdiction." Judge Buchen was elected, not appointed, to office. You can imagine, in Sheboygan County, where they closed down the whorehouses only yesterday but where cohabitation is still a living crime, what an opponent might have to say if Judge Buchen took a firmer stand.

In California, Decko wasn't faring well. No work turned up in recreation, possibly because prospective employers were checking back with the Sheboygan school board, possibly because California is a veritable outdoor gymnasium of recreation directors at least as well qualified as Decko was. He went six weeks without a job before accepting a position as a sales clerk, and he lost that job because he cashed a customer's bad check. In some desperation, he became a night guard at a factory, and one night, brooding over his decline, he drove to a California town an hour away from Los Angeles and parked in a parking lot and slashed his wrists. The police found him before he bled to death and returned him to L.A. and with some encouragement he committed himself to a mental hospital but stayed only a few days and then checked out. When the police found him again he had taken a bottle of tranquilizers and was passed out on a beach. He wanted no more institutional group therapy then. When he had slept off the tranquilizers he got in his car and drove to Ohio, home.

A movement is abroad in Wisconsin to clear the books of consensual sex laws, and gambling and prostitution laws, too. A year ago, Governor Patrick J. Lucey appointed a Citizens Study Committee on Offender Rehabilitation. That committee recommended removing criminal prohibitions among consenting adults for gambling, fornication, adultery, sexual perversion, lewd and lascivious behavior, lewd, obscene or indecent matter, pictures or performances, and prostitution. State attorney general Robert W. Warren takes issue with the committee's recommendations. "The repeal of our criminal statutes [in these matters]," he told a meeting of the Wisconsin district attorneys' association, "in no way improves criminal justice. It in no way represents a disciplined or professional response to social problems." Whatever that means. Attorney general Warren found the idea of repealing laws against prostitution "most shocking of all." The report said that legal prostitution would protect prostitutes from criminal exploitation. Warren cited a "kidnap-torture-prostitution ring" recently uncovered in Madison to prove his contention that prostitution is a sordid business not deserving of legal protection.

A Wisconsin circuit judge ruled this year that the Wisconsin law that finds only female prostitution to be illegal is not discriminatory against women. "No one but a female can be a prostitute," Judge W. L. Jackman of the Dane County Circuit Court wrote to explain his decision. "The female alone is capable of the repeated and indiscriminate intercourse which makes prostitution a profitable occupation." In fact, male prostitutes service far more clients in an average night than female prostitutes do. But law-makers and judges in Wisconsin, where intercourse even between men and women is proscribed, may not know that.

Jim Decko got a job managing a department in a Penney's store in Toledo, and for a time seemed to be recovering from his depression. He wasn't. He was quietly going mad. After a party on Halloween night in 1971 he cut himself up some more, tore a gas stove off a wall and swallowed another bottle of tranquilizers. Friends recommended treatment. He wanted no more treatment. He said he knew that after treatment his life would never be the same. Which is the point of treatment, but he didn't see that point. He wanted his life to be the same as it had been before Sheboygan, before he was publicly branded a criminal for a crime for which he had not yet been tried. He had been successful. He wanted to be successful again. Penney's fired him for lack of ini-tiative.

Ray Shrank is a Madison attorney. He was assistant district at-torney in Sheboygan when the Decko case came up. Lance Jones was his immediate superior.

"I think both Lance Jones and Oakley Frank had the attitude that they would enforce the law," Shrank says. "If someone called them they would send someone out. If a case came up it would be investigated and charged. I don't think it had a high priority with Lance. I suspect the reason for enforcing the consensual sex laws is to get convictions. Most people who are charged on a morals charge will plead guilty, so you get a lot of convictions. Eighty per cent convictions. That looks good. If they get 80 per cent convic-tions from arrests, that looks very good and that makes them feel like they're doing a job. Eighty per cent convictions makes the district attorney look good. He looks like he knows what he's doing. It makes the police look good when they apply for funds, when they apply for more officers, when they apply to the city or for federal funding. And morals charges are easy to get convictions on, because, first of all, so many people when they're arrested are probably guilty and, second of all, they're embarrassed by their ar-rest and so they plead guilty and get a thirty-five dollar fine or something like that and they'd just as soon get out of the court and not have anybody else know about it rather than drag it on. Plus, because it's a misdemeanor, these people do not have the right to court-appointed counsel. Consequently, unless they can afford an attorney they aren't going to get an attorney into the picture who's going to challenge the state either on the facts or the law in general. And so it's kind of like disorderly conduct, because police are going to use it because they're going to get a conviction on it.

"I think Sheboygan is a very bigoted town," Shrank concludes. "They can say, well, if people are violating the law then they ought to be prosecuted, but I assume if they were violating that law they wouldn't want to be prosecuted for it. When you have people like that who aren't hurting anybody and you destroy their lives, you aren't fulfilling your role. The court's not fulfilling its role. Nobody's fulfilling his role. Because you're destroying people's lives for no reason at all."

Late in November, Jim Decko got hold of a gun and walked out into a city park one night and fired one shot into the air, perhaps to make sure the gun worked, perhaps halfheartedly hoping someone would hear it and come and save him from himself. But no one came, no one would save him, and after a while, breathing despair, overwhelmed by grief, emptied at last of everything except dread, he turned the gun around and squeezed the trigger and shot himself to death. His body lay all night face down in the snow. The police found it the next morning. He died innocent even of a victimless crime. The charge against him was never tried.

Sheboygan didn't kill Jim Decko, but it is implicated in his death more than accidentally. Suicide, self-murder, comments violently on every experience the suicide has had of joy and sorrow and love and hate and indifference, back all the way to the nipple and the womb. Like a contract torn in anger, it shreds across the large print and the small. But because it is a sickness, and because it is constructed not of present pain but of past experience, it is not inevitable. Decko might have lived. The immediate focus of his conflict was Sheboygan's capricious decision to select him for public humiliation. All his life, his distorted inner voice had warned him to be a good boy. When he tried to be a man, looking for his own way, that voice sounded forth again in the voice of the community where he lived and thought he had earned respect. Sounded forth with considerable cynicism, by the way, and even now the principal officials in the case pass the buck. Many believe the consensual sex laws are wrong. Jim Decko thought *he* was wrong. Sheboygan rejected him. Perhaps sensing his despair, employers rejected him. Toward the end, his terrified girl rejected him. By then his anger had become pathological, and to control that anger and also to release that anger, he destroyed the only world he dared destroy: himself. And stilled his inner voice, but stilled his human voice too, forever.

Decko's case isn't even typical of Sheboygan. A law so banal that it is used to fatten police statistics ought to protect the public from banal behavior, and, by and large, that is what Wisconsin's consensual sex laws do. A typical Sheboygan case on the books involved a couple living together in a trailer near the outskirts of town. The woman called the police because the man had been beating her. The police arrived, discovered that the two weren't married and charged them both with lewd and lascivious behavior. They pleaded guilty and were each fined thirty-five dollars plus court costs.

Judge Buchen described another case to me, a low comedy. A Sheboygan woman on the outs with her husband picked up two men in a bar and, as the judge put it, "shacked up with them in the back of their car" and then was driven to her home where she "shacked up" with them again. While the men were taking turns with the woman, they also took turns relieving the house of her husband's gun collection. The police stopped the men because of the guns in their car; an adultery charge followed when they made their confession.

In both cases, the police stumbled onto the crime. That much at least is unusual about them, because the usual lewd-and-lascivious investigation in Sheboygan is initiated by a tip from a neighbor or a relative. The tip leads the police to conduct their own investigation, thereby relieving the tipster of the distasteful democratic necessity of confronting the accused.

A law that butts into private lives and sunders them with public humiliation is squalid enough, but Wisconsin's lewd-and-lascivious law is even more squalid, because it isn't really designed to stop cohabitation: it is designed to spare the sensibilities of neighbors who might better spare their sensibilities simply by minding their own business. The act of imagination required of police is also required of informers, who must construct, from the dim form of a parked car or the wink of a light going out, those unmarried bodies joined in criminal lubricity, and must wrench that construction across emotions of outrage and disgust, and then swell up indignantly and call the police. And people who can abuse themselves that way are the kind of people the laws encourage.

The consensual sex laws in the United States are backward and bizarre. Most of us agree on that by now. They enjoin behavior that even our churches, no avant-garde in such matters, have approved within the conjugal bed. They criminalize behavior that harms no one, and therefore they encourage blackmail, including the blackmail of one spouse by another at divorce proceedings. Even more dangerously, they stand on the books as an invitation to officials to use them to harass minorities: welfare recipients, blacks, activists, all those with whose opinions or life styles the officials do not agree. That is part of what happened to Jim Decko. Says Ray Shrank: "I think one reason Lance Jones issued against Jim Decko was because he could then say, look, I'm not just going after the little people, I'm going after the big people."

As in every city where the police use consensual sex laws for their own purposes, Sheboygan's enforcement of its laws is capricious. Even the most conservative application of Kinsey statistics to a town the size of Sheboygan indicates that far more people must be breaking the law than are caught. That is true of most kinds of crime, but people convicted of burglary may at least be assumed to have done some actual harm to someone else's property or person. Victimless crime does have its victims: the accused and their families.

Nothing is right about Sheboygan's enforcement of the consensual sex laws, not the laws themselves, with their pious horror of nonprocreative physical love, not the encouragement the laws' enforcement gives to self-righteous peeping toms, not the embarrassment or hardship or worse that capricious enforcement inflicts upon the laws' victims, not the cynical and despicable use of convictions to lard police and prosecutor statistics, and not the damage done to the tradition of law itself when it is used, as it has been used by state legislatures, to impose religious sanctions upon all of us whether we like them or not.

Sheboygan has made itself notorious, and the lesson of that notoriety ought not to be lost on us. Laws in the hands of unscrupulous men, and laws in the hands of men with so many scruples they would like to visit them upon us all, are never dead letters. So long as they are on the books they can be revived and enforced. No politician dares take a stand in favor of premarital sex or homosexuality or cunnilingus, nor should he presume to, those matters being private. But every politician ought to take a stand in favor of our right to privacy, a right that consensual sex laws violate. It is a right that is eroding in the United States of America. It is a right that is finally the source and support of all other rights. Without it we would live looking over our shoulders like retreating thieves, and that is a way no man can live. Not Jim Decko, not I, and not you. So don't mention your name in Sheboygan. Whatever it may be, it's not the greatest little town in the world.

The Great Memphis
Pornography Trials

The setting for this ethereal circus, this ecclesiastical, Cromwellian,
P. T. Barnum extravaganza, is the courtroom of the United States
District Court for the Western District of Tennessee, in Memphis, and here, as the sleight-of-hand artists like to say, nothing is
quite what it seems. The courtroom is spacious, as it must be to
contain its subdued but zany crew, but though admission is free,
the stands are nearly bare of spectators. Jugglers and midgets work
here, fat ladies and clowns, acrobats, bareback riders of noble proportions, sliders of poles and wires, sweepers of tanbark and dung,
and a dashing ringmaster calls the acts, but all are disguised
behind straight faces and business suits of the most ordinary cut.

Because it needs no spotlights to heighten the drama, the courtroom is lit like a mental ward by cold fluorescents recessed above
white plastic panels.The wall behind the judge's bench is faced
with gray marble, a feeble attenuation of symbolism alluding to
the mighty *Lex Romana* of ancient days, but the green draperies
drawn open before it reveal no windows at all. The bench, its
lines classically severe, is walnut, built in two tiers, the judge
dominating in his black robe above, the court reporter and the
clerk ministering below; the clerk runs his Middle English *oyesses*
in a Tennessee dialect, compelling the performers to stand and
bow their heads. The witness chair is placed to the judge's right,
under his magisterial wing, and no man may approach it except
by his leave. Beyond the witness chair extends the crowded jury
box, where one of the female jurors wears a bandage over her ear.
The prosecutor and his assistant ply stacks of incriminating
documents—telephone bills, canceled checks, a detritus of notes
torn from personalized memo pads—at a table cozily near the

jury, facing the bench. At a row of tables on the other side of the room, balefully confronting the jury, sit the angry defendants, those who haven't skipped the country, those at least who have physical existence (for corporations and the shells of corporations are also here on trial) and the presumption of guilt hangs heavy as cannon smoke in the air.

The First Amendment, libertarians say, is on trial in Memphis, Tennessee, in this severe, unlikely circus tent, but legally it is not: the First Amendment has been excused from attendance by prior decision of the United States Supreme Court. Not the First Amendment but one of its most impoverished representatives is on trial: *Deep Throat,* a reel of transparent acetate on which are reproduced images of the sexual organs of a species of mammal called *Homo sapiens* in the process of joining and unjoining to no apparent serious literary, artistic, political or scientific purpose. *School Girl* stood trial before *Deep Throat* (and was declared obscene), as did numerous other reels of acetate described variously as "hard-core," "pornographic," "sexually explicit" or "wet," and so will *The Devil in Miss Jones* after, if the longevity of judges, prosecutors and defendants allows—for these are dogged, complicated proceedings.

Deep Throat is on trial and with it Harry Reems—the young actor who played the crazy doctor who diagnosed the lady's ailment—and a hefty crowd of businessmen who purveyed the film to an eager America, earning an estimated $25 million or more for their pains, but Linda Lovelace, she of the wink and the girlish grin and the golden throat, is nowhere to be seen, nor has she been charged with the crime. The charge against the defendants, individual or corporate or fugitive, is conspiracy to distribute an obscene film interstate in violation of certain sections of the United States Criminal Code, a felony punishable by heavy fines and/or up to fifteen years in federal prison, and at the judge's express ruling, no one picked to be seated on the bored, bewildered jury has ever seen a sexually explicit film before.

The federal conspiracy laws are shotgun laws. They are designed to catch criminals whose crimes reach beyond local jurisdictions—drug distributors, for example, or interstate auto theft gangs. They are also complicated laws. To help the jury understand the trial, the prosecutor eagerly steps forward to explain.

He is only thirty-two years old, but he is six feet one, broad as a yeoman, dressed in a dark suit of conservative cut with his dark brown hair cropped close above his ears, and his face is puffy and pale despite the bully Memphis sun, because he has spent endless hours in windowless federal courtrooms pursuing conspiracies, pursuing military purchasing kickback schemes, insurance frauds, illegal bombings, Mexican drug pipelines, multistate prostitution rings. Behind his back some of the defendants call him "Potato Face." He knows and cherishes their hostility, and in the hall outside the courtroom, when they hiss him as he passes, he threatens with boyish humor to drop a "stink bomb" among them.

His name is Larry Parrish. He is an assistant U.S. attorney for the Western District of Tennessee. He was born in Nashville. He majored in political science at the University of Tennessee, where he also took his degree in law. He worked in Washington as a trial attorney for the Federal Trade Commission, specializing in consumer fraud. He was hired to his Memphis office in 1969, in the heyday of the Nixon years. He is married, the father of three, an elder in Memphis' First Evangelical Church. He has been officially commended for his prosecutorial skill by the Justice Department. His boss has described him as demonstrating "an almost instinctive ability to discern the true form and structure of perfidy."

He is pledged to enforce the law. He is also committed to the cause. He tells the press he "would rather see dope on the streets than pornography." He means, he says, that "the commercialization of sex in violation of a statute stands to have a more detrimental effect on society at large than heroin. The heroin hurts the addict, but obscenity hurts us all. And there's absolutely no question that there is such a thing as obscenity. The Supreme Court has said that there is and Congress has said that there is." He paces metronomically back and forth before the jury and explains the law:

MR. PARRISH: A conspiracy is simply a plan by people. It takes two to make a conspiracy, just like it does to tango. There can be two, a hundred and two, or a thousand and two, but it can't be one. Two people or corporations or legal entities make a conspiracy, and those people or entities have to have a plan and they have to plan to do acts, to engage in conduct, and the conduct that they plan to engage in has to be against the law.

Now, I make this distinction because this is very important. . . . It is not necessary that they know that what they plan to do is a violation of the law. . . . [The law] says "unlawfully combined, conspired, confederated, agreed and planned to engage in conduct against the laws of the United States. . . ." Notice it does not say that they planned to violate the laws of the United States, [it says they] planned to engage in conduct, that conduct which would be a violation of the law. The indictment alleges that the conduct that they planned to engage in was to distribute *Deep Throat* in interstate commerce. It alleges that *Deep Throat* was obscene, and being obscene it could not be distributed [legally] in interstate commerce in the manner alleged in the indictment. And what they planned to do was to distribute it in interstate commerce for the purpose of profit.

At which point, defense counsel interrupts to object that explanations of the law should be left to the judge, and the judge, Federal District Judge Harry Wellford, a short, handsome, athletic, impatient man with wavy silver-gray hair who came to the federal bench directly from private practice after a stint as Senator Howard Baker's Tennessee campaign manager, reminds the jury that he will instruct them in the law, and then the prosecutor continues:

MR. PARRISH: Now, obviously all of the persons who are represented in the courtroom here, and all of the other persons who you will hear from and hear about, did not join this plan all at the same time. Everybody didn't get in one big room and say that is our plan. A conspiracy is a plan conceived, it is put into operation and others can join in, and when others join in over a period of time they become responsible as if they had been there when it first started. . . . For that to be prosecutable [it will have to be shown] that they joined in and that they knew of the plan and that they participated as a co-conspirator in the plan.

Larry Parrish is not exceptionally articulate, but he is intelligent and exceptionally thorough, and the conspiracy charges he has brought in the *Deep Throat* case have far-reaching implications.

If the jury finds *Deep Throat* obscene, and finds that a conspiracy existed, then anyone involved in the film's production and distribution could be charged. The jury is a Memphis jury—eight black women, one black man, one white woman, four white men counting alternates—and it has never seen a sexually explicit film before; several of the defendants, including Harry Reems, have never been in Memphis before; according to the testimony later at the trial, one of the defendants, a Memphis theater owner, was muscled into paying for showing *Deep Throat* after being caught by the distributors with a bootleg print; but the jury could judge all these defendants conspirators. Linda Lovelace would be a conspirator too, but she has been given immunity from prosecution in exchange for her testimony (she never appeared at the trial; FBI agents were unable to track her down). Gerald Damiano, who wrote and coproduced and directed *Deep Throat*, would also be a conspirator, but under immunity he has come to town to testify, and from the witness stand he speaks of the requirements of art and fingers the defendants who put up money for his film and later bought him out.

Anyone, anywhere, who helped make *Deep Throat*, who handled a print, who paid money to the several individuals and corporations who produced and distributed it—the gaffer who arranged the lights; the Miami bachelor who loaned the *Deep Throat* crew his swimming pool and his house; the laboratory that processed the rushes; the many projectionists in Los Angeles and New York and points between who loaded the reels; the popcorn sellers; the ticket takers; anyone who had anything at all to do with the film except the hundreds of thousands of Americans who went to see it—was theoretically part of the conspiracy and could have been indicted. In fact, ninety-nine other citizens and corporations were listed on the indictment as unindicted coconspirators, including the agency that designed *Deep Throat*'s advertisements. The only reason the defendants don't fill all eleven floors of the Memphis federal office building is that Parrish and his boss, U. S. Attorney Thomas Turley, as Parrish explains, aren't after "the low people—we don't want the popcorn sellers and the ticket takers. The low people aren't the real people and prosecuting them at that level has no effect at all. It's analogous to getting addicts instead of pushers. So we resolved that if we were going to move in this area we wanted action on a high level, and decided to treat it as a national crime." And so they did: a national crime for which, had they so chosen, literally thousands of Americans might have been indicted, jailed, bailed, shipped to Memphis and required to remain there at there own expense for the duration of a trial that would prove to last a lengthy ten weeks, paying their counsel if they wanted better than a public defender. You see the possibilities.

The obscenity-conspiracy strategy, if it succeeded, would be a powerful new bludgeon for censors to wield (even as a threat it had already had a profound punitive effect: Harry Reems estimated the *Deep Throat* and *Devil* trials would cost him fifty thousand dollars in expenses and lost work). It had not yet succeeded for Larry Parrish at the time of the *Deep Throat* trial; the *School Girl* jury found that film obscene but found only interstate transport, not conspiracy. A Kentucky jury found conspiracy in a case involving *Deep Throat—United States* v. *Marks—*in 1975, and *Marks* had been upheld on appeal and accepted for review by the U. S. Supreme Court. An immediate question that defendants and reporters raised was where the strategy had originated.

U. S. Attorney Turley claimed the Memphis cases originated locally. He also claimed that the guidelines established for preparing them for trial have been adopted as models by the Justice Department, which knows a good thing when it sees one. Turley is a Nixon appointee who helped rebuild the Republican Party in Tennessee, and some have seen the heavy hands of Richard Nixon and John Mitchell, the law-and-order boys, in the Memphis prosecutions. Richard Kleindienst announced the *School Girl* indictments from Washington in 1973, and federal grand juries began working on the cases several years before, but the immediate indictments almost certainly originated with Turley and Parrish. Which is not to say that the ghosts of Nixon and Mitchell don't walk abroad in the Memphis courtroom, because they do: propelled by the decisions of the Nixon Supreme Court that make the trial possible; by the co-operation, since at least 1971, of the FBI, represented among other things by nearly one thousand depositions collected in most of the major cities of the land; by the approval by the Nixon and Ford administrations of grants of immunity, which are co-ordinated in Washington. Fred Grahame, the CBS correspondent and former practicing attorney, came to Memphis during the trial, talked to Turley and Parrish, and said afterward that he thought the conspiracy approach and the monumental series of trials had more to do with a climate of opinion in Washington than with any specific Justice Department scheme to crack down on "pornography," which nicely makes the point. Washington approves, and Washington is following and co-operating to give the strategy a chance. You see the possibilities.

The ten trials Parrish has scheduled are estimated to cost the government two million dollars. Since *Deep Throat* must be judged obscene before a criminal-conspiracy conviction can be sustained—if it isn't obscene, then conspiracy becomes business as usual—it might seem logical, and more economical, to test a jury's opinion of its obscenity first. Instead, Parrish has chosen to show the film to the jury at the end of his presentation, eight long weeks into the trial. Certainly he hopes to stun the jurors as close as possible to their time of deliberation. Certainly he also means to harass the defendants with expenses. These are standard, if deplorable, methods of attack.

But a remark Parrish made when I interviewed him at mid-trial suggests a further purpose. I asked him about the defendants. He said, with a touch of sarcasm, "It didn't surprise me to uncover *mafiosa*. It's that kind of business." Parrish denies using the obscenity-conspiracy strategy to get at organized crime. So does Turley, though he also describes the defendants as "some of the leading organized-crime figures who have taken over this industry." Both men believe that obscenity is crime enough. "We're going to get rid of all these perverted minds," Parrish chillingly promised a CBS producer during the trial. But he could hardly have failed to see the dramatic effect on the jury of the appearance and activities of the defendants, who were tough, physical, secretive men with Italian names. Or the dramatic effect on the jury of some of the testimony, which included allegations of violent threats made to witnesses to prevent them from testifying.

Consider the defendants listed in the indictment, most of whom now sit lined up at their row of tables facing the jury, alternating with their expensive New York, Florida, Atlanta and Memphis attorneys: Anthony Joseph Peraino, a fugitive in Italy from a federal warrant. Robert J. DeSalvo, a fugitive from a federal warrant, last located in Nassau. Michael Cherubino, business associate and trouble shooter for *Deep Throat*'s Fort Lauderdale

distributors. Louis Peraino, son of Anthony Peraino, coproducer
with Gerald Damiano of *Deep Throat* and principal in its distribution. Joseph Peraino, Louis Peraino's uncle, another principal, a
big man of nearly three hundred pounds. Carl R. Carter, a
Memphis theater owner already convicted of showing an obscene
film and sentenced to three years and fined ten thousand dollars in
the *School Girl* case. Mel Friedman, a Los Angeles distributor
who manages Tennessee theaters (Parrish remarks of him scorn-
fully in his opening statement, "There is one instance where it
will be shown that he engineered the film being seized by the
police in Atlanta in order to get publicity for the film, and then
raised the tickets two dollars so people would come and continue
to make money in that respect"). Mario DeSalvo, Robert De-
Salvo's brother and another principal in the Lauderdale operation,
formerly a bricklayer. Angelo Miragliotta, whom government
witnesses would describe as a "go-fer" at the Lauderdale office,
who suffered a heart attack during the trial the day after Judge
Wellford admonished him for laughing at a witness' testimony,
was awarded a mistrial and returned to a Miami hospital to recu-
perate. Anthony Novello, another Lauderdale "go-fer." And sitting as far away from the other defendants as possible, sitting not
at the line of tables but in a corner, on the first row of spectator
benches, looking wounded and forlorn, Harry Reems.

The witness whose testimony may be most damaging to these
defendants takes the stand in the trial's fifth week. His name is
Robert Bernstein and he has been chief booker for the Lauderdale
office. He has a badly, perhaps recently, broken nose. He wears a
green double-knit suit, a pale green shirt, a dark green tie. He is
balding, middle-aged, and he sports a deep Florida tan. His father
was a lawyer in the early motion-picture industry. He has owned
adult theaters—owns them now, and is still booking X-rated films
when he testifies, though he claims he's getting out of the business as fast as he can—but a few years ago his business failed and
the DeSalvo brothers picked him up and gave him a job.
Guided carefully by Parrish, he testifies under a grant of immunity.

Bernstein testifies that the system of distribution the defendants practiced was different from the industry norm and private to
the point of elaborate secrecy. The defendants, he says, shipped
Deep Throat around the country in the trunks of automobiles or

aboard commercial buses in boxes labeled "Projector Parts." They hired checkers who stood at ticket booths counting heads to make sure they weren't getting stiffed on the handle, and week by week they carted their 50 per cent of the proceeds back to Lauderdale in cash, as much as fifty thousand dollars at a time stuffed into their suitcases and their pockets. Bernstein tells of clandestine meetings at airports, of territories marked off for other operators, of salaries paid partly by check and partly in cash, of money—"green," he calls it—carried off to the Bahamas. He also tells of violent action against a rash of bootleg prints. In one case, he says, in Kansas City, some of the defendants roughed up a projectionist, seized an offending print and dumped it into the Missouri River.

The jury isn't allowed to hear many of Bernstein's allegations of violence; defense counsel argues outside the jury's hearing that such allegations don't show furtherance of the conspiracy but would prejudice the jury against the defendants, and for a change Judge Wellford, whose sympathies usually go to the prosecution, agrees. The jury does hear Bernstein charge that the defendants have threatened his life, the wife of one of the defendants telling Bernstein's wife that her husband is going to send Bernstein an "Italian kiss," whatever that is. The jury also, on cross-examination, hears Bernstein admit perjuring himself twice before the grand jury that investigated *Deep Throat*, at which point Parrish steps in and asks Bernstein if his present statements are true, and Bernstein swears that they are. The jury, which has listened to Bernstein's long testimony without expression, hardly bats an eye, and he leaves the courtroom as he arrived, nervous but defiant. How much weight the jury will give his testimony remains to be seen; if they weigh it heavily, it could be devastating, even though the allegations of violence have nothing directly to do with the conspiracy charges.

Parrish calls seventy-seven witnesses in a trial that lasts ten weeks, and one by one they index for the jury a textbook of office layouts, accounting systems, mail schedules, print-handling procedures, the comings and goings of various defendants—a short course in business management.

A few are more spectacular. Robert DeSalvo's secretary reveals herself to have been a secret informer for the FBI and the IRS, a role Bernstein also played after the government confronted him with his perjury. An expert witness, a physician, testifies that premarital sex is destructive, oral sex a perversion, and group sex sick. Only one-on-one sex with one's spouse is healthy and normal, he says. Another expert witness announces that sexual freedom and pornography caused the downfall of the Roman Empire and other ancient civilizations. Ninety civilizations in all, a Parrish expert had testified at the *School Girl* trial, including Rome, Greece, ancient India, Babylon, Egypt and the Syrian Empire.

The case that most observers at the trial find appalling is the case of Harry Reems. Reems, who borrowed his crazy doctor from an old and classic burlesque routine, who says that as an actor he has not yet "exposed" himself, who got into sexually explicit films for the money and the fun when he was studying acting in New York, who once did Wheaties commercials in Puerto Rico, who thinks sex films "a very mechanical, physical job," who decided to get out of the business after starring in nine of the eleven explicit films that grossed more than $1 million by the time of the trial, was called to Memphis from Rome, where he was beginning to find roles in Italian feature films. Trim, tanned, handsome, a legitimate actor with union cards to prove it and stints off Broadway and with the National Shakespeare Company behind him, he had worked as crew on *Deep Throat* for six days, earning twenty-five dollars a day, and as an actor for one day, earning one hundred dollars. He had not produced the film or distributed the film or promoted the film, but he was charged with conspiracy as certainly as the other defendants on trial.

His indictment was a direct threat to film makers everywhere. "I keep remembering," film critic Arthur Knight wrote in the *Hollywood Reporter* during the course of the trial (he would later appear to testify), "that soon after the Supreme Court's *Miller* decision, in 1973, the first film to be labeled obscene was not porno trash but *Carnal Knowledge*. Fortunately," Knight went on,

the charge was dismissed. But considering the climate in Memphis and our government's all-out determination to secure convictions, this might not be the case were that same film to go on trial today. Instead of Harry Reems it could just as well be Jack Nicholson, Art Garfunkle, Candice Bergen, and Ann-Margret standing in the docket—not to mention Mike Nichols, Joseph Levine, Jules Feiffer, Richard Sylbert, Sam

O'Steen and all the others who contributed to that watershed film. . . . [Reems's] conviction would imply that anyone—yes, anyone—connected with a picture that might conceivably be labeled obscene (Warren Beatty's upcoming *Hard Core*, for example) would be in jeopardy.

To underscore both the threat and the concern, Reems's Memphis counsel, an intensely competent young trial attorney named Bruce Kramer, who is also president of the West Tennessee chapter of the ACLU, arranged for Nicholson, Beatty, Knight, Buck Henry, Louise Fletcher, Tony Bill (producer of *The Sting* and *Taxi Driver*), Bert Schneider (who directed *Five Easy Pieces*, among others) and George Slaff (a Hollywood agent and attorney who once worked for Samuel Goldwyn) to come to Memphis to testify to the general question of an actor's limited control over the films in which he appears. Arthur Knight made the stand, as did Slaff and Bill, before Judge Wellford, livid with anger, sent the jury out of the courtroom and announced to Kramer that he was not going to allow any more expert testimony to this point, that the First Amendment didn't apply, that actors who performed in filth were not above the law. Only days before, Wellford had seen *Deep Throat* for the first time. Apparently the memory still stung.

"I never took this thing seriously," Reems said outside the courtroom. "I'd had many times when guys from out of town, FBI, would come busting through my door with the guns out. When the New York grand jury came around a few years back and subpoenaed me, the local morality squad talked to me about it. They said, 'We're not after you. We're not after the actors. We know you guys don't control it.' Actors have nothing whatsoever to do with the finished film. We do our work and sign away any control over editing or distribution. It's part of the standard contract. Hell, I've made soft-core films that people would later go back to and cut in hard-core inserts I didn't make. It's incredible." Reems also pronounced the last word on the technique that gave *Deep Throat* its title: "It hurts. Its not a very sensual feeling. It doesn't feel good at all. It's sort of like putting a ring on and off your finger. You don't feel anything up front, and then there's the ring, and then there's nothing." For doing something that hurts, Reems sits in a Memphis courtroom charged with conspiracy.

The appearance of the national press at the *Deep Throat* trial seemed to cause U. S. Attorney Thomas Turley discomfort. He was, at least, more defensive about his purposes than Parrish, who proudly identified his own standards with those promulgated by Congress and the Supreme Court. Turley, a tall, lanky, bald, weathered man of sixty-two who practiced law out of a one-man office for thirty years before accepting federal appointment, is colorful and articulate, quick with original turns of phrase. He once described a rural hoodlum whom Parrish prosecuted as "typical of a breed of cockleburr bullies" that infests the countryside. His explanation for the Memphis pornography trials is appropriately ingenuous.

"I came to his office with specific ideas on writing," he told me. "I would willingly stand up on Milton's *Areopagitica* and wave a sword. I always thought it was every man to his own taste, that some people prefer opera and other people prefer burlesque. I thought that since I was raised a country-town boy and served in the walking army and practiced law for thirty years I could say with the ancient that 'I am a man and a Roman and nothing human is foreign to me.' I thought I was a man of the world. But these damned films are *raunchy*. The *mafioso* were coming in to take over production and distribution and they were getting filthier and worse by the week. And they don't give me a problem. Responsible psychologists tell us that some of these things are destructive. We had a prostitution case here, and we found crude efforts to recruit prostitutes by photographing them and turning them out. Girls as young as twelve and thirteen are getting recruited, beaten, hooked on drugs and then shipped and sold around the country. Sometimes in bunches. You tell me about victimless crime!" Which has nothing to do with *Deep Throat*, but Turley does not find it easy to justify the Memphis trials, or perhaps he fears that out-of-towners will take him for a hick, which he is not. He is, rather, a clever and quite possibly an ambitious man. He was appointed to the Tennessee Supreme Court in 1971, but such complaint was raised that he asked that his appointment be withdrawn. He may have been more interested in the federal bench or in a federal appointment, though he denies personal ambition and insists that he continues to pay rent on his one-man office in case he gets tired of his federal job.

Nevertheless, he, not Parrish, authorized the Memphis trials, as he personally authorizes all trials in his district, and in boosting Parrish for the Justice Department's John Marshal Award—which Parrish received in the spring of 1975—he was also forcefully and even heavy-handedly boosting himself. Only one other U.S. attorney has successfully pursued a national obscenity conspiracy, and no other has assembled so large a list of indictments—in Turley's case, indictments against more than sixty individuals and corporations. Nor would any others necessarily find assistants willing to try them. "Tell most assistant U.S. attorneys," commented Fred Grahame, "that they'll have to spend the next two years of their lives trying skin flicks and they'd say, 'No way, brother!' Parrish is obviously a zealot." But since Turley is obviously not a zealot, what explains his decision to spend millions of dollars and thousands of man-hours on obscenity prosecutions? It had, as the trial ground on, all the appearance of a grandstand play designed to catch Washington's eye. If the *Marks* case passes muster with the Supreme Court, as the Court of Appeals in sustaining it obviously thought it would, and if the same maneuver works in Memphis, then it will work almost anywhere, and Turley and Parrish will be credited with a monumental victory in the obscenity wars. And credit, as we know, brings reward.

Yet the Memphis trials could not have been staged without the decision of the United States Supreme Court to retreat from its past liberalism in matters of First Amendment protection.

In 1957, under the leadership of Chief Justice Earl Warren, the Court decided a pair of cases collectively cited as *U.S.* v. *Roth*. The Court was asked to judge if antiobscenity statutes were unconstitutional because they denied freedom of speech. Mr. Justice Brennan wrote the leading opinion. It questioned "whether obscenity is utterance within the area of protected speech" and held that it was not.

The Brennan opinion then proceeded to define unprotected obscenity. In the course of that definition, in what amounted to an aside, Brennan wrote: "All ideas having even the slightest redeeming social importance . . . have the full protection of the guarantees." The phrase became the foundation for a new attack on the antiobscenity statutes, and by 1966, in the case of John Cleland's *Memoirs of a Woman of Pleasure* (*Fanny Hill*), it was accorded what appeared to be the full force of judicial law. Brennan wrote of *Memoirs* that "a book cannot be proscribed unless it is found to be *utterly* without redeeming social importance." Brennan again wrote for only a three-member plurality of the Court, however; the Justices who constituted the rest of the *Memoirs* majority found the book to be not obscene on other grounds.

The *Memoirs* decision did not eliminate the possibility of obscenity trials, especially where "hard-core" films were concerned, but it did make conviction appear to be less likely, and it deterred prosecutors and thoroughly confused the lower courts. The immediate effect of the decision was to embolden the makers of sexually explicit films. There were only anonymous skin flicks before it; there were *Deep Throats* and *Devils* and *Green Doors* after it, and Americans in great numbers went to see them, many taking their spouses, many for the first time. The New York *Times* announced the era of Porno Chic; Johnny Carson saw *Deep Throat*, and Truman Capote, and some of the Kennedys, and Ed McMahon stood outside the theater in New York one day quaffing his favorite beverage and waving pedestrians in.

But the justices of the Supreme Court hadn't really agreed on what constituted obscenity. They had written no fewer than five separate opinions in the *Memoirs* case. Lower courts didn't know which to rely on, and obscenity cases continued to work their way up to the Supreme Court on appeal. Between 1967 and 1971 the Court practiced justice by head count. The justices took a vote. Whenever five agreed on the obscenity of the material before them they refused to review the case; whenever five agreed on the redeeming social value of the material before them they summarily reversed the lower court. In effect, without providing guidelines for the lower courts, they set themselves up as a national board of censors. They dealt with no fewer than thirty-one cases this way.

They didn't like the role and they didn't like turning cases back without explanation. They obviously had two options: they must either find a clearer and more reliable definition of obscenity or get out of the censorship business entirely. Given the trend of their previous decisions toward increasing liberalism in matters of expression, they might well have chosen the latter option, but at that point the Warren Court became the Burger Court, and four new men came onto the court in the short space of four years, appointees of Richard Nixon, and Chief Justice Warren Burger, at least, had no intention of allowing the open circulation of sexually explicit material in the United States of America: he knew the Nixon administration's position on obscenity and basically agreed with it.

Nixon had announced it most blatantly in 1970 when he angrily rejected the liberal and enlightened report of the President's Commission on Obscenity and Pornography that Lyndon Johnson had appointed in 1967. "So long as I am in the White House," Nixon had said, "there will be no relaxation of the national effort to control and eliminate smut from our national life." He had compared "the pollution of our culture" to "the pollution of our once pure air and water." He had theorized that "the warped and brutal portrayal of sex in books, plays, magazines and movies, if not halted and reversed, could poison the wellsprings of American and Western culture and civilization. . . . American morality is not to be trifled with." Of the truth of the latter statement, at least, he would soon have reason to know.

Chief Justice Burger decided to try to find a way to assemble a clear majority of justices behind a new obscenity decision, and on June 21, 1973, he succeeded. The decision he announced that day concerning a number of cases generically titled *Miller* v. *California* expanded the definition of obscenity and made its prosecution a matter of local option, and for the first time in years a majority delivered a common opinion on the subject. Justices Burger, Blackmun, Powell, Rehnquist and White joined; significantly, four of the five were the Nixon appointees. Mr. Justice Douglas, who has consistently argued that the First Amendment means exactly what it says, predictably dissented. Mr. Justice Brennan, with Justices Stewart and Marshall joining, dissented separately on less absolute gounds.

Burger delivered the majority decision. He said that the Court was now undertaking "to formulate standards more concrete than those in the past. . . ." He repudiated the value test of the *Memoirs* case (*"utterly* without redeeming social value"), saying it "called on the prosecution to prove a negative . . . a burden nearly impossible to discharge under our criminal standards of proof." His emphasis on the problems of the prosecution was prophetic of the rest of the decision: he went on to redefine obscenity as "works which, taken as a whole, appeal to the prurient interest in sex, which portray sexual conduct in a patently offensive way, and which, taken as a whole, do not have serious literary, artistic, political or scientific value." The last clause, changing "*utterly* without" to "serious," changed everything. Burger justified it by emphasizing the force of numbers: "We do not adopt as a constitutional standard the '*utterly* without redeeming social value' test . . . ; that concept has never commanded the adherence of more than three justices at one time." The liberals, he said in effect, have finally been outvoted.

Burger expressed the local-option judgment this way: "Nothing in the First Amendment requires that a jury must consider hypothetical and unascertainable 'national standards'. . . . It is neither realistic nor constitutionally sound to read the First Amendment as requiring that the people of Maine or Mississippi accept public depiction of conduct found tolerable in Las Vegas, or New York City."

One of Burger's footnotes implicitly slapped the hand of the President's Commission on Obscenity and Pornography. It cited not the report of the commission's liberal majority, which recommended legalizing sexually explicit material for consenting adults, but the repressive report of its three-man minority, which had claimed that viewing erotic materials might lead to crime. And near the end of the *Miller* decision came a peculiar comparison between sex and drugs:

> One can concede that the "sexual revolution" of recent years may have had useful by-products in striking layers of prudery from a subject long irrationally kept from needed ventilation. But it does not follow that no regulation of patently offensive "hard core" materials is needed or permissible; civilized people do not allow unregulated access to heroin because it is a derivative of medicinal morphine.

Commercial depiction of explicit sexual behavior was thus made analogous to the heroin traffic, and the stage was set for Larry Parrish's more extreme formulation, "I'd rather see dope on the streets than pornography."

The justices of the *Miller* majority may have hoped that they had dispensed with the constitutional question once and for all, but they would soon discover that they had not, largely because their decision was inconsistent and even self-contradictory. Mr.

Justice Douglas' dissent raised one immediate issue that came up again in the case of *U.S.* v. *Marks,* the Kentucky conspiracy case that included *Deep Throat* and that the Supreme Court has recently agreed to review.

"Today we leave open the way," Douglas wrote at the beginning of his *Miller* dissent, "for California to send a man to prison for distributing brochures that advertise books and a movie under freshly written standards defining obscenity which until today's decision were never the part of any law. . . . A brand-new test would put a publisher behind bars under a new law improvised by the courts after the publication. That . . . has all the evils of an *ex post facto* law."

Deep Throat was filmed late in 1971 and released in 1972, before the *Miller* decision. The *Marks* attorneys therefore argued before the Court of Appeals that the retroactive application of *Miller* was effectively the application of *ex post facto* standards. The Court of Appeals ruled bluntly that *Deep Throat* and the other films involved in the case were obscene by any standards, whether *Miller* or *Memoirs.* Yet the Supreme Court justices weren't entirely convinced, or they wouldn't have agreed to review.

The *Marks* appeal also struck at the local-option portion of the *Miller* decision, arguing that a locally restricted jury couldn't constitutionally decide the issue of obscenity in a national conspiracy case. The Court of Appeals upheld the correctness of the jury's composition in the *Marks* case, but judges in at least three other obscenity cases coming on for appellate review have not done so. The Supreme Court apparently overlooked the possibility of combining the obscenity and conspiracy laws to force federal censorship beyond local jurisdictions; as a result, it must deal again with the issue of national versus local standards of judgment.

The *Miller* decision made the obscenity-conspiracy strategy possible, however, giving the people of Maine or Mississippi control over public depiction of conduct found tolerable in Las Vegas or New York City; and now in Memphis, on a sunny spring day, the *Deep Throat* jury, which has finally seen a sexually explicit film and been enlightened as to the true form and structure of perfidy, goes out at 4:30 P.M. to deliberate, having first been charged by Judge Wellford that neither the First Amendment nor cruel censorship are among the issues it must decide.

Since some of us are still free men, and also have opinions in these matters, perhaps we should constitute ourselves an imaginary jury and go out to deliberate as well.

By the force of both legislative and judicial laws, there exists today in the United States of America, one of whose most eminent founders, Thomas Jefferson, long ago swore "eternal hostility against every form of tyranny over the mind of man," a category of materials—inanimate objects—declared to be criminal and obscene. These materials may be possessed in the privacy of one's home, but they may neither be created nor distributed nor bought nor sold. They are not drugs of powerful and potentially asocial effect, nor government secrets whose loosing could precipitate distant wars or proximate humiliations, nor counterfeit bills that might debase the currency on whose bloating certitudes we depend. They are materials far more dangerous than these: they are photographs, still or motion-picture, of naked, priapic human beings at work imitating play.

Almost uniquely in American law, the criminality of such images has never been precisely defined. Such terms as "appeal to the prurient interest in sex" and "patently offensive," for example, describe not the criminality of these images but merely two possible responses jurors might have when they view them.

Yet the images that judges and legislators have consistently condemned as obscene can be simply defined. They are images of human beings engaged in sexual play or intercourse with engorged genitals fully displayed, images frankly offered for sexual stimulation and used by other human beings for purposes of recreation.

Authorities have chosen not to define obscenity in this straightforward way, because such definition includes no assertion of social harm. Without an assertion of social harm, without an imagined appeal to prurient interest, without patent offensiveness, images of sexual congress, no matter how casual, take their place beside other images—of human beings being born, eating, suffering pubescence, loving, voting, marrying, praying, dying, giving birth—as mute but eloquent expressions of the enormous glory and the tragic brevity of human existence. And such expressions, however lulling or shocking, are protected from limitation by the First Amendment.

No one goes to jail for taking baby pictures, but people have gone to jail for taking pictures of the plain connection whereby babies are conceived. The crucial term of the definition is "recreation." Its counterpart in legal phraseology is "prurient interest." Erotic images, the Supreme Court has repeatedly held, are freely available to scholars and scientists, and they are sometimes required viewing for judges and juries, as are images of accidents and violent death. They become criminal only when purveyed to the common man. Charles Rembar, the distinguished New York attorney who defended *Lady Chatterley's Lover, Tropic of Cancer,* and *Memoirs* before the Supreme Court, writes in his book *The End of Obscenity:*

> A curious phenomenon in censorship is the censor's personal immunity to the infectious [material]. The moral fiber in jeopardy is always somebody else's. In not one of these trials did the prosecution produce a witness—or his doctor, or his clergyman—who, as a result of his [exposure], suffered physical, moral or spiritual deterioration. But prosecutors are certain it can happen—to other people.

We may look at the obscene with impunity so long as we have our thinking caps on. Take them off, go out for a hot evening or a lazy afternoon, and we risk becoming criminal, we risk being doomed. The Supreme Court, having achieved its majority, is weary of these apparent scholasticisms, and would remand them to lower jurisdictions to reduce its burdensome load. Only Mr. Justice William O. Douglas saw the point, though even without his paralyzing stroke his age would not have carried it. He declared his exposure to such images a matter of taste, not of law, and being a man of taste he never bothered to look at them, and like a sovereign or a Jefferson he pronounced them free as the birds. He was busy with the business of the Court, and fertile with young wives. He had to hike the Appalachians. He had other fish to fry.

These erotic images, whether in written or pictorial form, have been the curiosity and the common entertainment of mankind throughout its history, and continue to be today. Most of us have seen them at one time or another (84 per cent of American males, 69 per cent of American females, according to the President's Commission report), and there is reliable scientific and statistical evidence that not to have seen them—or, more precisely, to have grown up in an environment where they were strictly forbidden along with any other open expression of sexuality—predisposes some men to vicious sexual crime. The majority of Americans do not believe these images should be outlawed among consenting adults. Americans who are older, who are less active politically, who have fewer years of education, who more frequently attend church, tend to favor outlawing them more than Americans who are younger, who are more active politically, who have more years of education, who less frequently attend church. An overwhelming number of professionals in such fields of science and social service as sex research, psychology, sociology and marriage counseling believe that erotic images are at least harmless and may even be beneficial to love, marriage and mental health. And yet they are outlawed, and for trafficking in them Americans are arrested and are sentenced to jail.

We came to this madness by so slow a progress that few of us now even remember the steps of our descent. The history of Western attitudes toward explicit sexuality—toward sexuality itself—is long, subtle, and complex. It is intimately connected to the rise and ultimate dominance of Christianity; obscenity is now and has always been a religious crime, though it is cast today in other words. The early Church found sexual pleasure to be a grievous sin by a subtle and most peculiar argument: because at the moment of climax, of orgasm, it suspended reason and temporarily blotted out man's consciousness of God. "It was as much the suspension of reason," writes the historian Wayland Young, "as the narrowing and averting of love from God which made St. Augustine look askance on desire and the pleasure of love. To St. Thomas Aquinas, it was the main objection." Outside of marriage, or for purposes other than procreation, it still is.

But the line of thought, even the line of terrorism, that leads most directly to Memphis is more immediately anchored in nineteenth-century England and America, in a body of pseudo-scientific medical theory, concerned primarily with the supposed evil effects of masturbation, that was taken over and exaggerated to the point of hysteria by clergymen and reformers. The theory, which paralleled early theories of capitalism, held that the body had a finite quantity of vital fluids, semen pre-eminent among them. Saving semen produced health; "spending" it produced sickness, mental illness, and eventually death. Sexual activity was thus stigmatized as a disease: "spermatorrhea." But since even the most continent of men had noctural emissions, the disease must inevitably be fatal. In the immensely popular works of the leading proponent of the spermatorrhea theory, writes Steven Marcus in *The Other Victorians,* "Sex is thought of as a universal and virtually incurable scourge. It cannot ultimately be controlled, and it serves as a kind of metaphor for death, as cancer does today."

One way that nineteenth-century doctors sought to control the disease was to eliminate a powerful source of infection, female sexual desire. Good women were raised to be passionless, but for those who were not, American gynecologists perfected surgical cures. Gynecology, the historian G. J. Barker-Benfield points out in his brilliant study *The Horrors of the Half-Known Life,* was the only branch of American medical science to achieve an international reputation in the nineteenth century, largely because a few leading practitioners honed their skills on submissive women, including female Negro slaves. Women who came to such practitioners complaining of excessive desire or compulsive masturbation found themselves treated by having their clitorises cut off or their ovaries removed. The last known clitoridectomy for psychological reasons was performed in the United States in 1927. The last known castration for psychological reasons was performed in the United States in 1946. The surgical expression of the quaint sexual theories of the Victorians reaches down almost to the present day. "It may be noted," Barker-Benfield writes, "that clitoridectomists and castrators tested women for indications of the disease of desire by inducing orgasm, manipulating clitoris or breasts." Rape thus proceeded mutilation in the name of medical science and mental health.

Medical violence against the disease of sexuality had its counterpart in movements of reform, and here the line that leads to *Miller* and Memphis grows taut. One man more than any other shaped the attitudes and lobbied into existence the laws that, duly revised but hardly improved upon, are the basis for the Memphis trials. His name is a joke today: Anthony Comstock. It was not a joke in the years between 1872 and 1915, when Comstock almost singlehandedly defined the obscene.

Anthony Comstock was a Connecticut farm boy whose mother died when he was ten. He grew up with an intense and religious desire to keep himself as pure as his mother had piously taught him to be. He volunteered to fight for the Union in the Civil War and afterward found work in New York as a grocery clerk. Images that stimulated sexual desire enraged him, and he began fighting them on his own. When he was twenty-eight, in 1872, he emerged to public notice by raiding two New York stationery stores with a police captain and a newspaper reporter in tow. That year, he acquired the backing of a group of powerful and reform-minded men, and with their financial and moral support he founded a Committee for the Suppression of Vice within the YMCA, the forerunner of the New York Society for the Suppression of Vice. With a bundle of obscene materials to display, he went to Washington in 1873 to lobby for legislation (which he wrote) outlawing the mailing of obscene matter interstate. He got his law; he also got appointment as a postal inspector with broad discretionary powers and free passage on the nation's railroads.

From that moment until the day he died, he scourged the land. He achieved such power that his word alone was sufficient to convict in almost every American court. He claimed once that he had driven thirteen people to suicide, and he boasted in 1913, near the end of his life, that he had personally arrested more than thirty-six hundred men, women, and children and confiscated hundreds of thousands of pounds of smut, including tons of contraceptives and wagonloads of printing plates.

Comstock believed fiercely that his purpose in life was to protect children from exposure to mental infection. He insisted that "a single book or a single picture may taint forever the soul of the person who reads or sees it," and from the diaries he kept as a young man it appears that the soul he knew to be tainted was his own: he was for much of his youth a secret masturbator, and he fought his "sin" for years before he brought it under control. He believed with the medical men and the clergy that desire was a disease that sapped the body and drove men and women insane. He was terrorized by his fear of his own infection, as someone would be terrorized who believed he had been deliberately infected with cancer, and he resolved that those who similarly infected others would receive the full measure of his revenge.

He promulgated not only federal but also model state laws against obscenity, and the Comstock laws are the immediate precursors to those under which Larry Parrish prosecutes in

Memphis today. They are thus founded on a species of illogic that would be merely a historical curiosity if it were not embodied in harsh, punitive laws: that erotic images sometimes stimulate men and women to masturbate, and masturbation is a fatal disease, and therefore the state must interdict erotic images as it interdicts pollutants or powerful drugs.

Yet they are also, like all laws, political, and the political suppression they mask has been of far greater consequence than the discredited theories on which they are based. Not for any artistic virtue that they may possess, but for the hard core of protected political expression that they mutely define, do such meaty images of sexual congress as *Deep Throat* deserve to be unchained, however much they may disturb us. Charles Rembar:

> Sex in literature provided the field on which the struggles [I have] recounted . . . took place, but the war was wider. The true censor has objectives beyond the masking of the erotic and the indecent. The end in view is an established principle of suppression, available anywhere in the world of the mind.

Steven Marcus discovers a similar and more insidious connection:

> We have in our own time been witness to a sexual revolution which has . . . been split off from what might have been expected to accompany it—impulses of a social revolutionary kind. . . . The socially radical impulses with which the sexually revolutionary impulses have, historically, been symbiotically connected seem to have been almost systematically thwarted in their search for legitimate means of expression.

Think of the connection between open sexual expression and social revolution and examples immediately come to mind: early feminism with its emphasis on free love (it was forced to disavow that emphasis before it could achieve female suffrage); the radical sexual reforms advocated by American and Soviet Communists in the 1920s and 1930s; the counterculture of the 1960s, with its rejection of middle-class moral values; the women's movement itself. "Those who have spoken out in defense of pornography from the expert realm," Larry Parrish told me in Memphis, "are speaking a political philosophy, not a scientific view." And again, more bluntly, his remark to the CBS producer: "We're going to get rid of all these perverted minds."

It should come as no surprise that the Nixon regime was fanatical on the subject of "smut," of denying radical—or, for that matter, even normal sexual expression. Nixon saw such expression for what, potentially, it is, a source of social revolution. Since he feared such revolution, he thought sexual expression could "poison the wellsprings of American and Western culture and civilization." It could also help them run clear again.

It should come as no surprise that Nixon appointees are trying erotic films in Memphis, or that the Nixon Court has rigged new standards to help police and prosecutors suppress what they consider obscene.

They wish to control expression, and sexual expression, whether in images or in person, is expression of the most radical kind. It distracts men and women from the love of God and from the love of the state, and it teaches them a fact that no fanatic and no fascist would have them know: that they are human, and beneath the clothing of circumstance have their humanity in common with others of their kind, and might, if they choose, assemble to defend it from all oppression. It teaches them not with words, which are paltry things, but with the immutable senses themselves, with sight and hearing and taste and smell and touch, beyond denial or contradiction. We had a long, hard task to free ourselves from political authoritarianism, and the central document of that freedom is the Bill of Rights. We have not yet freed ourselves from moral authoritarianism, and the authorities still seek to convince us that to do so would destroy what we have gained. Freedom didn't destroy us last time, in the political realm, two hundred years ago, in 1776.

But through the law out of spermatorrhea by way of Comstock, censors still belabor us. They strike today, in their increasing desperation, at the shock wave of the advancing revolution, at images that we have not yet admitted to our living rooms and therefore still suspect of danger and therefore still fear, though they are no more fearsome than the barnyard or the meat counter, though they are far less fearsome, and so also far less promising, than the bedroom itself and that mysterious other who voluntarily, out of love and lust, joins us there. They strike at a few of us caught up in cynicism and profit, but thereby they most certainly strike at the rest of us as well.

So the jury returns, the real one is Memphis, having deliberated for less than an hour on a Thursday afternoon and merely four hours on a Friday—at 2:30 P.M., Friday, April 30, 1976, our Bicentennial Year—and the foreman announces that he and his eleven peers "had to follow the law," and the brute verdict is guilty: Louis Peranio is guilty, and Mario DeSalvo is guilty, and Mickey Cherubino is guilty, and handsome Harry Reems is guilty, and the others, and the corporations with which they dressed themselves, of obscenity, of interstate transport, of conspiracy, and the clowns roll their barrels and the lion tamers crack their whips and the ringmaster affects a somber mien to disguise his righteous delight and they are all guilty, guilty, guilty all.

Coming Down Snow Mountain

Cocaine—coke, flake, blow and lady, the white crystalline compound that Sigmund Freud made famous in 1884—is also called snow, and now at the beginning of 1975 a blizzard of cocaine is blowing over us, little spoons hanging from our necks like crucifixes, snorting noises in the next room coming from people who don't have colds, people working twenty-hour days who used to work four. The United States Bureau of Customs seized only six pounds of illegal cocaine in 1960, but 907 pounds in 1974, and the Bureau estimates that each figure accounted for less than 5 per cent of the traffic. Both estimates are probably low. In the past two years, cocaine has spilled from the ghetto and the mansion to become the illegal drug of choice, second only to marijuana, of many prosperous, middle-class Americans. At sixty dollars to ninety dollars a gram, one user's evening's worth, it isn't likely to replace Jack Daniel's or Chivas Regal on the side table, but it is being used, socially and privately, in every major American city. Illegal laboratories in Chile, Bolivia, Peru, Ecuador, Colombia and Argentina are working overtime to satisfy the growing North American demand, a demand that must seem all the more surprising when you consider that cocaine is classed, inaccurately but legally, as a hard narcotic, and is subject to the same draconian penalties as heroin. Who, even as recently as five years ago, would have guessed that otherwise-straight people, doctors, lawyers and merchant chiefs, would take such risks? And what are we to make of that?

Late afternoon in a friend's apartment, the door locked, the sunlight slanting through the windows. I've never tried coke before, have hardly even smoked grass, am apprehensive, feel the tension

Playboy, January 1975.

of this fiercely illegal act in my arms and at the back of my head. The tension shapes itself into an uncontrollable grin, the facial equivalent of a giggle, a child's response to the forbidden, playing dress-up in Daddy's shoes. I grinned so when news of another friend's suicide reached me years ago, and was appalled until I understood that we sometimes respond by opposites, grinning with fear, crying with joy. My friend isn't grinning; he is grim with tension after a bad day at the office.

From the locked drawer of a low table he removes a glass one-ounce vial and a miniature spoon. The vial is half full of a powder not quite white, a tinge of brown to its white. The spoon, its bowl smaller than the nail on my little finger, has a ring attached to its handle and could be worn on a chain around the neck, though my friend prefers not to advertise his interest in cocaine by so wearing it. Others do, perhaps even some who don't use the lady, as once, as teen-agers, we carried a condom in our wallets when we had no ladies to use.

"This is it," he says, holding up the vial. "It's fantastic stuff. It can do things nothing else does. It doesn't send you off into a corner and it doesn't fuck up your head. You can use it and then go on with an ordinary day and all that happens is that you feel normal, feel straight. I'm tired right now and I'm pissed off and I'm down. After the coke I'll be ready for the evening." He unscrews the lid and dips into the cocaine with the spoon. "This is premium, better than you can get on the street. It's maybe 70, 80 per cent pure. I had it tested. It's cut with lactose. It's good shit." The spoon comes out of the vial mounded with the powder and in the late-afternoon light suddenly it sparkles, the small, flat crystals catching the sun. My friend sniffs to clear his head and then raises the spoon to one nostril and with a loud snort sucks the coke up his nose. His expression doesn't change but his eyes widen and he lets his breath go slowly out. His motion now more serious, more deliberate, he dips the spoon into the vial and withdraws another mound of coke and snorts again, then leans back in his chair and is silent, abstracted, as I have been silent and abstracted by the first taste of a fine wine. He returns from that distance and looks at me.

"That was a full hit," he says, more quietly than before. "You should probably start with less. Be careful not to breathe out as you bring the spoon to your nose or you'll blow the stuff away."

My hands are trembling, but not enough to spill the coke. I dip the spoon into the vial, tapping it against the side to level it, bring it to my nose and snort hard and feel a flare of powder brushing inside my head and then feel it dissolve and disappear. Carefully I return the spoon to the vial and scoop another hit and tap it level and bring it to my other nostril and snort again, spilling a few grains this time into my mustache. I hand the vial and the spoon back to my friend and settle on the couch, watching the motes of dust moving in the sunlight, watching what is happening to the inside of my nose. My friend comes out of his silence to ask me my favorite music and I say Bach, Mozart. He unwinds from his chair and finds a record and puts it on his stereo and returns and sits down. "Beethoven's last quartets," he says, smiling. The motes of dust in the sunlight remind me of times as a boy when I lay in the loft of the barn on cool autumn mornings, the alfalfa sweet beneath me, sparrows chirping in the peaks of the rafters, random lines and tubes and bands of light coming down from holes in the roof, dust from the hay dancing complicated patterns that I could change with the slightest motion of my little finger in the light, complicated patterns that played like silent music before my eyes. My head clears, my lungs, burred with smoking, clear, and I am breathing mountain air in a city apartment in the late afternoon. A taste I've never tasted before appears at the top of my throat, a taste bitter and medicinal but not unpleasant, the taste of cocaine, and I realize without concern that it's a taste I'll never forget.

So we sit, in the late afternoon, our eyes dilating, listening to Beethoven and the light, and when I come back from wherever I went I realize that the tremor in my hands is stilled and the grin has disappeared. I'm calm, I'm myself within myself, my friend has gone gentle, the way I enjoy him most, and after a while we take another hit and leave for an evening of good food and good talk in the company of good women. But I wonder, before I go, if the change came from the coke, or from the shared peace and music-framed silence, or from my relief at having done what I feared to do. My friend says the change comes from the coke, but that, after all, is why he uses it.

Coca—not cocoa but *Erythroxylon coca*, the native South American plant from which cocaine is refined—grows on the eastern slopes of the Andes, grows best between fifteen hundred and six thousand feet in the zone of mountain climate called the cinchona, the zone Peruvians call the *Montaña*. It is an evergreen zone, cool, humid, frost-free, the mean annual temperature between 65 and 68 degrees with little variation from day to day, mists blowing across the slopes, mists curling around the coca bushes in the small cleared plots, the *cocales*, that the Indians cultivate, Carmel weather all the way. Coca, in the language of the Incas, meant *tree*, without qualifiers, the primal tree, the preeminent tree, and left unpruned the cultivated plant would grow as tall as ten or twelve feet, but the Indians prune it down to three or four feet, keeping it within reach and forcing it to thicken and bush outward, forcing it to produce more leaves. The leaves, not the flowers or the berries or the bark, are the coca plant's crop, glossy-green on one side, silver-gray on the other, varying in size and shape depending on their maturity and on the subspecies of *E. coca* to which they belong but generally oval and pointed, one to four inches in length, half an inch to two inches in width. A prominent central vein runs from stem to point; pseudo-veins curve on each side of it from stem to point; between the pseudo-veins and the central vein the venous system is denser than on the margins of the leaf; held to the light, a coca leaf appears to harbor a ghostly miniature of itself, a leaf within a leaf, at its heart.

Manco Ccapac—rich Manco—and Mama Ocllo, whom Inca legend insists were white, appeared one day on the shores of Lake Titicaca, Manco Ccapac holding a golden wand in his hand. The wand was a divining rod and the two mysterious white people followed it north all the way to the site of Cuzco, where it struck and buried itself in the ground. "And here," writes a historian, "was built the palace of the first Inca." The year was 1021. Coca was there before the Inca rulers came, but they took possession of it: the Inca was divine, and coca was divine: coca came from God, and God was the Inca: the Inca controlled the coca, collected it in tribute and dispensed it for devotion, like the body and blood of Christ. The Inca had a thousand concubines and wore a headdress of gold surmounted by two white feathers. The people were divided by regions, north, south, east and west, and within regions were organized by tens, ten families making a *Chunca*, ten *Chuncas* making a *Pachaca*, and so on up to ten thousand, each rank of tens under an appointed leader who was re-

sponsible to the leader above him, the ultimate leaders responsible
to the Inca himself. So the kingdom was orderly, the Inca stern
but benign. The kingdom flowered into golden ornaments and
fine woolen tapestries, palaces and aqueducts of unmortared
stone, exotic festivals and bold celebrations, and on the hillsides
of the *Montaña*, the soil held in place by narrow terraces like
steps down the mountain carved for the feet of God, the coca
grew.

Francisco Pizarro, a soldier's bastard son said to have been
suckled by a sow, came down sniffing gold and destroyed the kingdom by lopping off its head. The administrators who followed
him suppressed the Indian use of coca until they understood that
without it the Indians could not perform their slave labor in the
gold mines, and then they supplied it contemptuously, a slave's
furtive pleasure, a weakness of brown and lesser men. The
poisoned gold floated across the sea and inflated Europe, and
sickened by it, Spain grew arthritic, Spain grew old. The Indians
abided, and eventually broke free. They use coca now, eight million of them, as they used it then, in moderation, as a tonic, part
of the continuity of their lives. They pick the leaves, dry them
carefully over a fire or in the sun, chew them mixed with a paste
made of ashes. The paste, which is alkaline, may serve to sweeten
the leaves or it may liberate their alkaloids. At least fourteen
alkaloids have been isolated from coca leaves, of which cocaine is
one. The Indians prefer the sweeter leaves, and the sweeter leaves
contain less cocaine. Cocaine is not the essence of coca, but
merely the most potent of its decoctions. The other alkaloids may
temper it, moderate its effects: so little research has been done on
coca that no one knows. The Indians know. "They carry an herb,
the leaves of which can sustain them two days without eating or
drinking, by merely carrying these in their mouths. The herb they
call *coca*." That is a Spanish chronicler writing in 1535. They still
do today.

Coca came to Europe at about the same time as coffee and tea,
two far more jagged tonics. Why it failed to achieve their popularity the record doesn't explain. The record registers a search for essences, for vital principles: to master the complexity of the natural world, young science sought simplicity: if man had an essential
soul, psychoactive plants must have an essential secret ingredient.
A German named Gaedicke isolated an alkaloid from coca in

1855. He named it *Erythroxylon*. A German named Niemann purified the alkaloid in 1860. He named it *cocaine*. It was white as the driven snow.

Cocaine—cocaine hydrochloride, in its legal and most of its illegal forms—is benzoylmethylecgonine, an ester of ecgonine and benzoic acid, chemical formula $C_{17}H_{21}NO_4$. In its refined state it is a crystalline compound, the crystals long, prism-shaped, needled. It is a powerful local anesthetic and a subtle general stimulant, two characteristics that sound antagonistic but aren't. It isn't much used for local anesthesia any more; that effect, discovered by a colleague of Freud's in 1884, was hailed as a boon to mankind, but the eye surgeons who were the primary recipients of the boon soon discovered that cocaine damaged the cornea and excessively dilated the pupil of the eye, and switched to procaine and other man-made anesthetics when they were developed in the early twentieth century. Ear, nose and throat men still sometimes use cocaine for nose surgery, spraying it onto the mucous membranes or applying it in liquid form, just about the only official medical use left for what was once a wonder drug.

Cocaine is usually described as a central-nervous-system stimulant, its stimulation beginning in the higher centers of the brain and, with increased dosage, working downward to the lower. That description doesn't distinguish cocaine from the amphetamines: it differs in its more generalized effect on the brain, and doesn't wire users up, string them out, as amphetamines do. Some researchers believe it also works by suppressing whatever in the body is responsible for depression, fatigue, the blues, bringing the body up to "normal" rather than raising it to "high." "The psychic effect [of cocaine]," Freud wrote, "consists of exhilaration and lasting euphoria, which does not differ in any way from the normal euphoria of a healthy person. The feeling of excitement which accompanies stimulus by alcohol is completely lacking; the characteristic urge for immediate activity which alcohol produces is also absent. One senses an increase of self-control and feels more vigorous and more capable of work; on the other hand, if one works, one misses that heightening of the mental powers which alcohol, tea or coffee induce. One is simply normal, and soon finds it difficult to believe that one is under the influence of any drug at all."

Freud was describing the effects of a .05–.10-gram dose. In such moderate doses cocaine increases pulse rate, increases blood pressure and respiration, dilates the pupils, and suppresses appetite by anesthetizing the lining of the stomach. Freud took cocaine by mouth in liquid form and so did not notice the effects that users today, who generally snort cocaine in powdered form, look for and cherish: the freeze that comes when the powder anesthetizes the mucous membranes of the nose, the flash that comes when the powder, dissolving in the nose and the upper throat, rapidly takes effect, the deep, open breathing that comes when the cocaine shrinks the mucous membranes and clears the sinuses and the bronchi. Before it became illegal, cocaine was enthusiastically endorsed by the Hay Fever Association. Despite the fact that it is an extremely effective vasoconstrictor, slowing down and even stopping the local circulation of the blood wherever it is applied to the mucous membranes, it is a short-acting drug, which helps account for its reported seductiveness: most people who snort it are up and down again in forty minutes, and therefore thinking about another hit.

Sigmund Freud began experimenting with cocaine in Vienna in 1884, when he was 28 years old. It lifted him from depression, he wrote at the time, steadied his mind, suppressed his appetite, strengthened his hand, and it seemed to him a wonder drug. He thought it might cure morphine addiction, one of the more grievous problems of his day, and he tried it on an addicted friend and it did. He thought it might cure neuresthenia—the condition he later called neurosis—and he tried it on neuresthenic patients with some success. He was young, working to arrange his life and his income so that he could marry the girl he'd been courting, and he hoped that cocaine might be a means to that end, a means to success and acclaim and the improvement of his prospects. He wrote to his fiancée, Martha Bernays:

> Woe to you, my Princess, when I come. I will kiss you quite red and feed you till you are plump. And if you are froward you shall see who is the stronger, a gentle little girl who doesn't eat enough or a big wild man *who has cocaine in his body*. [Freud's emphasis.] In my last severe depression I took coca again and a small dose lifted me to the heights in wonderful fashion. I am

just now busy collecting the literature for a song of praise to this magical substance.

By June he had finished, and immediately published, his "song of praise," a paper titled "Über Coca"—*On Coca* (Freud used the terms "coca" and "cocaine" interchangeably). "Long-lasting, intensive mental or physical work can be performed without fatigue," he wrote; "it is as though the need for food and sleep, which otherwise makes itself felt peremptorily at certain times of the day, were completely banished." He suggested the use of cocaine as a general stimulant, to treat digestive disorders of the stomach, to treat severe malnutrition, to treat morphine and alcohol addiction, as an aphrodisiac and as a local anesthetic.

In his enthusiasm for the drug, Freud all but ballyhooed it, sending doses to Martha, pressing it upon his friends. Only later, after he had taken his public stand, did he discover that the friend whom he had removed from morphine addiction with cocaine had begun using the new drug in massive quantities, had become, in effect, a cocaine addict, although cocaine is not addictive in the strict, medical sense of the word. Freud published five papers on cocaine between 1884 and 1887, in one of the later papers defending himself from charges that he had loosed "the third scourge of humanity" (alcohol and morphine being the other two) upon the world. He acknowledged that cocaine didn't cure morphine addiction after all, but he argued, in effect, that the fault didn't lie with the drug but with the head of the user—an argument as valid today as it was then, though in the 1880s it hardly added to his popularity. He also admitted that the drug turned him off: "There occurred more frequently than I should have liked, an aversion to the drug, which was sufficient cause for curtailing its use."

Between Freud and Carl Koller, the colleague who first used it as an anesthetic in eye surgery, cocaine became famous, and from 1884 until it was brought under government interdiction in the United States and in Europe in the early twentieth century it achieved such popularity that the era has been described by some medical historians as "The Great Cocaine Explosion." Doctors in the United States enthusiastically reported cures of alcohol and morphine addiction, usually within a few days after withdrawal was complete and usually without follow-up. Cocaine parlors opened in major cities and catered to a genteel clientele. Patent-medicine companies had a field day, packaging cocaine or coca extract or coca leaves in syrups, tonics, cordials, tablets, capsules, hypodermic injections, cigarettes, cigars and nasal sprays. Bartenders dropped pinches of cocaine into shots of whiskey for a little added zing; salesmen sold cocaine preparations door to door. Soda fountains first appeared in drugstores for a reason: among the many patent medicines devised in those days that contained cocaine, one remains famous, our very own Coca-Cola, which was flavored with coca extract, the pause that refreshes, until 1903, by which time a growing body of medical opinion held that cocaine was a dangerous drug, and the Coca-Cola Company decided to use only dealkaloided coca extract and substituted caffeine for the cocaine. Coca-Cola is still flavored with coca extract, by the way, though the cocaine is missing from the brew.

Freud never became "addicted" to cocaine, but others of his era used the drug to such excess that it hampered their work and their health. The pioneering surgeon William Halstead, of Johns Hopkins, developed nerve-block anesthesia, the kind of regional anesthesia dentists practice today, using cocaine, but spent three years on long sea voyages and confined to hospitals trying to free himself from his craving for cocaine, and then succeeded only by becoming a morphine addict. Arthur Conan Doyle was probably a user, and so was his alter ego, Sherlock Holmes, whom he portrays, in "The Sign of the Four," shooting up a 7 per cent solution as a counter to boredom: " 'My mind,' he said, 'rebels at stagnation. . . . I abhor the dull routine of existence. I crave for mental exaltation.' " Robert Louis Stevenson used cocaine as a tonic against the tuberculosis that shortened his life—his wife, Fanny, carried some in their medicine chest when they sailed to Samoa—and he may have been taking it when he wrote *The Strange Case of Dr. Jekyll and Mr. Hyde,* a story of bizarre personality changes induced by white powders and blood-red liquids: he produced the first draft, a manuscript of sixty thousand words, in six days, without benefit of a typewriter. Cocaine was cheaper in those seldom-chronicled days when Popes and princes turned on: an ounce came over the counter for $2.50.

Another apartment in another city. I am the guest of a psychologist and his dark, beautiful wife. Call them Aaron and Mara. They have another guest; all three are sitting in the living room of the apartment when I arrive; the second guest is also a psychologist: call him Jim. They are willing to talk about coke; we will do coke together through the evening and the night. The chairs in the living room are by Eames, the couch black leather, and on the walls hang framed drawings that look like the work of children, but Aaron explains they are the work of a young schizophrenic who was also a heroin addict. Aaron got him off the heroin, but the schizophrenia remains, flowering in drawings that might be the work of children.

Aaron had some coke in the apartment but had casually left it on the dresser that morning and the maid had as casually thrown it out. "Or took it home," Aaron grins. So the dealer is coming to visit us and we are waiting for Santa Claus. The dealer is Santa Claus and he carries a shoulder bag stuffed with snow. Waiting for the dealer, we talk, checking each other out, but I have come with good credentials and Aaron eventually says I'm cool. Mara listens intently, but her eyes are far away. Women, I've been told, are mystical about coke: I've never seen a woman use coke before. This woman is small and lithe; she wears a pullover I can see through, see the dark nipples of her fine breasts that repeat on a somber octave the dark pupils of her eyes. An air conditioner hums in the window, and beside it green plants grow.

The buzzer sounds and Aaron goes to the hall door and releases the downstairs lock and Mara and Jim look up and footsteps beat the stairs and the door is flung open and Santa Claus bursts in, two Santa Clauses wearing shoulder bags. Dave is tall, big, young, blond, dressed in chinos and a white button-down shirt rolled up at the sleeves, his body heavy and athletic, a man who plays tennis and moves fast, his voice incongruously loud and high, a wispy blond mustache adding a touch of comedy to a lively and yet shrewd face. Noah is dark, trim, a shadowed James Coburn in the sense that comes off him of reserved force and assumed superiority, wearing a polo shirt and comfortable pants and sandals. Both are lively, jazzed, talking fast, doing the amenities even as they move into the living room and take places in the circle, Noah on the couch beside Mara, Dave to the left of the couch on a chair higher than ours, and they are seated before I realize they're already coked up, having sampled their wares on the way over. Aaron introduces me and quickly explains who I am and why I'm there, and Dave does a long double-take and settles back to ponder. "Did I hit you too fast?" Aaron asks, and Dave says, "No, I just want to think about it for a minute," and Aaron says, "He's cool," and Dave then says to Aaron, "Look, I know you, and if you say he's okay that's good enough for me. I do this because I like to do good things for people and if you say he's cool that's good enough." So I am cool and the evening can proceed.

Dave isn't hurried and Noah isn't hurried and the two talk to their acquaintances, their clients, about the good old times and then about dry times in the summer when the coke gets low, when it's harder to shop south of the border because the tourist ranks are thin and an American stands out from the crowd. Dave just got some coke in, not a lot, not as pure as he'd like but good enough to stuff up his nose, good enough to share if anyone wants to share and does anyone want to share? Yes, we all want to share. Then is there a gram scale in the house? Yes, there's a gram scale in the house, coke people all keep gram scales in their houses, and many of them keep test kits too to see to the purity of the coke and the nature of the cut, which might be lactose or might be speed or might even be Spanish baby laxative, *mannite*, *cara mia*. Dave takes up his bag and Mara shows him to the next room and no one is hurried, what's there to be hurried about? And then Dave, his eyes how merry, is back in the room with a little bag of white powder and he looks around the room and his eyes light on the schizophrenic drawing hanging on the wall and he asks Mara for a kitchen towel and she fetches it and he takes the picture down, the frame 16×20 inches and the drawing covered with glass, and dusts the glass and sets the picture on his lap. He pulls his wallet from his hip pocket and extracts from it a fifty-dollar bill and his American Express card and puts the wallet away and dumps a pile of powder, a gram of white snow, onto the glass, and begins meticulously to chop it up with the edge of the American Express card, a fine touch that, lesser souls use a single-edge razor blade. There are rocks in the coke, and I have heard that rocks mean good coke—so says the dealer in Richard Woodley's book *Dealer*—but Dave disagrees. The coke gets lumps in it, he says, and the lumps aren't necessarily lumps of pure coke, just lumps, like lumps in damp sugar, but this is fairly good coke, he says, good enough for him to stuff up his nose and share with his friends.

As he talks, Dave scrapes the pile, most of it, out flat and begins to divide it into little lines, an eighth of an inch wide, an inch or an inch and a quarter long, looking up briefly to count the number of people in the room, six, looking back down to make twelve expert lines each the same length, spaced half an inch apart in the center of the picture. "Bobby would like that," Aaron says with amusement. "He'd like using his drawing to lay out the lines. He's off heroin but it would still make him feel good." Dave finishes the lines, leaving a small pile of powder in one corner of the glass. He balances the picture on his knees and rolls the fifty-dollar bill into a tube the diameter of a soda straw, tucking in a corner to keep it from unrolling, and then with the reverse good manners that obtain among those who use illegal drugs, for which there is no guarantee of quality or even of safety, he takes his own two lines first, deftly snorting through the rolled bill, not even setting his finger beside his nose, and up the chimney it goes.

Mara is waiting, expectantly, and Dave passes the picture to her and she curls her feet under her on the couch and settles the picture in her lap. She pulls back her hair with one hand, the fifty-dollar bill in the other, and then notices that I am watching her and seems to suppress a shudder, as if I were a rapist staring at her across a narrow street, which of course I am, though it is not her body that I am urgent to know. She looks at the lines again and forgets me, looks at the lines as if they were the oldest and most intimate of friends. The friend is back, and quickly she bends to it and sniffs it up, one line, the other line, and breathes deeply and widens, widens her eyes, and then almost nonchalantly wets her finger and cleans the dust of the two lines from the glass and presses it to her tongue.

Passes the picture to Noah, who takes his hit casually and passes it to me, and I am clumsy with it and embarrassed by my clumsiness, finding I have to hold one nostril shut to make the other one work, as my acquaintances do not. And the picture goes round, people pulling back into themselves after they take their hits, letting the coke work. Someone will say to me much later, in another town, someone who has never done coke, that snorting it up your nose sounds inelegant, but she did not see the ritual around the room that night, as formal in its own way as a tea ceremony, the expensive people who were also good and decent people, wives skilled at love, healers of the addicted and the mentally ill.

Dave and Noah compete through the evening, perhaps because

I am there to find a story to tell, perhaps because they do. The talk is guarded, the route of acquisition never explained except that Dave says he doesn't smuggle and Noah hints that he is off to South America soon. Most coke comes through Florida, some of it through syndicate channels, much of it through the Cuban community in Miami, a little of it, according to a Cuban doing time for coke, on Bebe Rebozo's yacht, but coke is so portable and its value so high that individual operations go on continuously, women often serving as couriers, stashing the powder in bras and girdles and vaginas. A man tried to bring coke through by swallowing it in plastic bags, Noah says, but one of the bags burst and he was dead on the spot, ODed on pure cocaine—panic, convulsion, all the synapses firing, terminal man, death. The coke comes from Peru, the coke comes from Colombia, you take risks all the way, but it isn't risky if you have a good plan, so says Noah, who has a good plan. There's coke everywhere, Dave says, never enough to go around, in San Francisco the market is so tight you can sell anybody anything, and were we ready for another hit, yes we were, and the little pile in the corner becomes six small lines and the picture drawn by the schizophrenic former heroin addict goes around the civilized room.

Risk-taking, Jim says, finding reasons for cocaine's growing popularity, and Aaron says getting out of your head once in a while, though it's a seductive drug and he's had to pull back from it because he found it becoming too interesting, consuming too much of his time, but tonight is the night before a holiday and patients get demanding before holiday time, and what a pleasant way to come together with friends. A little water then for our noses, dipping a finger into a glass and sniffing the water to rinse the nose, help the snow melt, my gums numb where I had rubbed the dust from my lines up above my front teeth, the coke working its anesthesia and my head high in the mountains again with the mountain air. "The Indians chew coca to help fight the altitude," someone would tell me later, "and we snort coke to help us fight the city air." And the city stresses, banashees, collywobbles, the city blackass, though coke has its blackass too.

From left field Dave says it looks to him as if we want to go on, and he's shared a gram with us but there is the question of cost, and Aaron looks around at the rest of us and says of course there is, let's go ahead and square it up at the end, and Dave goes out and comes back and the picture goes around and the night goes around without dinner, without drink except for cold grapefruit juice and iced tea, and Aaron takes off his shirt and Mara curls and curls on the couch. Dave says his money is carefully laundered but the IRS audits him every year nonetheless, and Noah says he knows a dealer who sometimes has so much cash that he can cover his living room floor with it to the depth of six inches, small bills, and who sometimes has nothing at all, who has no septum in his nose and would drown if he stuck his head under water, the coke having eaten the septum away. Dave says he went to college, more than one college, not to graduate but to study the things that interested him, and Noah says so did he, and Dave says he made his first connection dealing grass with his tuition money, running grass up from Texas to his Great Lakes college town, his father was a corporation executive, he was twenty-four years old, there had always been money in his life, he wanted to get out of the business someday because the risks in the long run were too high, too much running around, he didn't smuggle and he didn't deal on the street, he liked arrangements like tonight, high-level people who used coke socially and made their connections privately and could be relied on, he is filling a need, he likes to be around good people, likes to help them acquire this pleasant and, in moderation, entirely healthy and decent high, and what could be more harmless than a night like this one in the lives of busy, responsible people. And everyone is doing it, he says, from teen-agers to elder statesmen, he wouldn't be surprised if there had been coke in the White House in the Watergate days, not Nixon maybe but the gang around him. He had heard of a judge, a distinguished judge of seventy years, asking a busted dealer if he'd been dealing in coke, and when the dealer said yes the judge said, well, coke was indeed the queen of drugs. That's where it's at, Dave says, whatever the laws. And the picture goes around, and I noticed myself measuring the small variations in the size of the lines, debating taking two of the larger ones and then rejecting the thought as unworthy and taking one large and one small, as the others seem to do. Joints pass around too, as the night goes on, and later Noah feels strung out and borrows a tranquilizer, and I consider a drink and reject the idea.

Morning, the sun just rising, the light pulling up through blue to green, and Dave has to leave to pick up his wife and take her to work and it's time to settle accounts and does anyone want a gram to take along? Some of us do, and with the four we'd done that night, four grams among six people, that almost makes up a quarter ounce, so someone says he'll take the rest to fill it out, and while Dave in the other room weighs up the carry-out orders Aaron cuts squares from the cover of a medical journal, fine thick calendared stock, and folds them into small precise origami envelopes and in the other room Dave pours the coke in, and at $60 a gram the night, for four people since Dave and Noah are partners and do not pay, comes to $420, $105 each, and because I was there as an observer and had my mental cameras running I never left the room, I got no kick from cocaine.

After cocaine became effectively illegal in the United States, with the passage of the Harrison Narcotic Act in 1914 which erroneously classified it with true narcotics, it disappeared from sight, surfacing again in the twenties and thirties as the favorite drug of musicians and actors, going underground again during World War II, turning up again among musicians in the rock years and among entertainers and film people since, so that Sammy Davis Jr., for example, the same who hugged Richard Nixon at the 1972 convention rally, wears a coke spoon, and the nasal inhalers some of the better-known rock stars flaunt onstage contain not phenylephrine hydrochloride, like yours and mine, but liquid lady.

Why cocaine has returned to vogue, and especially why it is becoming popular with otherwise-straight people, no one really knows, but the reasons people give are interesting, if only because they say so much about the people giving them. The official line of the Drug Enforcement Administration, the federal agency that in 1973 replaced the Bureau of Narcotics and Dangerous Drugs, is that cocaine came in to replace heroin when the BNDD successfully shut down the heroin supply. Well, the BNDD didn't shut down the heroin supply, so street people say, and the likelihood that a junkie would exchange a hundred-dollar-a-day heroin habit for a sixty-dollar-a-gram cocaine habit isn't very great. The DEA is tooting its own horn and insuring its survival: if it stopped all the heroin, which it hasn't, it would thus have prepared the ground for a campaign against cocaine. The DEA thinks that one drug leads to another, and it thinks that with bigger budgets, more manpower, faster planes, and better informants it could control the traffic, which is approximately what organized crime is thinking these days, though of course we understand that the control is to different ends.

Jerry Strickler, a trim, snappily dressed official at the DEA who is in charge of Latin American operations, offers his own theory to explain cocaine's growing popularity. "We saw an increase starting in the middle sixties," he says, "when Cubans settled here in large numbers. Cuba had the greatest per-capita use in the world. Very little cocaine came into the United States before then. But the Cubans brought their habits with them, and some of the political groups that opposed Castro found that they could finance their operations by selling the stuff." Snorting coke thus becomes an act of defiant anticommunism. In the next breath Strickler makes a statement I've heard before from a cocaine dealer, drugs making strange bedfellows: "Where drugs are concerned, demand creates supply." Which doesn't exactly jibe with the theory that dissident Cubans turned America on.

Chilean couriers, Strickler says, used to bring coke to the Cubans in Miami, but when they saw the money the Cubans were making they decided to cut out the middleman and deal themselves. By 1971, federal narcotics agents were arresting more Chilean dealers than Cubans. Then the traffic shifted again and the DEA found itself arresting more Colombians than Chileans. Today a new shift is underway. "In the last two years," says Strickler, "we've begun seeing the gringo going down to buy a kilo or two and we find white American middle-class types active in organizations. They may also deal in hash, heroin, marijuana, they think in terms of running boats, good communication systems, they're at home anywhere in the world. But most of the mules, the couriers, are foreign nationals. They account for one third of our arrests." Strickler describes the eccentric routes couriers take to avoid an obvious approach to United States ports of entry: Chile to Argentina, for example, and then Argentina to Senegal, Senegal to Spain, Spain to London, London to Canada, where they are frequently met by Colombians from New York. But the point of the changing nationalities of suppliers is Strickler's second point—that demand creates supply—and that point returns us to the original question: why the increasing demand?

There is an increasing demand for all drugs in the United

States. The two most important factors in that increase are probably affluence and education. Alcohol consumption is up, tobacco consumption is up, marijuana consumption is up, why not cocaine? People of affluence, having been turned off alcohol, the most dangerous psychoactive drug of all, by marijuana, would turn to cocaine logically enough. One drug doesn't necessarily lead to another, but people do search, some people, when choice is available, for their drug of choice. We are all learning to dose ourselves anyway now that the doctor no longer comes to our door, now that his armamentarium largely consists of pills, pills that purge disease, pills that purge melancholy. I haven't met an adult American in years who didn't have his own little pharmacy stashed in his medicine cabinet—tranks, sleeping pills, nose drops, antihistamines, antibiotics, aspirin, you name it—and liquor on the side bar and sometimes grass in the freezer. Having learned that alcohol isn't the only game in town, having learned that chemicals can change our moods up and down and sideways, should we be surprised that some Americans believe that the locked medicine cabinet of the physician and the pharmacist is the gateway to paradise? Ah, God, the nation's becoming a head shop, and did you know you can get a megalomaniac high on intramuscular cortisone? That a heart transplant can make you feel immortal?

As with all psychoactive drugs, what cocaine does to the head depends on the head. Effects have been reported ranging from nothing at all to euphoria, excitement, a conviction of great mental clarity and physical strength, on down the tunnel to paranoia and hallucinations. Early users and researchers such as Freud were generally enthusiastic about cocaine's mood-changing properties. Modern writers manage to convey a sense of discomfort and even peril, though how much that sense relates to the drug and how much to sixty years of official, legal and medical condemnation remains to be seen. It's clear from the literature, at least, that there's no such thing as an unbiased opinion where cocaine is concerned.

I found no unqualified praise of cocaine after 1920. Bruce Jay Friedman's celebrated story "Lady," for example, begins:

When it was good, it was of a smooth consistency and white as Christmas snow. If Harry Towns had a slim silver-foil packet of it against his thigh—which he did two or three nights a week—he felt rich and fortified, almost as though he were carrying a gun.

But ends:

But anyone who stuck so much as a grain of that white shit up his nose on the actual *day* of his mother's funeral had to be some new and as yet undiscovered breed of sonofabitch. The lowest.

Thomas Skelton, the hero of Thomas McGuane's novel *Ninety-two in the Shade,* thinks of "that pale cocaine edge pale like acetylene flame," but he also worries about "that voluminous hollow rush inside, that slippage of control systems, the cocaine express. Mild enough on the face of it, he had known it in other days to be the first step on the ride to the O. D. Corral." William Burroughs, in *Naked Lunch,* says of cocaine: "When you shoot coke in the mainline there is a rush of pure pleasure to the head. . . . Ten minutes later you want another shot . . . intravenous C is electricity through the brain, activating cocaine pleasure connections. . . . There is no withdrawal syndrome with C. It is a need of the brain alone." But Burroughs has spent his later years proselytizing against all drugs except the apomorphine that he believes cured him of heroin addiction.

A young East Coast writer I talked to told me that for him cocaine was *Walpurgisnacht,* the witches' sabbath—"Pure evil, man," he said, grinning—but he described nights that started with coke and graduated to whatever he could find at hand to drink, smoke, swallow and snort: those would be witches' sabbaths indeed, and he said he had spent a hard year fighting the feeling and had finally come through, though his girl friend, there at his side asking for my astrological sign, inquiring after my karma, dealt coke.

Or consider Paul Kantner in *Rolling Stone:*

Cocaine is a really great drug, it's a great way to feel good, and you can function and work clearly on it, like for 12 or 15 hours straight, without losing your perspective the way you do on uppers or speed. But it's not controllable. It's not that you have an increased need or tolerance, it's that it's so pleasant you can't control your use of it. And when you're heavily into it, it makes you cold toward people, in the sense that you're thinking of so many other things that you can't possibly accomplish them all, and you're thinking of how to do all the things and you don't think about all the people you're around. . . . Also, it can get you physically fucked up.

Which is one of the more ambivalent testimonials I've seen.

Think what you want of these qualified wisdoms, of this wonderful chemical that is too wonderful to be good; here at least are facts about cocaine's physical and psychological effects on the body and the body politic:

•Cocaine, as it is used recreationally in the United States, has not been responsible for any reported deaths by overdose in recent years. A few deaths have occurred during medical administration of the drug, and any drug, taken in sufficient quantity, can cause death. Dr. Robert Byck of the Yale School of Medicine, who is studying the acute effects of cocaine in man under a 1974 contract from the National Institute on Drug Abuse and who is qualified to be called the leading U.S. expert on cocaine, said in a recent trial affidavit, "There are probably more deaths each year attributable to aspirin overdose than can be attributed to cocaine throughout history." There is certainly a lethal dose of cocaine, but none of the experts I talked to were willing to put a number on it, because they didn't know what the number would be. According to the U. S. Census Bureau, alcohol killed 15,326 people in 1969, heroin killed 454 and cocaine killed 0.

•Cocaine takes effect most rapidly when it is injected, slightly less rapidly when snorted or packed (rubbed into the gums or the lining of the nose), least rapidly when swallowed, because the stomach immediately goes to work breaking it down. In recreational use in the United States, most people snort or pack cocaine. Injection of an illegal drug is always risky, since users rarely know its purity or its cuts and seldom know how to maintain the sterility of the equipment.

•Long-term snorting of cocaine can destroy the tissue of the nose, especially the partition that divides the two nasal passages, the septum. Cocaine can also produce some of the nastiest sore throats known to man. I had one and it felt like the hole left when a tonsil is removed.

·A small percentage of people who try cocaine are likely to be allergic to it and will react by going into fatal or near-fatal anaphylactic shock. So will a small percentage of people stung by a bee or injected with penicillin.

·Like all stimulants, cocaine is not addictive. It is also not habituating, nor do users develop tolerance of its effects. There is no evidence that cocaine produces, even in heavy users, any physical "craving," though users may well experience a psychological craving, as do some users of alcohol, money, sex, food and fingernails.

·It has been an axiom of antidrug literature for more than fifty years that long-term cocaine use results in paranoid psychosis. The most reliable U.S. experts on cocaine have not found, in hospital admittance records and in the memories of clinical psychiatrists operating psychiatric wards, any instances of psychosis directly attributable to cocaine. The best that can be said, on the evidence, is that psychotics who use cocaine are likely to be psychotic.

·Similarly, traditional antidrug literature emphasizes that coke users frequently experience deep and even suicidal depressions when they run out of coke. Such depressions have not been reported within recent experience even among Colombian users who consumed coke daily for years.

·Many users report a dramatic sexual rush, though users of almost every drug report a dramatic sexual rush at one time or another, and it's likely that the rush comes from sex and setting, not from the drug. Men consistently told me that women turn on with coke, but the women I talked to were vague on the subject. If coke gives some users a sexual rush, the reason may be that it loosens their inhibitions: after you've shared some coke, after you've set yourself up for five to life in the penitentiary, why be modest?

·In the days before Masters and Johnson reported a simple mechanical method for developing ejaculatory control, some men applied cocaine to their glans to anesthetize it and thereby extend intercourse. Some men, not knowing any better, still do.

·Coke cures hangovers, sort of, relieving the headache and nausea and attendant general depression, but the trade-off is temporary, especially since coke suppresses appetite and discourages sleep, and food and rest are still the best hangover cures known to man.

·Illegal cocaine is usually cut, though it cannot be cut as drasti-cally as heroin without losing most or all of its effect, which is so subtle in the first place that many people don't recognize it until it's pointed out to them. Street coke, sold by the spoon—a spoon is about a gram—may be cut as much as 80 per cent, which means it will do very little more than numb your nose, and fifty to one hundred dollars a gram is a high price to pay for a numbed nose and watering in the eyes, and are more reason to suspect usually goes up accordingly, as does the quantity you must buy. Lactose, milk sugar, is the best and safest cut commonly used. Dextrose is sweeter than lactose but equally safe. Various amino acids, simple proteins, are safe and have no taste, but they're harder for dealers to come by and aren't often used. *Mannite*, the Spanish laxative, may add to the diarrhea that cocaine sometimes causes. Quinine lowers body temperature but not significantly in the quantities anyone is likely to blow. Procaine—Novocain—and lidocain are occasionally used as cuts because they increase the freeze, but their presence is reason to suspect the quality of the coke. Amphetamine cuts are worst of all, causing burning in the nose and watering in the eyes, and are more reason to suspect the quality of the coke, because amphetamines mimic the effects of cocaine.

·Cocaine is made by packing coca leaves in gasoline drums with kerosene and other solvents and allowing the alkaloids to soak free. After the soaking, the fluid is drained off and the leaves re-moved, leaving behind a brown paste that smells like tobacco. Since the leaves contain about .5 to 1.2 per cent cocaine by weight, one kilo of paste to one hundred kilos of leaves is considered a good extraction. The paste is subsequently converted to crystalline cocaine by reaction with hydrochloric acid. One hundred kilos of leaves sell for about $110, producing one kilo of paste that sells for $600; a kilo of cocaine 90–98 per cent pure, delivered in Latin America, sells for $3,000 to $4,000; cut to 50–80 per cent and delivered in New York, a kilo of coke sells for $30,000 to $40,000—the kilo is expanding, of course, with the cut. Cut to 20 per cent and sold in New York by the spoon, the same kilo might earn as much as $200,000 to $250,000. Illegal cocaine returns bet-ter profits than legal diamonds, which is why the DEA and the Bureau of Customs and probably God Himself can't stop the co-caine traffic. Cocaine has been smuggled in artificial legs, banana boxes, wine bottles, brassieres, girdles, vaginas, rectums, diplomatic pouches, baby carriages, plastic tubes, false-bottomed suitcases, mouthwash bottles, shampoo bottles, Instamatic packs, and water skis, to name only a few, to name only the containers that didn't work. Cocaine can be smuggled as a liquid or as a powder. No one has yet gotten around to smuggling coca leaves. Like marijuana, they are bulky and they have a characteristic smell that dogs can detect. So does cocaine, by the way, and recently Customs has been training dogs to smell it out. The dogs are very alert and easily work twenty-hour days.

·In America's major cities, an ounce of cocaine sells for anywhere from $400 to $1200, depending on its purity (an ounce contains 28.3 grams). In Latin America, an ounce of 85 per cent pure cocaine costs from $50 to $100. A gram dealer in the United States sells 40–50 per cent coke, an ounce dealer 70–80 per cent coke, a pound dealer 85–98 per cent coke. There is no simple way to determine precisely the percentage of the cut.

·Blacks have been into coke a long time, Latin Americans even longer. Before coke became illegal, Southerners feared black use of coke as much as Westerners feared Chinese use of opium, believing without evidence then or since that coke would lead to uprisings of plantation workers and attacks on white women. Blacks in big-city ghettos maintained the community of coke use through the dry years of World War II and after, and coke is the drug of choice today among black dealers, hustlers, pimps, musicians and entrepreneurs. That world is described in Woodley's remarkable *Dealer*. The scene is changing now that New York has installed its severe new laws: dealers there now carry guns and intend to use them against police, since life imprisonment makes the issue one of get the cop before he gets you.

·Controlled scientific research on human responses to cocaine began only last year, 1974, 115 years after cocaine's discovery. The best available evidence is that cocaine in moderate use is a mild drug, similar in action to the amphetamines but without their more serious effects. It is certainly not in a class, in terms of any clear and present danger, with heroin, alcohol or the barbiturates. Several lawsuits are under way in the United States that ask the federal courts to remove cocaine from its present classification as a dangerous narcotic, subject to the most severe penalties, and place it in the same classification as the amphetamines or marijuana, subject to far more moderate penalties. Those lawsuits have been supported by affidavits from distinguished scientists and physicians, all of whom emphasize that cocaine is not a narcotic, some of whom emphasize that cocaine is a mild drug and some of whom also emphasize what is today the central fact about cocaine: that despite its growing popularity on the one hand and its condemnation and prohibition as a dangerous drug on the other, very little is known about its effects on human beings. Cocaine can kill you; so can aspirin. Cocaine acts on the central nervous system; so does caffeine. It's possible to overstimulate the central nervous system, and you can't do that forever without damaging it. Cases of cocaine "addiction" were reported in the past, usually among patients being treated for morphine or alcohol addiction, hardly the most reliable test population, and are not reported today. Cocaine psychosis and suicidal depression upon withdrawal were reported in the past, and are not seen today. Violent assaultive behavior by cocaine users was reported in the past and is not reported today. At least two conclusions seemed reasonable: that the greatest danger connected with moderate, recreational use of cocaine is legal, not chemical; and that not nearly enough is known about cocaine's effects on human beings.

If, as it appears, cocaine in small doses is only a moderate euphoric, but if, as is certain, it comes with severe criminal penalties attached, how are we to account for its increasing use by the middle class, which has so much to lose by conviction? And how account for the seductiveness of cocaine that users so frequently report?

Cocaine's effects may match some pre-existing cultural bias, a point made nicely by Drs. Gay, Inaba, Sheppard and Newmeyer of the Haight-Ashbury Free Medical Clinics in a recent paper:

> In its pharmacologic action, cocaine, perhaps more than any other of the recognized psychoactive drugs, reinforces and boosts what we recognize as the highest aspirations of American initiative, energy, frenetic achievement and ebullient optimism even in the face of great odds.

A more pedestrian possiblity is that cocaine use is increasing because the federal government has succeeded in dramatically reducing the illegal supply of amphetamines in the United States. The amphetamines got tight about the same time that cocaine began coming in, and cocaine is, among other things, a "better amphetamine."

Cocaine may be increasing in popularity because, besides producing a state of mind that users perceive as pleasant, its dosage can be controlled. Because it is a short-acting drug, cocaine doesn't blow people away, as marijuana and LSD notoriously do. Middle-class users, accustomed to controlled doses of alcohol, apparently perceive controlled doses of cocaine to be a less physically disruptive high.

But the seductiveness of coke may be the seductiveness of danger. Unwilling to risk physical addiction by playing with heroin, but willing and even eager to risk breaking some very stiff laws for a new high they perceive as desirable, middle-class coke users may like the heavy taste of the illegal that is part of coke's thrill, may like the smell of fear mingled with the caresses of the drug itself. It cannot be without significance that coke came into fashion in the later years of the Nixon administration, when respect for law and order reached a new low. As risks go, those seem to me to be among the more useless and even infantile, but my opinion is only one. I took a few infantile risks of my own coming down snow mountain.

Here, see: coming down snow mountain: in a large Eastern city I meet a married couple, Bill and Sherry, for dinner at my hotel. Bill knows coke; he's been a dealer, been busted, been in jail and back out again on parole, isn't dealing any more but knows the street. Sherry is just in from an out-of-town party and hasn't slept for twenty-eight hours, doing coke, and looks as fresh as morning, a knockout woman in a halter top and jeans who reduces the waiters to adolescence: they bring our orders one at a time, one waiter per order, to get a close-up of her. We eat, drink wine, talk coke. Bill says there's no shortage of coke on the East Coast because more people than ever are dealing it up from Florida and South America. Who's doing coke? I ask him, and he says men do it to give them that extra surge of power, that extra flush of confidence. "It's like taking a deep breath," he says. "If you look at these different industries where coke is most used, they're all high-pressure. Superfast industries—music, the garment business, film, entertainment basically. And then unpleasant businesses.

Prostitutes do a lot of coke. Pimps do it for the glamour of it. But with women it's different. It really has a mystical effect on women." I ask Sherry if it has a mystical effect on women and she grins. "Yeah," she says, "look at me. Mystical tonight."

Up to my room after dinner and Sherry produces a small bag of coke and a bag of grass. Bill isn't doing any coke, because he gets a surprise urinalysis every now and then, one of the terms of his parole. He's feeling good anyway from the wine and the joint now going around. Sherry produces a small black compact that opens up to a mirror, a compartment for a single-edge razor-blade, and a compartment for a silver soda straw, the kind they sell at Tiffany's, and she dumps the coke onto the mirror and pulverizes it with the razor blade and lays out six lines. She does two and I do two through the silver straw. The joint and the coke work together and the boundaries of the room begin to shift and wobble, but despite the warping of the grass I also feel completely clear-headed, thinking fast, concisely, even profoundly but noticing that I forget Bill's words as soon as he says them, they go through a tunnel and don't come out.

We talk on and smoke on. Bill shows me a vial of white, crystalline amino acid and asks me to taste it and I do and it has no taste at all. He says it's the best cut for coke he's ever found, adds bulk without any taste or effect. Sherry says more than once that her coke supply is almost gone and begins to hint that she might stay after Bill leaves and Bill asks questions about the people I've seen while working on this story, who and where and when, and I think about Sherry staying and what that might be like and I know where I can get some coke and then I think about a husband going off and leaving his knockout wife with a near stranger in a hotel room and I think about Bill's questions and suddenly I'm struck with the absolute certainty that these two people are entrapping me and I sit up straight and the urge to giggle I've been feeling goes away and I tell them, Bill and Sherry, that either I'm having a paranoid trip or they're narcs.

Embarrassed, flushed, Bill asks what's happening and why do I think that and Sherry becomes silent, both of them reacting the wrong way, it seems to me with my conviction racing around my head, reacting with embarrassment when I would have reacted with anger to a similar charge, and their responses convince me that I'm right and abruptly I stand up and say that, trip or narc, the party's over and it's time to leave. Bill quickly snorts the two remaining lines of coke, he's that nervous, and at the door, following Sherry, he says he's really sorry and I say so am I but I have to trust my instincts and then they are gone and the door is closed and I slip the chain lock and collapse into my chair with the room still blowing back and forth like a bellows and the certainty still certain and then the whistle, the whistle like the song of the meadowlark on the telephone wire outside my apartment back in Kansas, begins sounding in my ear, the whistle that says I know where I can get some coke and the coke might bury the enormous load of anxiety I'm suddenly carrying and I listen to the whistle, the birdsong, the cokesong, for ten minutes by the clock before it occurs to me that if my guests were narcs and they thought I had coke in my room they could come back and break down the door and I'd be off in the pokey for years and years and who would support my children while I was away? And coke lost its enchantment then and forevermore and I went to bed, knowing that the worst part of the entire experience, whatever the experience had been, was the fact that it took me ten long minutes to get beyond the feeling that the coke would set me free.

The next day, I call people who need to be called, going carefully to a pay phone in case my hotel phone is tapped—Bill made some calls and took one on my phone during the evening, he could have installed a tap—and I end one call from the pay phone abruptly when a black man enters the next booth and I don't hear the money ring in the slot and as I leave the booth I glance warily at him and he glances warily at me. Only when I am home clean, a week later, when I have thought about the experience, when a mutual friend has supplied reasonable proof that Bill and Sherry aren't narcs, only then do I decide that my reaction was paranoid, a bad trip, and even then I'm not entirely sure, they could have been narcs, the other people I met could have been narcs, my next-door neighbor could be a narc, anyone could be a narc, couldn't he, couldn't she?

I decided even later that my reaction wasn't to the coke at all but to the joint. And I decided later yet that my reaction wasn't to either: it came from my head, as all reactions do. Apologies to Bill and Sherry, wherever they may be.

Between dark and dark we float free. Dreams consume us; the simple perception of the natural world dazzles our eyes; we comprehend edges, corners, boundaries, lines, and beyond them we

sense spaces and times larger than Leviathan, more teeming than
the sea. Out of signals, cues, sets, codes we construct a reasonable
world, knowing and trying to forget that our construction is only
approximate, reduced, is not substance but modality, is not form
but a screen before form. Every ecstasy we know, every art we
have devised, points to rents in the screen, points out beyond the
flesh and the stage and the page and the canvas to the ultramun-
dane, where we are lovers and murderers, children and ancient
crones, athletes and paralytics, dead and unborn, rock and fish
and fowl, where we are also forms out of flesh, where we sail forever to Byzantium. We go mad through the screen and come
back towing gods behind us. We go burning through the screen
and come back flayed and spent and still. We go toying through
the screen and come back brimming with the formulae that activate the stars. We are not the only race of creatures that thinks,
but we are the only race of creatures that voluntarily, periodically
and perhaps necessarily seeks out disorder, madness, chaos, knowing that only through those terrifying passages can order, sanity
and creation be enriched and sustained.

The ecstasy of the dream, the ecstasy of sexual union, the ecstasy of art are merely orders and suborders of the greater ecstasy
all of us glimpse spiraling at the boundaries of our structured per-
ceptions, and we have searched since the beginning of time for
substances that would produce that ecstasy upon demand. The
search is quixotic: the essence of that ecstasy is that it cannot be
induced, because it comes from within. But it is the work of years
to learn to call it out, and we are busy at other work; we would
have our ecstasies scheduled and ordered, like the other parts of
our lives, though ecstasy cannot be partitioned, because it is not
part but whole. So we nod and buzz and dizzy and faint, playing
with our minor magic, we drink and smoke and snort and fire,
playing with our minor magic, and the play brings a sort of relief,
but it is the relief of substitution, as the neurotic symptom is a relief of substitution: anything that any drug can do for you you
can do for yourself, as the mystics of East and West have demonstrated for thousands of years. Chemicals seem to imitate because,
using them, we permit ourselves to let go, but it is the letting go
more than the chemicals that turns us on. We all of us sense that,
and use the chemicals anyway because their limitations are known
and socially accepted, so to speak; turning on without them, we

fear, may be limitless: that way, we fear, madness lies, and sometimes it does.

Perhaps the drugs can lead us. Good men have suggested that in more trusting societies than ours, they do. They cannot take us all the way. There we must go alone, or go accompanied by others who have been there before us, and that is not news: it has always been so. Art has served such purpose, and religion, and sexual initiation, and every kind of learning. "What man is he that liveth," John Donne asked the King and the Court in a sermon long ago, "and shall not see death?" That is one side of the coin of our lives, but Donne might equally have asked, "What man is he that liveth, and shall not see transcendence?" The question we struggle with today is what quality that transcendence shall be. Freud concluded eventually that the great requirements for life were love and work: the man who once thought cocaine might redeem us discovered later that reality was the most extraordinary of all highs. It still is.

V
CLOSER TO HOME

Credences of Summer

1. The Seduction of Mrs. Callaghan

Beads, drops, pearls of sweat glistened on the fine down of Mrs. Callaghan's upper lip like passion on the lip of a woman in love, but Mrs. Callaghan wasn't in her passion and wasn't in love. She wasn't even Irish and her husband was dead. She was sweating in the 95-degree heat of a Missouri summer in the dormitory of a boys' home where I had just finished scrubbing the terrazzo floor, not at all to Mrs. Callaghan's satisfaction.

She was such a beautiful woman to me. Not more than forty, tall, her skin of that pastel umber range between cream and olive so that it turned brown as a high colored woman's in the sun and with definite beautiful veins in her hands that would glow in the lamplight and a hint, no more, of wrinkles at her throat, her eyes, her elbows and in unexpected places where bones join together, her wrists, her clavicles, her ankles when she turned quickly upon them. Long, firm legs not a day over eighteen. Big hips, the pelvis beneath the flesh jutting out on both sides so that her skirt, a peasant skirt gathered from a full circle with elastic at the waist, sat high on those arrogant bones. I've thought it over. Sloping butt, the shape and the weight of it low, something to get your hands into. Something of a belly too, although hard enough from the muscles under the splurge of fat, the kind of belly you don't easily distinguish from the mound it joins a little way down. Big, pendulous breasts, the only breasts that should be allowed at a boys' home, and I could imagine their dark nipples big at night as thumbs. Yet fine long feet and slender hands. Fine long head and spiritual eyes, wide and brown and somehow fluid, as if Mrs. Callaghan were always on the verge of tears. A loose but not a slack mouth, the looseness an illusion because the mouth was wider than the average and with a fuller lip. And the lip perspired, measuring my floor.

"You haven't cleaned this floor. You can't just run a rag around a floor and expect to get away with it. That's just dusting. Look at those corners! Here, I'll show you once how to get into those corners and then I expect you to do them right."

She got down on her hands and knees with me then in a white peasant blouse that let her breasts swing as she worked and showed me herself cleaning corners, wringing out the rag above the gray iron pail spotted with tin like a sawed-off organ pipe, water running from the rag and gliding over her hands into the pail on a rising melody. She left the rag dripping and sloshed it into a corner, building a puddle of soapy water to soak away the dirt and old wax. Wrung the rag again drier this time and poked a long finger into it and with the rag mounted happily on the finger poked it into the corner and scraped away the gray wax, using one of her sharp fingernails as a scraper. The room contained twelve beds, that big, with wooden chests between the beds marking off each boy's territory, but to clean it she would scrape away a line thin as a fingernail in each corner and then scrape another and another until she had cleaned one of the room's eight or ten corners (the corners formed not only by the four sides of the room but also by the junction of the double frosted glass doors that led into the hallway and at each side of the two radiators at the ends of the room which coughed up, in the winter, their rust-loaded heat), that scraping as exciting to me, watching her swing and lean, as if she were scraping my back. She flushed now from the effort of scrubbing and scraping in the heat but determined that I would learn how hard I must work if the floor would meet her standards, and determined behind that subterfuge that no lolling orphan who had discovered his first pubic hair only a few months before would loll around her, but knowing also that by descending to the floor with me, sweating with me, scraping away the corners, she had compromised her high purpose beyond salvation. And knowing also that I knew, which, in a dim, inexperienced sort of way, I did.

"Now, I want you to do this dormitory over again and do it right. And you'll keep on doing it as far as I'm concerned until it's done the way I want it done."

Tossing her head—limp strands of brown hair against her

cheeks with their high Indian bones—in disdain and stalking—
was she barefoot? and did I see the roundness of her heels which
would so perfectly fit my hands?—out of the long dormitory to
her own room, full of sounds like intimate secrets. I could hardly
bear to be in the same building with her; she was safe only within
her own room, a room within a room really, an apartment built of
purple-brown lacquered redwood in the hall between the two
wings of the dormitory, god a hotbox it must have been in
those days before air conditioning, and with two strange windows
each opening into the wings of the dormitory covered over with
wallpaper yet with ill-fitting cracks that admitted her light into
the dormitories at night. We crowded those windows on hot summer nights, peeking through the cracks of light, breathing through
them, beasts of the night forest watching in silence Snow White,
eager if necessary only to touch her long cool feet. Strange creature, mother and beloved, the only thing female in that hard child-
ish forest, eager imagined smells and springs welling from cracks
of yellow light that might have been floods of peace and love, one
long-boned body that answered our questions, one shape that
shadowed absently our staring eyes, one sound upon the sounds of
the night that called us like moths to her windows, one shape of
sweating curves that fitted our loneliness and filled it out to a
dream of presence, of sleep without floors or walls or the edges of
beds over which we might forever fall. How could she bathe, how
could she breathe, how could she move to her bed and sleep with
the gigantic din of our bodies and our urgent eyes thrown against
the thin wood of her walls? I never questioned her irritation with
us, I understood her constant anger with me, because she must
have known the frail barriers between her privacy and our need
and must have known that of all those who pressed against her
windows at night I pressed most urgently. And she pressed—this
was Mrs. Callaghan's exception, the reason she more than any
other housemother lives in my imagination now—she pressed
back, scraping out my corners with her sharp nails.

2. Canning Tomatoes

If you have fresh tomatoes, new potatoes and sweet corn on your
table in Missouri on the Fourth of July you're a good farmer. At

the home we canned tomatoes, twenty acres of tomatoes every summer.

The canning house had been an army barracks. We got it army surplus from a camp in the center of the state and hauled it back in pieces on the truck and reassembled it on a new concrete floor we had poured. In the southwest corner of the building stood an eight-burner stove made of black cast iron. Beside it was a deep sink. Beside the sink a chicken plucker, a revolving drum with rubber fingers ringing it. Two stainless steel rendering kettles, double-walled and fed with steam from a boiler outside. Meat-hooks on a rail overhead—we also butchered here—and in the center of the building a canning table, a waist-high trough of wood painted white and two wings of wood jutting out from the edges of the trough.

Outside in the sun you walked down the long rows of tomato plants dragging a bushel basket behind you, holding onto one of its wire handles or onto the slatted brim if the handle was gone. The plants had not been staked. They spread in their profusion of vines all over the ground and into the rows themselves. You picked each plant clean of its ripe tomatoes, easy enough for the tomatoes on top, harder—bending down your back and trying to avoid kneeling in the damp black dirt, saving your jeans, bending down and lifting up the heavy vines—for the tomatoes underneath, hoping your fingers would not plunge into a tomato that had rotted where it sat on the wet ground, looking, as the work became monotonous, for rarities of tomato: two grown together like dumbbells, one grown enormous in that soil that had been for fifty years a feedlot, one no larger than a cherry and fully ripe, one with a navel like an orange; and, looking, picked until your basket was full.

Inside the canning house you set your basket beside the others, eight or ten of them at a time, near the cookstove on which two vast kettles boiled, and the boy in charge of scalding them unloaded them into a wire basket and dipped the basket into one of the kettles and timed the scalding. In the other kettle on a rack boiled Mason jars. The boy lifted the basket of scalded tomatoes out of the kettle and carried it to the trough and dumped the tomatoes onto the wings, shelves. I stood there, with other boys, and as the tomatoes, red as blood, their skins wounded now and peeling, came rolling my way, I picked up the first one in my left hand, a paring knife in my right, juggling the tomato to avoid burning my hand, and began to peel and core it, revealing its velvety meat, the pink juice running down my hands, down my arms, dripping off my elbows, making them itch so that I constantly bent them inward to wipe them on my white tee shirt, staining it red, working in a rapid rhythm, dropping the tomato into the trough, picking up another, peeling it, coring it, molding its plumpness in my hands, remembering its sweet tart taste, smelling its pungent smell of gardens and summer, in love with tomatoes fresh from the garden after the winter of canned food, in love with velvety meat sprung somehow from black dirt and water and sun, unbelievable resurrection that gave us work and food and unrelenting love, the air its transformer but I its shaper, I the lover who peeled its skin and cored its stem and dropped it into the trough (from which, at the open ends, other boys plucked the juicy meat and forced it into the hot jars, capped them with a rubber ring and a glass top, snapped a metal clamp over the glass and moved the jars to the cooker where the meat was cooked and the jars were sterilized).

And at noon and again in the evening, though we had seen and smelled a universe of tomatoes by now, we sat on baskets turned upside down to make stools and sorted among the tomatoes fresh from the garden, found the best, the juiciest and most perfectly formed, and gone mad on tomatoes covered them with coarse cattle salt and ate them gravely one by one.

3. White Worms

In the terrible heat of summer, amid caecal dust, I cleaned the chicken roosts with a hoe. Scraped away the night's accumulation of manure, piles of gray and brown capped with white, dropped them into a bucket that once held tractor oil. Hated the work, hated the chickens, old hens with glittering eyes forever purritting, clucking, cackling. Hauled gravelly oyster shell to line their craws, corn to yellow their yolks, water to plump their albumen.

The faucet, outside the door of the chicken house and to the right, rose up waist high from the ground, a rusted pipe capped by an outlet rigged to a lever that snapped up vertically on. Before the faucet a puddle of leaked water and in that puddle, in the terrible heat of summer, white worms shimmering, worms fastened, hundreds of them, to the mud like trunks of time-maddened trees, worms writhing, asking, always these questions from the beasts, mute, dancing questions, they dance their questions, beasts, writhing dance in puddlesway, worms sprung from caecal slime to accuse, infinitude of insect accusations without regard. They frightened me: I knew no insect like them but had to stand on the cornice of dry earth between the puddle and the faucet to fill the buckets of water to water the chickens and stood with whirling frightened head, the puddle deepening to a lake, to a sea and white worms like deathly fingers beckoning and knew I would fall, would join that entropic dance, worm in a white wormery, would sway to . . . and fro . . . to . . . and fro, and beckon as they beckoned. For light? For food? For wind to speed the sway?

Finally I got gasoline and burned them.

4. Ramming Time

The ram in ramming time we kept penned in a lot behind the south barn. He waited all day in his dignity, his legs folded under him in the shade by the wooden fence, his massive head nodding as he panted quietly in the heat.

The ewes grazed in the north pasture. At four-thirty I went to get them; they waited then at the gate, a graceful herd. I had checked the gates in the lane and found a stick to instruct laggards. I opened the gate and they surged through, anxious for water and rest. They moved in a crowd through the lane, remarking a boy pushing a cart to the north barn. They herded again outside the gate to the lot where the ram stood, on his feet now and alert but no less dignified than before. I moved him away from the gate with the stick, opened the gate inward, and the ewes trotted in. I closed the gate and watched. The ram moved from one ewe to the next, sniffing their labia. When he found a ewe in heat he mounted her skillfully, moved in her briefly and then for one moment wildly and got off. He mounted five ewes in a row before, dazed now, he contented himself with sniffing others, with walking among them, with resting, his legs folded beneath him, at the place beside the fence where he had rested before. If I had brought him the evening paper he probably would have found spectacles in a pocket in his wool and read it while the ewes settled before him. We had painted a solution of red chalk on his belly, and thus he marked with red rumps the ewes he had mounted. They wore their markings proudly, dignified flags the color of brick.

5. A Noiseless Patient Spider

When there's no other work—no radishes to pull, no barns to mend or potatoes to dig, no hens to slaughter for stew—we hoe field corn. That summer the Sergeant marched us out to the field. The Sergeant walked on the balls of his feet, light in army boots, a tall man, rangy, with a long bald forehead and yellow eyes and a thin mouth and that look of insanity that is the birthright or defect of so many southern men. He could hunker down on his heels like an African and sit there for hours, swaying like grain in a breeze, chewing on a stalk of seed grass and watching us with yellow evil in his eyes, waiting as a dog or an idiot boy waits unminded for the moment to pounce. We marched smartly across the plain downhill dry creek uphill level of the first forty-acre pasture. Billy Densing opened the gate—reaching through the planking to lift the latch on the other side, then lifting the gate off the ground and carrying it back halfway, guarding it with his copperplated hoe at casual parade rest until we had all marched through, carrying it back then and shifting to the other side and hooking the latch. Then we faced, at the end of a mounded terrace, curving rows of field corn taller than we by half and no green ears yet showing. Modern farmers spray herbicides onto their field corn to retard weeds, but at the home, with such urgent manpower, we cut the weeds by hand as if the tall corn we would shell for cattle feed were some domestic vegetable in a truck garden.

We started at the left, each boy taking a row, the rows half a mile long down a section line but curving with the land, a lesson in touch and feel, a map you could lie on, could walk over. You plunged into your canopied row for a reason: the morning hung cool under the leaves of corn, hung cooler than the sun outside the rows, the dew not yet evaporated from the leaves, and in your white tee shirt and blue jeans and black high-topped work shoes you were already sweating and holding your breath for that cool air. With any breeze at all the leaves of the cornstalks rustled like crowded satin skirts and whispered about your undone appearance between their rows, a reception line you must traverse, torn among alternatives: to go slowly and be cooled by the air trapped under the leaves, to go quickly and find rest at the other end of the row, to leave tall weeds and make better progress but perhaps to be called back to do it over after the Sergeant's regular inspection, to cut all the weeds but risk falling behind the others and hearing the Sergeant's ridicule despite your conscientious effort. To go quickly meant also to be nicked by the knife edges of the leaves of corn, edges not only sharp but serrated like a saw. To go slowly meant finding yourself alone in your row, unable to see the sky or the entrance or the exit, alone in a field that looked then suddenly like an endless expanse of jungle, alone with weeds that grew as if they had no shame in rows that had no end so that you would hoe and hoe and hoe, a vegetable Sysiphus in the alien corn.

I chose, as I so often chose, the middle way: fast but not too fast, clean but not too clean, enjoying the cool, shaded row but looking forward to flopping down in the wet grass at the other end, keeping up too because some of the boys you hoed with devised contests to see who could get through his row fastest, and even though the Sergeant wanted to believe in thoroughness (since we were after all there to get rid of the weeds, the weeds that would stunt the corn and decrease the yield), yet he was all-American and believed most fervently in a contest, any contest, a pissing contest if it came to that, so that the boy who did the best job of hoeing but finished last on his row could count on little more than a grudging salute from the Sergeant and a few surreptitious kicks from the other boys. So I chose the middle way. You are usually safe in the middle of a crowd.

And choosing the middle way, I worked at a half run with my head down, alert to any weeds, my fine new hoe with the square corners adept at weeds, gashing them with its edge and pulling them away, tripping a tall ragweed the way you would trip a man running for his life if you kicked his feet out from under him, the weed coming down with its severed butt and its leafy top hitting the ground at the same time, that something of a private art too, because in the boredom of hoeing you develop artworks like that, never chronicled but part of every day for those who devise them, as hitting two ducks with one pass of the double-barreled shotgun is an art form most high for duck hunters, as sewing a regular and fine stitch is an art form most high for those who sew. For me in the cornfield the art form was dropping the weeds in one swift cut and one horizontal fall onto the ground, at a half run that would get me out of the row and into the lounging crowd in the middle third of the group, safe and inconspicuous.

So I didn't even notice the web until I was almost on top of it and the huge black-and-yellow spider had rushed to the middle of it strung between two rows of cornstalks and big as a wagon wheel and thrown herself back and forth to set up a pattern this lumbering monster might see before he—it—tore it away. Spiders are always female. This one—I had seen her sisters many times before, watched them weave their beautifully symmetrical nets among the tomato and potato plants—displayed calm benevolence compared to so many smaller and more aggressive spiders I have known (the trapdoor spider the most frantic of them all, peeking out of its lid of sod like a shy workman appearing from under a manhole cover, darting out to catch a passing bug and dragging it back into the manhole or spiderhole as if the entire act violated some church-sponsored public law, as if the spider were in fact kidnaping children from a school yard), and this yellow-and-black spider patiently building her web in plain daylight, warning all neighboring insects if they were smart enough to heed the warning that she was setting up shop in the area and expected to welcome a few select customers soon, and now faced with the threat of destruction, her shop and her laces alike to be torn down, a veritable German invasion of her Paris, and she had no intention of defending herself from me, knew better, knew me, my god, as a natural force, I become despite myself a whirlwind, an accident of fate like an avalanche or a falling tree so that a voice might have spoken to this plump and graceful creature saying, *Canst thou tame Leviathan?* but Leviathan would have been merely me, such is the scale of life and the chance of life's violation in this enormous and yet enormously minute universe.

So she threw herself back and forth in her web as if playing with her whole body some giant harp, and I, hearing more than seeing the hum of that vibration—hearing it first—I looked up and there, bare inches from my eyes, in the very center of her white web, was the spider herself, big and plump—so close to my eyes—as a baby, but marked with the primitive mask of these ordered breeds of creatures, the zigzag stripes of yellow on her black fur that you find on African but not American mammals and otherwise only on insects and fishes and imitated among primitive tribes and not recalled again until man invented the football helmet and the racing car, and looking I froze, not merely in fear—a wasp I would have feared, his needle so near my face—but in fear mixed with desire for the plump abdomen that scant inches from my eyes thrust itself back and forth before me to call me from my mechanical work of tripping up ragweed, to show me that a fellow creature and a most pregnant and female fellow creature needed my attention. And no such appeal—the mare whinnying from the burning barn, the cow down with milk fever, the woman in childbirth, the firefly winking her green light, my spider throwing her web—can go unregarded by any male of any species unless instinct completely interdicts, as it often does, all intelligent response. I saw her belly and her eyes; I saw her eight legs softened by a fine black down; and though I feared her as spider, I felt her as female, with shame that I should have failed to notice without being told that I would quickly have violated the business of living represented by her web, a business that goes on with different rules, with different equipment, along different lines of thought, and to different and most opposite ends from the other business, my human but most inhuman business of working, of remaking the world in the image of a machine.

So I jumped back. She was after all a spider and I, immediately upon seeing her a glimpse before me, realized that she could jump easily to my eyes and then I jumped back. Then I broke into a sweat, fearful of spider, but even then I realized I had done something more in the moment before my panic: lusted for a female outside my race and species and size and time scale and successfully resisted destroying her world because I could in no way except in imagination ever hope to be a part of it. That was growth, the kind summer gives, no textbooks and no grade cards and hardly anyone in the world even to remember. My god, we experience so much more than we understand.

A Bicentennial Minute

In its utopian sense—inspired nonsense—America might be defined as a concatenation of souls. Like most utopiana, the definition fails: a utopia is nowhere, a concatenation is a chain, a soul is lost. For a foot on definition, I have in mind something historical: the coastal Atlantic, episcopal lands, tidal exceptions; the Appalachians, the Cumberland Gap, Boone loping on; the conquest of the gloomy inland forest, sycamores athwart, in a litter of passenger pigeons stinking of Rome; eventually the Middle West, which is to say the depth of field mediate between assertion and regret, and there among lenses and cohorts settlement paradisiacal on the ecotone between forest and prairie. As, for example, the Osage. Where I live. And the Pacific arc shaking beyond. I know that others believe. Midway between time zones and with no demonstrable clock I notice the coming and going of the sun. Where merely highways are now were animal trails before.

Lacking but the modicum of cultured experience, we went to school. We sat in classes talking. Books, sometimes venereal and Jacobean, were fifty cents an hour overdue. Sol warmed our torsos and the great library recalled. We drank milk in dining rooms. I grew up digging in the earth with shovels and tractor-drawn plows and forgot digging for the foppery of madras belts. Measuring with his nose, a fraternity initiate flipped a sanitary napkin across an intersection. Classmates returned from field trips praising calculus or the fossilization of hyena dung. I learned the Heisenberg uncertainty principle and the concept of time in the early twentieth century, and fossilized hyena dung occupied the Smithsonian and the undergraduate years were fine.

In those days there were whales. No one commanded them but

Previously unpublished (1976)

they were guided by dolphins. Their trajectories split infinitives, however, and under the wrack of the New Frontier they were lost.

I came back to the land to the extent of crabgrass above a lake, and the dearest friend I have ever known put a bullet through his chest. The bullet remembered by mother and I distinctly heard it apologize. These were the sixties, when lacking all other graces we forgave. Lyndon Johnson and the American Dream displayed their scars.

We suffered the hours of daylight. A man long before us, in a gout of definition, wrote that "there are ideal types of brothels as well as of religions," and in pursuit of an ideal type beyond judgment I contacted certain children who longed for release from the fancy they had of parenthood. Their shoes smelled and they were given to unresolvable paradoxes but hardly knowing their eyes from their appetite for Victorians I took them in. Hidden in a closet, we preserved tomato jellies against a later time. They grew against me as a love nest grows, sparing only my numerals, and an unnamable force taught them school.

The woman I had loved went lame. Her lameness was in an eye rather than a limb and I longed to cure her affliction, but at last her habit of spitting after micturition unnerved me and I discovered the mole-like disturbance of crocuses. "You are no more to me than the filter of a cigarette," she wrote, "and in a measure of your precious children I butt you out." Stung, I returned to the Smithsonian and searched the ground for stairs.

Dusky Sally brought me alive again. Her dung was pinched like the hyena's, but fresh, and though brown she precisely remembered gray, level-headed Paris. Her head was shaved to a stubble that she willingly exposed on early-morning television and her thighs were thick as thieves. I was red-haired like Jefferson and counted the brood I spent her to by the pendulum that descended through my floor. I gave her lime and she darkened and on an unforgivable morning she shot grama through my veil and created the Continental Divide.

Lincoln slipped by me, wearing his shawl, and West Virginia. The first human being alive in North America closed a valve.

You see the acceleration. Despite the forgiveness of sins, despite the circadian rhythms of insects, black holes, the delicate stroke of pacemakers on the American heart, no one need apologize. There are colors presumptive of certain fishes that defy description, while the exploits of the Donner Party, parents and teachers coming together for mutual improvement, have been explained. What remains is what was formerly called the love of the land. I recall a beaver whose dam forced me to sequester my billfold in my hat, like the beaver his browse in the silo of his dam, and I learned that when he splashed I'd best also splash. Once, a finger beside my hand, I saw a cottonmouth water moccasin sunning on a rubber tire. The place where I had walked was virgin except for the tire. There was a man of the early West who once hid out for twenty-eight days behind a rock. He might have bashed a skunk and eaten even its fur but fastidiousness prevailed. In what is called America there are caves that percolate in tune or sing, and I have personally seen a salamander as vicious as a peccary. If you go up into the mountains you brave meeting skiers with accents, German politely most of all.

I like to remember when I was suckled when I was young. The milk was immense above the diving buttocks and the semen was strong. The ewe and the mare were no better: a darkness of labia behind that promised thunderstorms. Oxen pulled wagons, dropping wedding cakes of thick nitrogen, and eggs hid cool and ovoid in flour barrels. Hoops of hickory ascended to the throne.

In Minnesota, runes violate an ordinary stone. In California, one of Elizabeth's many suitors, abroad for his health, abandoned a belt buckle. The Spanish alchemied gold into artichokes and beef and turquoise-and-silver tacos. The English pulled up ginseng, the homunculus screaming for its jewels to give court. This list could of course go on to Puritans and Portuguese. In America one avoids the predictable.

Ma Bell has fancies. Nixon got off. There are satellites that drop their load by parachute and are captured with clotheslines for the nasty pleasures of the lost and found. The Mars Landers violate a hymeneal source. I learned my grammar with you and I. With the brother of the woman I love I play chess by mail. There was never any forgiveness. Ten thousand years ago, plus or minus a hundred, men waded the straits and murdered the mastodon. You must forget social security and the incontinent George Wallace to imagine murdering a mastodon.

Huge, hairy, a warehouse guarded by dogs of all the stink and guts of the zoo, a mastodon. Men, barely, bare women walking or running on the bones of unavailable horses. God, God, Great

Splay of Temple Sunset, the smell! The special stink of ruminants elevated to a principle, great steaming piles of holy manure. You saunter down, being young and untried and therefore unafraid, counting cadence by the old man who walks a cakewalk to a limp, and you don't only smell the holy manure but slurp it up, two hands streaming, and to show your certainty wipe it over yourself like a Masai, glory the manure raked over your pectorals, if you are a man, or drowning your breasts if you are a woman and it slowly falls, ample time to set your foot carpeted in antelope on the soft ground, wade it, slop it, eat it, stink it and come back to the hunting party noising and grinning, *Dat dere mastodon am mine, old boy, chop chop!* Take a flint from your pouch with awe for its sacred spark, strike it, set the bluestem afire, scourge the Indian paintbrush, the old bastard hairy in its bulk grazing with an ear cocked and an eye open, screw your grass. Watch the fire start on a stalk and kindle, hate its slow assembly, tear the bluestem out by its roots and feed it over to the line, the line on one hand and then the line on the other, blow on it, fan it, scream on it, jerk back to gather the old men's approval who are watching with shaking legs and growling bellies and one hand playing with themselves in their mounting frenzy, and then scream to Jack and Abraham and Franklin and George, *Go!* and feet sooting on the running burn you sprint down the fire to the trumpeting mastodon, the outrigger bull beyond the female society with your Arizona point on your pitiful spear attending and like lust and your jetting ejaculate you jab your narrow spear home and see blood ooze between the hair and stand back and the others, Ulysses and Woodrow and Cal and Jerry whom you hate jab on after you usurping your geek show and to snuff them you mount the beast, a smell like perdition, and haul out your flint knife long and chocolate as a bat's wing and erect again and stabbing drink the bucking beast's minor blood humping on its back like a mouse on a mountain and screeching like an eagle anyway. And the mastodon runs on as if you never were and hanging onto its hairy mane you pull yourself up and ride, ride, erect in glory you ride and the fire chases after, will-o'-the-wisp orange licking high, the mastodon giving no quarter, the mastodon not even aware you're riding its bleeding back until it coughs, lung-shot cough, pink foam bubbling out its side around your spear. It collapses, settles like a stew, you squat down before it falls and watch the kicks and painful spasms of its great gray marrowed legs, know inside its skin its liver like a tent green and slick and lugubrious with gall, and then screaming again you assault it and it struggles to get up, the huge face with pitiful opposite eyes glaring at you like a drunken executive and garishly you twist your spear out of its lung and plunge it into a globular jellied eye and wince, and bubbling foam, pink foam against the sovereign brown grasses and pissing a creek beneath you it dies, its final legs flailing like great Jehoshaphat.

Home with your woman a decade later, Eleanor Roosevelt, she feeds you marrow mush on a horn spoon.

The women in the Donner Party, for example, outsurvived the men two to one and the best of them never ventured human flesh. Women forgive me I don't know how to praise you. Forgive me the embarrassment of finding you beyond praise. Dusky Sally mixes with ancestral lime and brings forth Jeffersons without number blunt as you and extends them onto this wild land among gynecologists and sorry politicians contending for trees of walnut and live oak. Men in Massachusetts roll stones like coconuts and a flower in Nantucket drips bees on the Great Salt Lake all the way to Crescent City. Mellowed by Missouri, I revisit my mother's grave on a bluff above the river. She was beautiful, I've figured that out, and young, I've figured that out, and she died in the hard times. My Daddy died later almost unforgiven and was buried beside a man-made lake. Skeletons calcine the ground all over America. Lost souls. Waxes that avoid impressions. Deaf Dalmatians abide in vacant lots and buildings boom and all overruns everywhere resurrect.

With this I have expiated candor and may speak directly.

What else is there to say?

I'm Richard Rhodes and that's the way it was today and yesterday and a million years ago.